ECONOMIC SANCTIONS AND PRESIDENTIAL DECISIONS

Advances in Foreign Policy Analysis

Series Editor: Alex Mintz

Foreign policy analysis offers rich theoretical perspectives and diverse methodological approaches. Scholars specializing in foreign policy analysis produce a vast output of research. Yet, there were only very few specialized outlets for publishing work in the field. Addressing this need is the purpose of **Advances in Foreign Policy Analysis**. The series bridges the gap between academic and policy approaches to foreign policy analysis, integrates across levels of analysis, span theoretical approaches to the field, and advances research utilizing decision theory, utility theory, and game theory.

Members of the Board of Advisors

Published by Palgrave Macmillan

Integrating Cognitive and Rational Theories of Foreign Policy Decision Making
Edited by Alex Mintz

Studies in International Mediation
Edited by Jacob Bercovitch

Media, Bureaucracies, and Foreign Aid: A Comparative Analysis of the United States, the United Kingdom, Canada, France, and Japan
By Douglas A. Van Belle, Jean-Sébastien Rioux, and David M. Potter

Civil–Military Dynamics, Democracy, and International Conflict: A New Quest for International Peace
By Seung-Whan Choi and Patrick James

Economic Sanctions and Presidential Decisions: Models of Political Rationality
By A. Cooper Drury

ECONOMIC SANCTIONS AND PRESIDENTIAL DECISIONS

Models of Political Rationality

A. COOPER DRURY

First published in 2005 by
PALGRAVE MACMILLAN™
175 Fifth Avenue, New York, N.Y. 10010 and
Houndmills, Basingstoke, Hampshire, England RG21 6XS
Companies and representatives throughout the world.

PALGRAVE MACMILLAN is the global academic imprint of the Palgrave Macmillan division of St. Martin's Press, LLC and of Palgrave Macmillan Ltd. Macmillan® is a registered trademark in the United States, United Kingdom and other countries. Palgrave is a registered trademark in the European Union and other countries.

ISBN 1–4039–6725–3

Library of Congress Cataloging-in-Publication Data

Drury, A. Cooper, 1967–
    Economic sanctions and presidential decisions : models of political rationality / A. Cooper Drury.
        p. cm.—(Advances in foreign policy analysis)
    Includes bibliographical references and index.
    ISBN 1–4039–6725–3 (hc)
        1. United States—Foreign relations. 2. Economic sanctions, American.
    3. Presidents—United States —Decision making. I. Title. II. Series.

JZ1480.A5D78 2005
327.73′009′0511—dc22   2005045962

A catalogue record for this book is available from the British Library.

Design by Newgen Imaging Systems (P) Ltd., Chennai, India.

First edition: November 2005
10 9 8 7 6 5 4 3 2 1

Printed in the United States of America.

For my wife, Melanie Taylor Drury

Contents

List of Tables

Preface

My original interest in economic sanctions dates back to an international political economy seminar I took while working toward my master's degree at Michigan State University. Initially interested in effectiveness, I soon found that I was more puzzled by the difficulty scholars had explaining why economic coercion was used when it so often failed. This curiosity led me to study the conditions that led to the use of economic sanctions while working on my doctorate at Arizona State University.

My dissertation provided me with a spring board for several articles on economic sanctions, but I had never brought together a comprehensive study of the use of economic coercion. With the encouragement of several colleagues, I returned to my dissertation to attempt writing such a study of the use of economic coercion. This book is the culmination of that effort.

Like most scholarly enterprises, this one has benefited from the generous input of others over the years. Several colleagues have provided both direct and indirect input on this project. My conversations with Steve Chan about economic coercion have helped clarify and expand my thinking on the topic. Additionally, Steve's generous suggestions for this book have been extremely helpful. I am also indebted to Rich Olson for pushing me to turn my ideas into clear and more exact prose.

My colleagues at the University of Missouri have also been very helpful with providing a sounding board and reality check. Susan Allen, Jay Dow, Joe Hewitt, and Marvin Overby have all cheerfully greeted my knock at their door and answered questions about methods, theory, and data. Several of them would also kindly ask "how's the book going?" and then listen politely over our ubiquitous trips for a cup of coffee. I will always appreciate their intellectual, friendly support and the often needed break from writing that came from the question "coffee?"

Two others at Missouri deserve special note. Pat James has provided not only intellectual guidance but also practical and professional advice that has helped me navigate the writing process. Though always busy, Pat never hesitated to put down his own work and listen and respond to my questions. Vanya Krieckhaus has been a sort of brother-in-arms as we have both written books at the same time.

Vanya has listened to and answered every sort of question over the past year, as well as often sharing the same harried look of someone writing Stata code or revising another chapter. I am deeply indebted to both of these fine scholars.

The Department of Political Science has given me resources and time to complete this project, as well as a very positive academic environment. I have benefited from the able research assistance of Imran Demir, Dursun Peksen, and most especially Yitan Li. I am also very thankful to Kim Elliott for her suggestions, comments, and data. She provided an updated list of sanction cases that made the analyses more feasible. Erick Duchesne provided Section 301 data which considerably limited the number of cases I had to enter by hand. I must also thank my editor David Pervin. His encouragement and quick response to my questions has proved to make this process an enjoyable one.

One person in particular has gone well above and beyond the call of duty. As my dissertation advisor, Steve Walker always showed tremendous patience and support, though I imagine I pushed his limits at times. His constant questioning of my assumptions and theory forced me to think more clearly and critically about research. The pen he used to write comments on my dissertation made it bleed blue. This book has also had a fair amount of his blue ink spilled on it, and it is better thanks to his tireless efforts.

Finally, I am eternally indebted to my family. My two boys, Abraham Taylor Drury and Alexander George Drury, continue to teach me that smaller powers can outsmart and outmaneuver bigger powers, even when the parents claim hegemony. In addition to being my unwavering ally at home, my wife, Melanie Taylor Drury, has been a crucial part of writing this book and of my career. She has read and edited every word I have written, put up with my complaints, and engaged in regular discussions of economic coercion, foreign policy, and even statistical methods. The intellect, grounded perspective, humor, and support she gives are more than I could ever have wished for, and it has made this project possible. To her, I dedicate this book.

Chapter 1
Introduction

Introduction

A 1997 article in the *New York Times* titled "Converting the Dollar into a Bludgeon" reported that in 1996, the United States alone used 22 new economic sanctions against various target states.[1] The author asserts that sanctions "are an irresistible, relatively risk-free and inexpensive way of assuaging America's sense of outrage" (Myers 1997). While suggesting that sanctions are used more for domestic political reasons than for foreign policy efforts, the journalist also points out that sanctions have been generally successful in influencing the target nations at which they are aimed. The economic sanction literature's conventional wisdom partly disagrees with the *New York Times* analysis. Most studies of sanctions focus on their lack of effectiveness. Without mention of the goals or the conditions that lead to their use, the scholarly literature shows that sanctions are largely ineffective—a result that is often blamed on domestic politics in the sender state, particularly domestic demands for action. The *New York Times* article is correct in saying that sanctions are used to make the public feel better. However, scholars argue that sanctions are driven by protectionist impulses and rarely work because they are used to supply domestic special interest groups with rent.

Both of these views are plausible. The brief sanctions against China following the Tiananmen Square violence certainly had no real economic bite nor did Beijing change any of its policies (Drury and Li 2004; Li and Drury 2004). The *New York Times*' interpretation of this episode would be that President Bush expressed America's outrage at the violent suppression of the pro-democracy movement but little else. The conventional scholarly wisdom would emphasize that the sanction effort was in response to lobbying by labor groups unhappy with Chinese competition (and use of prison laborers) and by industries suffering losses from intellectual property right violations. Economic coercion failed to achieve its objectives thanks to lobbying efforts by groups, such as Boeing, which were attempting to deliver products to China.

The problem with both interpretations is they are simply anecdotes. Neither the outrage nor the rent-seeking explanations are more than assertions. Those making these claims have not systematically studied why President Bush initiated the sanctions, and evidence can be marshaled in support of either assertion. Consequently, we do not know whether sanctions are used to "assuage America's outrage," respond to domestic lobbies, or actually coerce the target.

Although single case studies of economic sanctions provide important information, they lack generalizability. Previous quantitative studies of effectiveness typically have very poor ability to explain sanction effectiveness. I contend that this inability is the direct result of the literature's inattention to the reasons sanctions are used. Without a strong understanding of the reasons or goals, any study of sanctions would have difficulty explaining why a sanction could or could not attain those goals. This lack of attention to the conditions that lead to sanction use constitutes a gap in the general understanding of economic coercion and, more specifically, limits our ability to understand what makes economic sanctions work.

The goal of this book is to fill that gap in the understanding of economic sanctions by answering the question: What conditions lead the President of the United States to initiate and then modify an economic sanction? The first step toward this goal is to reassess the question of sanction effectiveness in order to highlight both the limitations of our understanding of sanction success and identify the reasons that sanctions are used. Once the reassessment has shown that the sanction literature's conventional wisdom is unable to explain accurately sanction effectiveness, the next logical step is to investigate the conditions that lead to sanction use. The remainder of this book is dedicated to that investigation.

Baldwin (1985) argues that most scholars do not accurately understand economic sanctions because they do not consider them a normal type of foreign policy. Instead, scholars portray them as economic issues, not foreign policy tools. Baldwin develops a typology of statecraft, or coercive diplomacy, to remedy this problem. The typology, he argues, is a continuum of options available to the decision-maker: propaganda, diplomatic, economic sanctions, and military sanctions (Baldwin 1985: 13–14).

Because many scholars have studied the decision to use military sanctions, and Baldwin effectively argues that economic sanctions are members of the same set of policy alternatives, the literature on the decision to use military force should shed light on the president's decision to use and alter economic sanctions. Therefore, to explain the conditions under which the U.S. president uses economic sanctions, I draw from three decision-making literatures: coercive diplomacy, domestic imperatives, and cognitive processes. Similar to conflict analysis, coercive diplomacy portrays sanctions as the result of dyadic relations. Domestic imperatives draw upon the diversionary theory of war to include domestic political considerations that affect the president's view of what is a feasible coercive diplomacy option. Furthermore, the domestic and dyadic conditions that lead the president to use economic sanctions are tempered by cognitive process—the idea that information, beliefs, and cognitive biases affect the president's decision-making capacity and ultimately the decisions themselves.

I single out the United States for study because it accounts for more than 68 percent of the sanctions since 1966 (Hufbauer et al. 1990a, 1990b). Although it is certainly important to understand the circumstances that lead other nations to use economic sanctions, the fact that the United States accounts for the large majority of sanctions and is currently using them with such great frequency suggests that understanding American sanctions alone is important. In fact, the United States has a special penchant for economic coercion that dates back to its founding. Alexander Hamilton held a strong belief that a nation's economy could and should be used not only to increase its power but also as a form of influence. Influenced by mercantilist ideas, Hamilton's belief that commerce was a weapon used to gain power had a critical impact on George Washington and, therefore, has become a key element of American foreign policy (Gilpin 1984; see also Gilbert 1961; Feis 1950).

More recent historical circumstances also explain the frequent use of economic coercion by the United States. Following the Cold War, there was a strong incentive to realize the "peace dividend" and yet the increase in ethnic violence increased the need to be able to coerce other nations. This incentive, coupled with a desire for nonviolent alternatives to the use of force, increased U.S. sanction efforts (van Bergeijk 1994). Further, as the United States seeks to expand its influence to combat terrorism and keep from overextending its capabilities, it will try to accomplish more with economic sanctions. The recent attempts to threaten China with sanctions for the proliferation of nuclear technology to Iran and to buy off North Korea suggest that understanding U.S. economic coercion in the coming decade will be a key element to understand U.S. foreign policy.

This study of the presidential use of economic sanctions also provides an interesting addition to the literature on the presidential use of coercive foreign policy measures. Most quantitative studies of presidential decisions to use coercion focus on military force. This analysis provides a look at coercive decision-making short of military force, allowing the two kinds of decisions to be compared. By comparing the differences between the decisions to use military and economic sanctions, we will understand each decision better as well as have a more complete picture of presidential foreign policy decision-making.

Plan of the Book

To assess the conventional wisdom regarding economic sanctions, I survey in chapter 2 the scholarship regarding economic sanction effectiveness and examine the reasoning given to explain their ineffectiveness. This analysis pays particular attention to how scholars have defined economic sanctions and how that definition affects their analyses. Many scholars do not include economic coercion used for foreign economic goals, such as sanctions aimed at opening the target's market or ending a domestic subsidy in the target state. I argue that these goals should be considered along with sanctions aimed at improving human rights, ending nuclear proliferation, and so on. Instead of excluding these sanction efforts a priori as many scholars do, they should be examined as part of the data to determine what differences exist between them and their more politically oriented relatives.

From this discussion, I derive an understanding of the conventional model of sanction effectiveness as well as a working definition of economic coercion. Chapter 3 goes further and evaluates empirically the conventional explanation of sanction success and failure. By revisiting the actual data along with the scholarship, I show that the current understanding of economic sanctions still contains considerable gaps. The data analysis only supports a handful of the conventional wisdom's claims, and it shows that the regime type of the target and sender and the involvement of international institutions—largely overlooked variables in the literature—have significant impacts on the success of economic coercion.

In chapter 4, I develop three models of political rationality to explain the president's decision to use and alter economic coercion. Beginning with international influences and drawing from theories of conflict, crisis, and coercive diplomacy, the first model explains presidential action as a function of relations with the potential target nation. There are three specific factors in this model of coercive diplomacy: (1) the magnitude of tension between the United States and the target, (2) the rate of escalation of the dispute, and (3) the level of provocation by the target. The first two factors are positively associated with the president's use of economic sanctions—greater tensions and escalation in the dispute lead the president to be more likely to employ a sanction. Provocation, however, acts as a deterrent to the president who sees the target's bellicose statements and actions as a sign that any sanctions deployed against it will be resisted at all costs. As a result, the president either backs down from the demand or steps up the level of coercion. In all, these factors should have a major influence on the president's decision to use economic sanctions.

Next, I develop a model of the domestic political incentives and constraints facing the president regarding a decision to use economic sanctions. Building on the scholarship from diversionary theory, public choice theory, and poliheuristic theory, I contend that the president's decision to initiate, increase, decrease, and lift economic sanctions is influenced by his popularity, the economy, electoral cycles, and his party affiliation. Each of the factors have different effects, depending on the decision before the president (initiate, lift, etc.). Although these factors will be less critical in the president's decision than factors in the coercive diplomacy model, they still show the impact politics has on the decision to use economic coercion.

The last section of chapter 4 adds limits to the president's decision-making ability by discussing the structure of his advisory system and the president's beliefs. I begin by arguing that the way the president organizes the information flow within the White House limits the options he considers or to which he is exposed. The advisory system's structure affects the decision to use a sanction by influencing the options open to the president—more formal systems are slower to deploy economic coercion. In addition to the advisory system, the president's operational code affects his decision-making. Presidents who view foreign relations as more conflictual will be increasingly likely to use economic sanctions quickly in a dispute. Like the domestic factors, these cognitive constraints have more of an impact at the margin. Essentially, there must be some dispute with the target before these factors can come into play. If no dispute with another nation exists, the president does not seek out a nation to target with economic coercion. The significance of this point is that domestic politics and cognitive constraints do not create disputes; however, they do influence the president's decisions if the United States is in a dispute with another nation.

The empirical analysis begins in chapter 5 by delineating the hypotheses that explain the president's decision to initiate economic sanctions against another country. I then turn to a discussion of the data. By using both the World Event Interaction Survey and Integrated Data for Events Analysis databases, I create two separate time series cross-section data sets—one from 1966–1992 and the second ranging from 1991–2000 (merging these data is not a viable option). The data encompass 28 nations that were sanctioned by the United States at some point in the 35-year time series and another 22 randomly selected nations that were never sanctioned. I then begin with the analysis of the president's decision to initiate a sanction policy against the target.[2]

The results show that international factors play the largest role in the White House's choice to deploy economic coercion during both the Cold War and the post–Cold War periods. Tension between the United States and target increase the likelihood that sanctions will be deployed, but extremely provocative targets deter the White House from acting. Domestic politics and cognitive constraints are also shown to have a significant impact in the midst of a dispute, although the effect is rather small. Presidential approval and economic performance have some influence on the decision, but only at the margins. The trade relationship with the target becomes important, but mostly for sanctions aimed at foreign economic goals. Sanctions directed at political goals are more the result of international pressures, while sanctions aimed at foreign economic goals are influenced more by domestic imperatives. The discussion of the results includes not only estimated probabilities and marginal effects from the model but also brief illustrative case discussions.

In chapter 6, I expand the analysis further by assessing whether or not a bias exists when a president chooses a nation to sanction. Although disputes are required before sanctions are considered, I test to see if the president is more likely to sanction one type of nation versus another. The United States sanctions Latin America more during the Cold War and democracies less after the Cold War, even after controlling for the dispute.

Once sanctions are in place, the president can increase, decrease, or lift the coercive policy. Modifying the initiate model slightly in chapter 7, I assess the decision to modify an economic sanction with ordered logit estimation. The results show that domestic political factors become significantly less important once sanctions are in place. Given that the American public pays little attention to foreign affairs, a continuing sanction policy is very unlikely to garner any coverage, and therefore, the president is unlikely to consider domestic concerns when deciding to modify a sanction policy. However, cognitive constraints in the form of the president's information preferences influence the decision to alter the sanction policy. Illustrative cases highlight the results.

Lastly, I return to the question of domestic politics and sanction choice in chapter 8. Using prospect theory, I show that some aspects of sanctioning are influenced by domestic political considerations. The severity of the sanction deployed is determined partly by the president's domestic strength. The timing and manner in which sanctions are lifted is also affected by politics. Presidents pay closer attention to party affiliation when removing a failing sanction policy.

Overall, the analysis in this book establishes that the current understanding of economic sanctions is significantly limited by its narrow focus on effectiveness. It then attempts to create a more complete picture of the role of economic sanctions. In addition to economic coercion, the book also sheds light on presidential foreign policy-making in an understudied area—the employment of coercion short of military force. The conclusion in chapter 9 of this argument covers four themes. First, I review the analysis of the president's decisions to levy and then alter economic sanctions against a target. Second, I discuss the differences between foreign policy and foreign economic policy sanctions. Next, I contrast the sanction decisions made during the Cold War with those made after it. Fourth, I discuss the implications for our understanding of economic coercion and foreign policy analysis.

Chapter 2
Economic Coercion in Theory and Practice

Defining Economic Coercion

Before turning to the task of defining what constitutes an economic sanction, I first indicate what is *not* an economic sanction by contrasting economic coercion with economic incentives. I then turn to a discussion of the instruments and then goals of economic coercion.

Economic Incentives

Some scholars have argued for the importance of incentives or inducements as "positive" sanctions. These payments can include preferential trade agreements, aid, or loans (Baldwin 1985; Crumm 1995; Newnham 2000). There is no doubt that these foreign policy tools are important in influencing potential targets. Alexander George (1991) points out that coercive diplomacy is most effective when both carrots and sticks are used on the target state. George Kennen's original concept of containment at the start of the Cold War was based on just that idea—that both carrots and sticks should be used on the Soviets to moderate their behavior. The logic is that targets face punishment if they do not alter their policy, but they also will gain some tangible benefit or reward once they do acquiesce. In addition to the obvious tangible benefits, the target can claim it did not back down but simply exchanged its policy preference for the incentive. To its domestic population, the target regime can also spin the incentive as a sign it actually coerced or tricked the incentive out of the sender. For example, prior to the Suez Crisis, Nasser was able to acquire significant aid from both the Soviets and Americans by vacillating between the two superpowers. While Eisenhower may have thought he was buying allegiance, Nasser thought (correctly) that he was swindling the United States.

Several scholars have shown that economic incentives tend to be more effective than economic coercion. Randall Newnham shows that incentives were more productive for West Germany during the Cold War. Specifically, it was able to get more concessions from East Germany by offering incentives (Newnham 2000). Eileen Crumm (1995) argues that negative sanctions often have problems with implementation, especially in market economies, which make incentives more attractive. She asserts that non-replaceable, nondurable goods offer the best, most effective source of incentives. However, as she points out, negative sanctions require a more difficult implementation that must affect the decision to deploy them. That is, incentives can be simply transferred, while sanctions must be monitored and enforced. These higher implementation costs make incentives quite different in the decision-making process that leads to them. Thus, incentives differ both in how they work and how they are implemented relative to sanctions.

Jason Davidson and George Shambaugh (2000) show theoretically that incentives should be more effective than sanctions on opponents because economic relations between two opponents are usually not very strong, subsequently making the impact of the incentive greater. Allies, on the other hand, would react more to sanctions since they already have strong trade ties with the sender and would prefer to keep those benefits. The problem with using incentives on opponents and sanctions on friends is the political costs associated with each. Offering an economic inducement to an opponent may send a signal of weakness to the international community. It may also invite blackmail attempts.

For example, the 1994 Agreed Framework that supplied North Korea with heating oil and the promise to build a light water reactor in return for Pyongyang's promise to end its nuclear program failed miserably. North Korea violated the agreement by 1999 by demanding more payments with the threat that they would restart their nuclear weapons program. This logic is akin to a protection racket where people must pay criminals to keep them from attacking. To be blunt, Pyongyang was running the protection racket against the United States and its allies. Newnham (2004) argues that the Agreed Framework worked because the payments delayed the North Korean nuclear program. Since this was obviously not the purpose of the Agreed Framework, the conclusion is wrong. Instead, the DPRK was trying to extort more money from the United States, South Korea, and Japan (the primary states involved in the Agreed Framework). Not only did Pyongyang initially demand more payments, but it scrapped the entire agreement in 2002 by restarting its reactor in Yongbyon to process fissile material.

Costs are also associated with sanctioning friends or allies. Since future relations with friendly states have significant benefits, threatening those benefits with sanctions can be costly. The issue under dispute between two allied states must clearly be important enough to jeopardize the future benefits of the relationship. If not, as is most often the case with allies, the sender will prefer less hostile actions such as incentives rather than risk a more serious conflict with an ally. Thus, incentives are not commonly offered to adversaries, and sanctions against allies are rare (Davidson and Shambaugh 2000).

Like Davidson and Shambaugh, Daniel W. Drezner (1999/2000) makes the case that adversaries will be much more likely to use coercion rather than incentives, but he makes a different argument for why incentives are rarely used. He asserts that economic inducements entail significant transaction costs and are, therefore, not a commonly deployed foreign policy tool. These costs include monitoring the target state's compliance with the quid pro quo attached to the payment, whether the target is actually in control of the outcome, or any potential situation that would allow the target to cheat.[1] Even though these costs can be mitigated by international institutions and democratic regimes, Drezner states that "[e]ven in cases where the two states have harmonious relations, senders may prefer using economic or military coercion instead of inducements as a method of extracting concessions, because it is more cost-effective" (190–191). The result is "[t]he transactions costs posed by partially observable actions and unenforceable agreements prevent a full-fledged international market for political concession from developing" (194). Further, because incentives cost the sender when they succeed while sanctions only cost the sender when they fail, leaders will prefer coercion over inducements if they believe they have a chance of succeeding.

Both Drezner and Davidson and Shambaugh point to the potential uses of carrots, but they also raise a question about the factors that influence a leader's decision to use them. The potential costs associated with incentives (reputation, monitoring compliance, etc.) are not the same for economic coercion. Although a target can cheat during a sanction episode and claim it has fulfilled the sender's demand, the sender can maintain the pressure for as long as it sees fit rather than make a payment to the target and hope for the best. Of course, sanctions require monitoring firms and third-party states doing business with the target. The point is that those costs are different.

More importantly, sanctions do not have the same appearance of weakness that an incentive might, and they certainly do not provide the target state with the ability to extort payments from the sender. It is not that incentives are useless or cannot be used in conjunction with economic coercion. Instead, it is important to see that these are distinctly different policy options and therefore not the same as sanctions.

Instruments of Economic Coercion

To understand what does constitute an economic sanction, one must consider both the means and the ends or goals of the coercive policy. There is no real debate over what instruments can be included as an economic sanction. However, these means do vary considerably and are worth discussing in some detail. Sanction tools can include restrictions or cessation of imports from the target or exports to the target. Examples of these common trade restrictions include the initial quota on sugar imports from Cuba following the communist revolution and Castro's rise to power. President Eisenhower set in place by executive order what has become one of America's longest sanction policies. Rapidly following the sugar quota, more harsh and complete bans on all forms of trade were initiated creating a complete U.S. embargo of Cuba (Schreiber 1973; Losman 1979; Doxey 1980; Hufbauer et al. 1990b). Other examples include Indonesia's "Crush Malaysia" campaign from 1963–1966 and President Carter's sanctioning grain sales (exports) to the Soviet Union following their invasion of Afghanistan (Hufbauer et al. 1990a, 1990b).

Financial sanction tools include the freezing of assets, denial of loan rescheduling or guarantees, the limiting or cutting off of military or developmental aid, as well as pressure on banks and international financial organizations to deny loans and debt relief (Olson 1979a; Hufbauer et al. 1990a). This type of economic pressure is more varied than trade sanctions. For instance, the United States froze $12 billion of Iran's assets after Iranian students stormed the U.S. embassy in Teheran and took hostages (Hufbauer et al. 1990a). In another example, the Eisenhower administration blocked a World Bank loan to Egypt for the construction of the Aswan High dam because Cairo purchased Soviet weapons through Czechoslovakia. The sanctions were one of the sparks that led Nasser to nationalize the Suez Canal, a move that started the

Suez Crisis. Similarly, Richard Stuart Olson shows that the Nixon administration covertly blocked several attempts by Allende's Chilean government to reschedule or defer loans. These sanctions, combined with a covert campaign to destabilize Allende's government, made it impossible for him to govern the country (Olson 1979). In addition to the covert actions, Nixon also suspended nonmilitary aid to Chile—yet another type of economic coercion.

Other examples of aid sanctions include the terminating of aid to countries supporting international terrorism.[2] While this type of aid sanction seemingly occurs automatically when the target state fails to meet some requirement set out by legislation, the mechanism that determines whether the target meets or fails to meet the criterion is the State Department. As part of the executive branch and led by a politically appointed secretary, the certification process is far from automatic. In 1997, the United States decertified Colombia for failing to effectively fight the war on drugs but certified Mexico. That same year, however, the top Mexican antidrug official was arrested for being on the payroll of a Mexican drug lord. Clearly, the United States felt it could not punish Mexico for its transgressions but did not have the same inhibitions about Colombia. Thus, in practice, these automatic aid sanctions involve the same decision process as other sanctions. In all, these financial sanctions are meant to harm the target's economy, the same purpose as the trade sanctions discussed above.

Travel bans on the target's leadership or general population are also considered a form of economic coercion. An example of this type of sanction is the restriction put on the Haitian military junta that first deposed Jean Bertrand Aristide. In a policy that seemed to be inspired by the Greek comedy Lysistrata, not only were the junta members not permitted to visit the United States, but their spouses were also included in the ban.[3] Clearly, the hope was that the wives would pressure their husbands since their ability to vacation and shop in the United States had been curtailed.[4] The vacationing and shopping of a few elite members of the target state could certainly be interpreted as more a symbolic or diplomatic sanction than an economic one. However, these bans put direct economic pain on the ruling elite. Although the Haitian ban limited the access to luxury items, it was still economic pressure and therefore should be considered a sanction. Other travel bans have a more tangible economic impact. For example, the ban on direct flights to Cuba from the United States clearly decreases the tourism and a potential source of significant economic activity for the island.

Each of these economic tools can be the instrument for an economic sanction. These means are not controversial within the literature. However, the ends or goal at which a specific sanction aims is far more debated and is the key to defining economic coercion.

Goals of Economic Coercion

Economic Warfare

The first goal of economic statecraft that must be considered is what scholars commonly refer to as economic warfare (Baldwin 1985; Hufbauer et al. 1990a; Naylor 2001). Economic warfare is when the sender state initiates some kind of economic sanction against the target for the purpose of weakening its capabilities prior to a conflict. Examples include "trading with the enemy" laws, by which the government controls economic relations with an enemy and its allies, and the British sanctions against Germany in 1914. In the 1914 case, Great Britain restricted and then blockaded shipping to Germany as part of the war effort. As both these examples show, the idea is not to coerce the target, but to weaken it.

Not all scholars agree with this classification. Margaret Doxey (1980: 9; see also 1971, 1987) asserts that sanctions outside of an international organization constitute economic warfare. Conversely, R. T. Naylor (2001) argues that there is no difference between economic sanctions and economic warfare because they both place significant human costs on the sender and the target, regardless of their purpose or goal. These definitions are too restrictive for an analysis of sanction effectiveness and decisions. Economic sanctions are a type of coercive diplomacy; they are economic pressure that seeks to alter or deter some policy of the target state. Therefore, economic pressure that aims simply to weaken the target prior to military hostilities has no coercive properties. Instead, it is akin to using bombing to soften a target prior to invasion.

Economic warfare should not be confused with an arms embargo that attempts to limit the capabilities of one or more combatants in hopes of leading to a ceasefire and peaceful resolution to the conflict. This type of arms embargo, such as the one placed on Yugoslavia during the Bosnian conflict, does not seek to limit the target's abilities to gain the upper hand in a future conflict. Instead, it attempts to drive the party or parties to negotiate a settlement.

Economic versus Political Goals

Thus far, I have defined economic coercion as some form of negative economic pressure that the sender uses to coerce the target into either altering its policy or deterring the target from changing its policy. It includes neither negative economic pressure used to weaken the target prior to military hostilities nor positive economic incentives. One final distinction is the actual policy the sender wishes to alter. That is, does the sender seek to alter one of the target's foreign economic policies, such as a trade barrier or subsidy, or is the sender aiming at a more purely political goal? Most studies of economic sanctions only consider political goals but not economic ones, at least on the surface.

At first blush, this distinction makes sense. One can certainly see why day-to-day trade negotiations that include threats to increase tariffs and the like are not economic sanctions. What the U.S. trade delegation says during WTO meetings hardly seems to rise to the level of a sanction. While they are attempts to pressure a target to alter one of its policies, these actions are more a strategy of negotiation than a sanction. In the U.S. case, the president does not have the resources to be involved in such common trade negotiations. While presidential involvement does not define a sanction, it does indicate that these actions are simply part of a general strategy taken by bureaucrats in the different economic related departments such as Commerce or the U.S. Trade Representative's Office.

Closer inspection reveals there are problems with the application of this logic. Hufbauer et al. (1990a, 1990b) include cases of expropriation and even specific product pricing in their economic sanction data. These are not issues concerning U.S. government property being taken by the host country but the property of private American firms. Therefore, including expropriation disputes with other political issues but not other economic disputes is contradictory. While expropriation can be seen by the sender as an issue of theft, and therefore not a purely economic issue but a criminal one, at a minimum it constitutes a grey area. Even more contradictory is the inclusion of the U.S. sanctions against Chile in 1965 that attempted to force Santiago to lower its copper price by $0.02 and resist future increases. It seems very clear that the U.S. attempt to control copper prices is a foreign economic policy, not a political one. While one could argue that the Hufbauer et al. data are only one study, most quantitative research on sanctions uses their data. Therefore, these cases are included in more than simply one analysis.

These contradictions are one of Robert Pape's (1997) main contentions with the sanction literature, particularly the studies by Hufbauer et al. Pape takes an even stronger stand against the inclusion of these economic goals. He argues that the demands associated with trade issues are much less intense compared to those associated with political issues. As a result, the likelihood that the sanctions will succeed in a foreign economic goal is much greater.[5] Marcus Noland (1997) offers another potential difference between economic and politically oriented coercion—the difference is that trade is an ongoing relationship that can be and usually is regularly negotiated, while political issues are not so much a relationship as a policy or policy change within the target. Thus, the tariffs and trade balance provide perfect information and gradual changes. Political issues can literally change overnight and with no information. More importantly, the target decides whether or not to concede to an economic demand based on economic utility, while it decides political demands based on a calculus that includes political costs. Further, the difference in intensity of demands may also influence the sender's decision to use sanctions and what type to deploy. In the United States, the president tries to satisfy domestic industries when sanctioning over trade disputes, but in politically oriented sanctions, the president seeks to limit the anger of those firms. Therefore, the decision calculus may be very different.

So should economic goals be excluded from the definition of economic sanctions? Daniel Drezner (2001) says no. He refutes Pape's claim that the intensity of economic and political issues is significantly different by pointing to Congress's expanded definition of labor regulation to include human rights as an example of the blurring between economic (labor regulation) and political (human rights) issues. The inability to untangle these issues weakens the argument that they should be kept separate. Additionally, the target will perceive that "altering any domestic laws helps create a system amendable to the growth of domestic interests sympathetic to the sender" (Drezner 2001: 387). Thus, the target could interpret any demand, be it economic or political, to have important political consequences.

For example, in 1978, the United States sanctioned Canada under Section 301 auspices because Ottawa was denying U.S. broadcasters tax deductions (Bayard and Elliott 1994: 394–395). Although the issue could be interpreted as purely economic, that view is shortsighted. The Canadians see U.S. broadcasting as nearly hegemonic. If Ottawa does not protect its native industry, it may cease to exist. This failure of Canadian broadcasting could limit Canadian cultural and news outlets and possibly weaken support for the government because of a lack of Canadian presence in the airwaves. While these outcomes are clearly at the extreme end of possibility, they illustrate the political nature of seemingly nonpolitical issues. Even if Canadian broadcasting did not vanish, there is the perception that there would be a loss of culture—an issue that is clearly political and not simply economic.

Although some issues certainly have higher importance or intensity than others (e.g., territory is more important to a state than an agricultural subsidy), the point is that economic issues have political costs and consequences that cannot be easily separated from each other. Klaus Knorr also points out that economic goals, such as opening markets, affects the sender's future ability to coerce the target. That is, as trade between two countries increases (especially if it asymmetrically benefits the sender), so does the opportunity for economic coercion.

Drezner goes on to argue forcefully that sanction effectiveness theories are designed such that they can explain economic coercion with political or economic goals. By including economic goals in the definition of an economic sanction, we expand our understanding of coercive diplomacy. Too narrow a focus runs the risk of not adding to the knowledge base. "Theories of economic coercion have the potential to explain a wide variety of coercive bargaining situations in international relations. Sanctions scholars should be willing to see whether their mid-range theories can be used to inform grander theories of politics" (Drezner 2001: 381). Thus, Drezner and Knorr accurately show that any decision by the target concerning a sanction aimed at altering its economic policy has political consequences for its foreign relations. Therefore, I include both foreign economic goals and political goals as part of the definition of an economic sanction.

Two additional points must be considered regarding foreign economic goals. First, while too narrow a focus limits our understanding of economic statecraft, too wide a focus has drawbacks as well. As mentioned above, day-to-day trade bargaining may have coercive elements, but it is a routine aspect of diplomacy. Including routine behavior adds too much noise to a theory of foreign policy behavior. Economic sanctions are discrete foreign policy actions that involve more than mid-level bureaucrats in the decision process. Therefore, only nonroutine cases are defined as an economic sanction.

Second, even though sanction effectiveness and decision theories should apply to both economic and political goals, it is possible that the two are different enough that models estimating these theories would diverge across these two types of goals. The president may initiate sanctions aimed an economic goal when the dispute with the target is at a much lower level of intensity than when political issues are at stake. This issue is an empirical one, however, and will be addressed later in the book.

The preceding discussion provides the framework for the definition of an economic sanction. *Economic coercion is defined as the use of an economic instrument to cause a target nation some harm or economic loss with the purpose of coercing the target to cease, reverse, or not adopt some policy.* These policies include both political and economic issues. This coercive attempt does not include routine bargaining, negotiation, or compromise. While this definition is not completely shared by the extant scholarship on the effectiveness of sanctions, it is more encompassing so that it provides more to our understanding of economic coercion. I now turn to that extant scholarship.

The Question of Success or Failure

The literature on economic sanctions tends to agree quite strongly on a conventional wisdom of the effectiveness of economic coercion. Although there are certainly plenty of minor deviations and disagreements within this literature, there is general agreement over the big issues. This conventional wisdom takes the form of a focus, an assumption, and two conclusions.

First, there is a very strong tendency by scholars to study the effectiveness of economic sanctions, while only alluding to the reasons or the conditions under which they are used. These scholars may or may not agree with the conventional wisdom's assumptions, but regardless, they either do not focus on the decision-making process at all, or they merely suggest that sanctions have diverse goals and proceed to evaluate their effectiveness without further specification. Of course, scholars are not so single-minded as to never discuss or contemplate the decision-making process leading to economic coercion. However, the only studies that systematically explore the decision to use economic sanctions take a decidedly economic approach, slighting the politics involved in the decision.

Second, as a consequence of the focus on effectiveness and lack of attention to the reasons or conditions sanctions are used, the conventional wisdom assumes that economic sanctions aim solely to change a policy or policies in the target nation. Some scholars do raise the possibility that sanctions have goals other than simply coercing the target, for example, setting an international precedent or reinforcing an international norm. However, less than a handful of studies have included these nontarget related goals in their analysis of sanction effectiveness.

Third, almost all studies of economic coercion argue and show empirically that more severe sanctions (those causing greater economic damage to the target) are more likely to succeed in getting the target to alter the policy that the sender found objectionable. While this is certainly not the only finding in the sanctions literature, it is one common to almost all studies. It is also a logical consequence of the accepted definition of economic sanctions: economic *pressure* to coerce the target.

Fourth, the overwhelming conclusion of these analyses is that economic sanctions tend to fail in coercing the target nation. This conclusion leads to a consideration of the potential reasons that sanctions are used nonetheless, in an effort to explain their common use and typical failure. The common explanation is that sanctions fail because the sender initiates them for domestic political reasons. This so called do something hypothesis suggests that leaders facing domestic pressures to do something about the target's actions or policies use sanctions to placate their public while never expecting the economic coercion to succeed. A variant of this conclusion is that sanctions are used for domestic economic reasons—to placate not the public but rent-seeking firms.

Examples of the Conventional Wisdom

Margaret Doxey's scholarship helps form the core of the mainstream sanction research. She defines economic sanctions as economic measures levied by "a constitutionally authorized" international body seeking to compel the target nation to alter its policies so they no longer conflict with international norms. Economic measures imposed by single nations are considered economic warfare or coercion (Doxey 1980: 9; see also 1971, 1987). Although this definition is far more limiting than that found in other sanction scholarship, she still sees the purpose of these efforts as getting the target to change a given policy. This definition of an economic sanction leads Doxey to explore the problems of cooperation among sender nations. In particular, she investigates issues of goal-setting, selection of measures and the costs they inflict on the sender nations, scope of the sanctions, and sanction maintenance.

All of this analysis is driven by the question of whether sanctions work or not. Doxey argues that the effects of economic damage done to a target nation are conditioned primarily by the goals they intend to achieve (Doxey 1980: 125). In making this argument, she then points out the limited power economic sanctions often have. Throughout her analyses of different cases, she asserts that if economic sanctions are going to be effective, they must put tremendous pressure on the target (77–79). So even while sanctions may be functionally limited, they become more effective as they visit more economic pain on the target nation.

While she concerns herself almost completely with effectiveness, Doxey does allude to why nations resort to economic coercion. For example, she points out that during the 1980 presidential campaign, Ronald Reagan promised grain farmers that he would lift President Carter's grain embargo against the Soviets (Doxey 1987: 101). As President Reagan's famous reference to the Soviet Union as the "Evil Empire" indicates, he was vehemently opposed to the Soviets. Clearly, the campaign promise was also made to placate the farmers and win their votes. Thus, Doxey suggests that economic sanctions may fail because they are aimed at sending messages to the domestic populace rather than influencing the target. Unfortunately, Doxey takes this discussion no further; instead, she limits her analysis to effectiveness.

In *Economic Sanctions Reconsidered*, Hufbauer et al. (1990a) also contribute to the core research on economic sanctions. Solely focusing on effectiveness, they show that sanctions are effective in getting the target to alter its policy approximately 33 percent of the time. They deduce several policy recommendations and produce the most commonly used data set of economic sanctions. These data are the most comprehensive set of cases available. While not uncontroversial, their wide use makes them very influential in the study of economic coercion.

Using the Hufbauer et al. data, T. Clifton Morgan and Valerie Schwebach (1997) slightly alter the effectiveness question by asking *when* sanctions will work, instead of *if* they will work. They use the cost of the sanctions to both the target and the sender to test sanction effectiveness. Their findings show that sanctions are rarely successful, but that there are two conditions that lead to sanction effectiveness. First, high costs to the target increase success.[6] Second, high costs to the sender decrease effectiveness. Morgan and Schwebach (1997: 47) conclude that sanctions are so often ineffective because the conditions for their success are so stringent. However, they only specify the cost calculus to sender and target without surveying the possible conditions that can influence the cost ratios for sender and target and determine sanction effectiveness.

Noting that the conventional wisdom asserts that the more damaging sanctions are, the more effective they will be, Morgan and Schwebach (1996: 248) develop a more closely specified model that abandons the state level of analysis and looks at that portion of the target's domestic population affected by the sanctions (Morgan 1995: 25). Their model contends that the more economic pain that is inflicted on the target's ruling coalition, the more likely the sanctions are to succeed. This same model holds for the sender nation as well. The more the sanctions cost a powerful domestic group (e.g., a particular industry), the more likely the sender will end the sanctioning effort. However, if the costs of the sanctions are diffuse, then the sender may maintain and the target may resist the sanctions for longer (Morgan and Schwebach 1996: 253). While these two authors propose that domestic influences on the decision to use sanctions will vary with each case, they do not develop this proposal further, nor do they analyze it. Instead, they analyze the effectiveness of sanctions aimed at Latin American nations (Morgan and Schwebach 1996) and sanctions aimed at China (Morgan 1995).

In his study of the sanctions against Rhodesia, Johann Galtung (1967) takes exception to the idea that increased economic pressure is associated with more successful coercion. He argues that economic sanctions against a nation actually produce political integration within it because the population perceives the sanctions as foreign meddling in their domestic affairs. Galtung specifies three conditions that tend to favor increased political integration instead of disintegration: (1) when the sanctions are seen as aimed at the whole population, not just the ruling coalition, (2) when the population tends to have negative feelings toward the sender prior to the sanctions, and (3) when the population believes their country is right, and there are no better alternatives to the ones they currently follow. These three conditions should enhance the political integration within the target country and help it resist the sanctions.

In a direct response to Galtung's (1967) argument, Green (1983) argues that political integration is not a sufficient condition for evading economic sanctions. He criticizes Galtung for ignoring the possible leaks within the international system that a target country such as Rhodesia could use to its advantage.[7] Green's criticism of Galtung is typical of the conventional wisdom. He argues that without a leak, a nation cannot survive the pressure of economic sanctions. Therefore, complete trade cessation must correspond to effectiveness, and thus, increasing levels of sanction severity must also lead to success. Galtung's view is, of course, not consistent with the conventional wisdom because he suggests that increased severity may lead to increased political integration and thus, sanction failure. Neither scholar really addresses why the sanctions are put in place. They both simply assume that (1) the sender is attempting to change the target's policy in some way, and (2) only the economic components of the sanctions will affect the target.

In a refinement and defense of Galtung's argument, Eland (1995) argues that the target government's control of information will dramatically affect whether Galtung's effect will occur. That is, if the target government controls what the people know about the sanctions, there is a greater probability that they will rally behind their government. Additionally, any opposition a regime may have will be unable to be heard because of the government's control of information. He further argues that while total sanctions may cause an increase in political integration within the target, minimal or selective sanctions may have the opposite effect. This effect holds because the opposition will not ally itself with the government for economic survival (Eland 1995: 35; see also Wallensteen et al. 2004).

Richard Stuart Olson takes a very different approach to studying the effectiveness of economic coercion. Instead of analyzing direct or overt economic pressure, he assesses the impact of what he calls covert economic sanctions (see 1975, 1977, 1979a, 1979b). These sanctions are defined as efforts by the sender to destabilize the target by cutting aid, loans, loan guarantees, and so on. Olson's argument asserts that this type of sanction is more successful than overt types. He shows that if the target nation's population does not know that sanctions are being applied, there will not be an increase in political integration (Galtung 1967). Olson's cases, and the thrust of his argument, focus on nations in Latin America. He shows that the United States denied loans, loan rescheduling, and so on, to Brazil, Ceylon, Chile, and Peru. The result in each case was increased political disintegration. None of the targets knew or could prove the United States was denying them access to funds in order to destabilize their government. Thus, the leaders could not blame the United States for foreign meddling and were unable to secure political integration.

Consistent with the conventional wisdom, Olson suggests that even overt sanctions must be more economically damaging to be effective. He also suggests that there are domestic political reasons for using economic sanctions. In fact, he proposes that because overt sanctions tend to fail, they are probably domestically driven. Others are even more pessimistic about the prospects for success. Philip Levy (1999) argues that the sanctions against apartheid South Africa, often cited as a success, were, in fact, failures. Market distortions caused by the labor system, constant pressure from the opposition, and a realization that compromise with the African National Congress would not result in the conversion to a communist system were responsible for the downfall of the apartheid regime. Robert Pape extends this critical assessment by arguing that almost all of Hufbauer et al.'s sanction cases are failures. Pape (1997, 1998a, 1998b), who puts sanction success at around 5 percent instead of 33 percent, argues that most successes were not the result of the economic coercion but of military action or the threat of military action. As a result, he argues that sanctions are a miserable failure.

Modifications to the Conventional Wisdom

Peter Wallensteen (1968) takes a slightly different approach to the study of economic coercion. Instead of assuming sanctions seek to influence the target, he argues that most nations enact sanctions as a way of expressing disapproval of the target nation's actions. Wallensteen derives this conclusion from a content analysis of the sender nation's stated reasons for enacting the sanctions. He finds that most reasons contain emotive terms, such as outrage, and argues that they are expressive and not instrumental in nature. The balance of Wallensteen's analysis is devoted to understanding sanction effectiveness. He argues that sanctions are quite effective at expressing the sender's rejection of the target (Wallensteen 1968: 265). However, he asserts that they are almost completely useless as tools aimed to change target policies. In his evaluation of sanction effectiveness, therefore, Wallensteen supports the conventional wisdom. Although he rejects the idea that sanctions are only used to change target policy, he does not consider the possibility of domestically driven sanctions for instrumental goals.

Robin Renwick also suggests that sanctions can have goals unrelated to the target: "A decision to impose sanctions may be taken less on its intrinsic merits than because of its attractions in relation to the alternatives" (1981: 1). Thus, sanctions become a way for a nation to do something without resorting to more extreme actions. This conception of why sanctions may be imposed is essentially based on the idea that the sanctioning government is taking action to placate either its domestic population or various international actors. The first possible reason alters the goal of the sanction from one of changing the target's policies to satisfying the public's demand for action. The second possible reason shifts the sanction's goal from affecting the target to sending a message to international actors. These international actors could be allies whom the sender wanted to reassure, or opponents whom the sender wanted to deter. In either case, Renwick discusses these possible goals as reasons sanctions tend to fail. That is, because the goal of the sanction is not a change in the target's policies but a symbolic message, they are never expected to cause the target to change its policies. When the sanctions are evaluated on the grounds of policy change, they are seen (incorrectly) as abject failures. Renwick further points out that a sanction may just be punitive. That is, the sender may not expect the sanctions to force the target to change its policies, but instead, it may only want to punish the target. Kim Richard Nossal (1989) and David Deese also suggest that economic sanctions may be punitive; that their purpose is ". . . to punish, discredit, or embarrass" (1983: 156).

Schwebach (2000) also emphasizes the expressive or symbolic nature of economic coercion. She argues that the symbolic nature has an instrumental value—it can signal the target of the sender's resolve. However, clear signals require that the "sanctions are too costly relative to the issue at stake for irresolute actors to employ them, and . . . the target is predisposed to believe that only resolute actors engage in sanctions" (2000: 203). Most sanctions are "muddy" signals, ones that may or may not indicate a resolute actor. As a consequence, most sanctions fail. Either the target resists an irresolute sender that lifts the sanctions or a resolute one that maintains the coercion. The outcome of the latter case is an enduring sanction episode such as the U.S.–Cuba sanctions.[8]

In his study of sanction effectiveness, James Barber also expands the possible goals sanctions may be used to attain by creating a tripartite typology for the different goals: (1) primary—goals aimed at altering the target's policies, (2) secondary—goals aimed at the sender's domestic "behavior and expectations," and (3) tertiary—goals aimed at affecting the international system (1979: 370–373). This typology is an important conceptual advancement in the sanction literature, but Barber does not back it up with empirical testing because of the difficulty in determining and evaluating secondary and tertiary goals. For example, evaluating the success of a tertiary objective may require determining whether an international norm has been upheld and internalized by one or more nations—a next to impossible task (382). He argues further that just because primary objectives tend to fail, it does not mean that secondary objectives will (381).

Barber concludes that sanctions are used for a variety of reasons. Because a better and more rigorous understanding of secondary and tertiary objectives has not been developed, scholars evaluate sanctions on their primary goals. This emphasis on primary goals leads to the conventional wisdom's assumption that increased pressure should increase effectiveness. On these grounds Barber and a large number of other scholars see sanctions as essentially failures. Thus, it seems as though his argument suggests that the conventional wisdom is partly derived from necessity. That is, it emphasizes policy oriented goals partly because they are the only goals that can be evaluated and understood.

James Lindsay (1986) analyzes sanction effectiveness, but instead of examining only policy change in the target, he looks for changes specific to the sanction's goal. That is, if the sanctioning effort was attempting to create a rally effect in the sender nation, then he looks for a rally effect—not a change in the target's policies. Lindsay (1986: 155–156) identifies five goals sanctions may have: compliance, subversion, deterrence, international symbolism, and domestic symbolism. Each sanctioning episode has one or more of these goals. Lindsay identifies the goals of 19 different sanctioning episodes and proceeds to analyze their effectiveness for those goals. He finds that sanctions aimed at compliance, deterrence, and subversion are rarely effective. Economic coercion aimed at international and domestic symbolism tends to fare better. This finding does not reveal that sanctions are often effective for symbolic reasons, only that they tend to be effective more often than sanctions aimed at producing a change in the target's policies.

Lindsay identified the different goals by examining the publicly stated reasons, as well as case studies and memoirs; ". . . only the goals that officials consciously articulated as objectives were taken, though where information about the decision was scarce, these goals were imputed" (156–157). While this procedure seems to be quite rigorous, there are problems with it when determining domestic goals. It is unlikely that Eisenhower consciously attempted to increase his approval when he sanctioned Cuba. Yet Lindsay (167) identifies one of the Cuban sanction goals as just that: an attempt to bolster the president's approval. Thus, using case studies, it seems very difficult to systematically determine if the sender was attempting to use the sanctions for domestic symbolism.

Turning to the question of why sanctions fail, William Kaempfer and Anton Lowenberg are the strongest proponents of the idea that domestic political conditions in the sender are to blame. They use public choice analysis to explore the relationship between conditions in the sender's domestic arena and the decision to use economic sanctions. Kaempfer and Lowenberg (1992) make the case that interest groups within the sender nation will influence not only whether sanctions are used but also what kinds are used. Specifically, firms seeking protection from foreign competitors will pressure leaders to economically coerce those states. Thus, sanctions become protectionist trade barriers. This effect is most powerful in legislatively enacted sanctions, although executives are not completely immune from this interest group pressure. Their insightful analysis fleshes out the "do something" domestic politics explanation for sanction failure, but it is still incomplete because it looks only at the economic conditions that affect the decision to sanction. While the domestic economics and politics of sanctions are intertwined, there are political motives for the decisionmaker unrelated to economic benefits for the domestic constituents.

An example may be helpful. The U.S. sanctions against Cuba have been in place since 1960. Although the economic impact to U.S. businesses was costly in the 1960s, trade with Cuba has been virtually nonexistent for more than four decades. Sanctions against Cuba have become the status quo in the United States. While U.S. businesses are not suffering any direct monetary losses, they are suffering a loss of economic opportunity. On the other hand, American politicians are gaining electoral advantage, especially from politically active Cuban expatriate populations in Florida and New Jersey, by supporting the continuation of the economic sanctions. It is this strictly political argument that explains the sanction's maintenance. Because Kaempfer and Lowenberg's model only considers the economic benefits the sender may gain or lose, it cannot explain why these sanctions are maintained. Thus, while trying to address the political aspects of economic sanctions, the authors only scratch the surface of the domestic imperatives that influence the decision to sanction.

Simon (1996) and Smith (1996) partly remedy this problem by including domestic political benefits in their respective analyses.

Simon attempts to develop a better understanding of sanction effectiveness by calculating a theory of moves the sender and target may go through when deciding to use, resist, or comply with economic sanctions. Similar to Kaempfer and Lowenberg (1992), it is the actors' economic preferences that determine the use of, and resistance to, economic sanctions. That is, Simon bases the preference orderings of the sender and target on the economic costs and benefits they derive from the sanctions. For senders, his results show that they will tend to use sanctions under two basic conditions: (1) there are domestic economic (a la Kaempfer and Lowenberg) or political benefits to be gained; (2) the sender is willing to accept the costs involved (Simon 1996).

Smith (1996) focuses on the use and effectiveness of economic coercion. His formal analysis shows that there are certain conditions under which sanctions will be used and may be effective. One of two basic conditions must be met for the sender to initiate economic sanctions: (1) the sender must believe that the sanctions may be effective; or (2) the sender derives political benefit without excessive economic domestic cost. His analysis points out that sanctions that do little to the target country and demand great policy changes are probably used to satisfy domestic constituents. Although both Simon (1996) and Smith (1996) include domestic political benefits as part of the sender's reasons for sanctioning, they do not empirically measure what these benefits may include. Instead, they simply model them such that if they are greater than the costs of sanctioning, the sender will initiate and maintain economic sanctions. Thus, while their analyses increase the understanding of economic sanctions, they do not explicitly explain the conditions under which a nation uses economic sanctions.

Not all scholars are so negative about the effectiveness of economic coercion. In *Economic Statecraft*, David Baldwin (1985) explores why decision-makers continue to use economic sanctions when they appear to be ineffective foreign policy tools. To answer this question he does not look into the various reasons sanctions may be used; instead, he follows the conventional wisdom's assumption that policy change is the goal. He argues that the effectiveness of economic sanctions is underrated and, in the process, develops a conception of sanctions that portrays them as one option along a continuum of coercive foreign policy tools. The continuum includes, in order of increasing severity: propaganda, diplomacy, economic sanctions, and military sanctions. Baldwin (5) points out that his study does not include any consideration of domestic politics or economics, but he also asserts that its absence should not alter the analysis.

According to Baldwin, the conventional wisdom underrates economic sanction effectiveness for two main reasons. First, it does not consider all types of economic statecraft. That is, trade, foreign aid, and the like are not considered a part of statecraft. Second, scholars tend not to take a foreign policy perspective. Baldwin (60–61) argues that these two characteristics lead scholars to consider economic statecraft as being abnormal, unusual, and so on. Thus, they do not evaluate economic statecraft in the same way they evaluate other types of statecraft, a research strategy that Baldwin recommends.

The second reason the conventional wisdom has given economic statecraft such a poor report card is, according to Baldwin, the complex nature of the goals a decision-maker may have. First, means-ends analysis is problematic because most ends are intermediate in nature (16–17) and therefore, cannot be evaluated without considering what the next end may be. Second, the decision-maker may have multiple goals and targets for each sanctioning effort. He cites Barber's (1979) threefold classification of sanctions but points out that these categories will vary. He uses the illustration of a teacher making an example of a misbehaving student to deter other students. The real target is more the class as a whole than the misbehaving student. This type of sanction is a variation of Barber's (1979) tertiary goal.[9] With such complexity, it is very difficult to evaluate the decision-maker's goals, which in turn means that it is very difficult to evaluate the sanctioning effort's effectiveness.

Baldwin's argument is very persuasive with regards to effectiveness. Further, his insights into the complex, multifaceted nature of the goals decision-makers may have are very astute, adding considerably to our understanding of economic sanctions. However, he does not discuss the conditions under which economic coercion is used. Additionally, Baldwin does not consider domestic politics or the nature of the decision-maker as influencing the use of economic statecraft. Unfortunately, the omission of these considerations hurts his analysis. Baldwin calls for economic statecraft to be considered and analyzed as a foreign policy tool. However, he limits his consideration of foreign policy by excluding domestic and personal influences on the decision to use sanctions. Thus, while *Economic Statecraft* does answer many questions, in fact all those it sets out to answer, it does not provide us with a satisfactory understanding of the conditions under which sanctions are used.

Economic Sanction Threats

An emerging area in the study of economic sanction effectiveness is the analysis of the threat to initiate an economic sanction. In the theoretical exposition of this argument, Dean Lacy and Emerson Niou (2004; see also Eaton and Engers 1999; Morgan and Meirs 1999) illustrate how sanctions should be more effective when they are simply threatened and not fully deployed foreign policy instruments. The logic for why coercive threats should be more effective suggests that if the target is willing to acquiesce to the sender's demands, then the target will concede before the threats are actually imposed. For example, if the United States threatens Mexico with a sanction over some immigration policy and the Mexicans prefer changing their policy to the sanctions, then they will prefer to give in to the demand before the United States imposes the sanctions so that they can avoid the economic pain. Why endure the economic hardship caused by the sanctions if you plan to agree to the sender's demand. As a consequence, the cases of enacted sanctions over represent those sanctions likely to fail, while they under represent successful attempts at coercion appearing only in the threat stage. It is argued that this selection bias leads to the inaccurate conclusion that sanctions are very ineffective.

Framing the question specifically as a selection bias in the data, Ifran Nooruddin (2002) disaggregates the Hufbauer et al. data into U.S.–target dyads and adds all other dyads that include the United States. He then uses a censored probit model to correct for the selection effect and shows that there is a bias in the selection of economic coercion cases. Nooruddin shows that not all factors commonly held to influence the success of economic coercion do so once the selection effect is corrected. However, the economic cost to the target still increases the likelihood of a favorable outcome for the sender.

Drezner (2003) takes a more direct approach to determining whether threats to sanction are more effective than actual sanctions themselves. Adding to Hufbauer et al.'s data and including Section 301 cases, Drezner compares sanctions that were merely threatened to those that were imposed.[10] He shows that the cases of threatened economic coercion are almost effective twice as often as deployed sanctions. His results support his assertion that "[a] target that prefers conceding to deadlock and believes that the sender will carry out its threat will acquiesce before imposition to avoid incurring the cost of the sanctions" (648). One potential problem with Drezner's analysis is the issues over which the United States attempted to coerce the target. The United States sought to influence regulatory and economic policies of the target; goals that are often considered low politics. As Doxey and others have pointed out, the sender's demands must be commensurate with the cost it threatens or imposes, in order for the target to even consider acquiescing. Thus, it is possible that Drezner finds greater effectiveness in his cases because they demand less of the target than in many of the Hufbauer et al. cases. For example, it is easier for a target to enforce international money laundering regulations than for China to reform its human rights policies. As Yitan Li and I (Li and Drury 2004) argue, the human rights issue for Beijing is one of sovereignty. As such, the demands made by the United States following the Tiananmen Square uprising were far more radical and costly than the ones Drezner tests.

In a quantitative analysis of the U.S. threats to remove or condition China's MFN status, Drury and Li (2004) show that not only were the threats ineffective but also counterproductive. As the United States—particularly the Congress—became more bellicose toward Beijing, fewer prisoners were released, curfews lifted, and so on. However, when Washington took a more cooperative stand, the PRC tended to react by loosening political restrictions in China. Thus, it is not entirely clear that threats should be any more effective if the target has no desire or sees no utility to give in to the sender's demands.

Drezner (2003) does address this issue and points out that he is comparing threatened and actual sanctions that have similar ends, namely, changing a target's policies. Thus, the comparison is not between high and low politics sanctions but between threat and implementation. Drezner's case is convincing, but the issue is one that must be considered when assessing sanction threats. For example, it may be that threats are more often used on low politics issues, and senders tend to pull the trigger on sanctions more quickly for issues that concern national security.

Summary and Conclusion

In this chapter, I have attempted to define sanctions and then show that the extant literature on economic coercion concerns itself almost exclusively with evaluating the effectiveness of sanction policies. Some consider economic incentives as a type of "positive" sanction, however, these incentives have none of the qualities of coercive diplomacy, and therefore, are not economic sanctions. Economic sanctions are defined as the use of an economic instrument to cause a target nation some harm or economic loss with the purpose of coercing the target to cease, reverse, or not adopt some policy. The extant literature assumes, for the most part, that sanctions are used to coerce the target state to alter one or more of its policies. Concluding that sanctions often fail, this conventional wisdom suggests that domestic politics are the primary culprit without testing this conclusion. The convention wisdom has avoided assessing the domestic politics link to failure by (1) avoiding the inclusion of or not distinguishing economic goals (Hufbauer et al.), (2) not controlling for domestic political goals (Doxey), (3) modeling but not measuring domestic costs (Barber; Simon; Lindsay; and Morgan and Schwebach), and (4) arguing for spurious connection without demonstrating it. Modifications to the conventional wisdom have (5) introduced symbolic or expressive goals without including domestic instrumental goals (Wallensteen; Renwick; Schwebach), (6) limited the measurement of domestic reasons to domestic economic conditions or goals of economic interest groups (Kaempfer and Lowenberg), and (7) raised "complexity" as a barrier.

To sum up, most of the sanction literature deals with the question of effectiveness. This chapter has explored more carefully this focus on effectiveness by first arguing that there are several other characteristics of economic sanctions that are either not mentioned or, more commonly, assumed by the literature. These characteristics begin with the basic definition of what constitutes economic coercion. The first part of what defines a sanction is what is excluded; that is, what foreign policy tools are *not* sanctions. Several scholars discuss positive sanctions, also referred to as incentives or inducements. While these are important in influencing the target, they are a different form of diplomacy and are not considered as a form of economic coercion. A sanction is defined less by the specific economic instrument that actually puts pressure on the target state (e.g., an import restriction) and more by the goal that the sanction seeks to attain, such as stemming nuclear proliferation. Most studies of economic coercion assume that the economic instruments can include import, export, and financial restrictions. Additionally, travel bans are often included as a type of economic rather than diplomatic coercion. The key to what defines as an economic sanction, then, is the goal leaders have in mind when they initiate the coercion attempt. Sanction scholars also regularly exclude what is referred to as economic warfare—the use of economic instruments to weaken the target prior to hostilities or expected hostilities. Another category of instruments that are not regularly incorporated into the mainstream definition of economic coercion are those seeking to alter the target state's foreign economic policies. That is, sanctions aimed at opening markets seek an economic goal, not a political one and are therefore not normally considered in the economic sanction literature. The conventional view of sanctions is some type of economic pressure used as a means to a political end. I have argued that this definition is too restrictive. Instead of excluding sanctions seeking foreign economic policy goals a priori, they should be assessed to see if and how they differ from more politically oriented sanctions.

Research on the effectiveness of sanctions tends to explain success as a function of the economic pressure put on the target. Some studies do include the symbolic or signaling properties of sanctions, but the most common focus is on the more measurable economic pain visited on the target. More recently, sanction threats have been included in the assessment of overall sanction effectiveness. Scholars argue that threats are more effective because if the target is going to acquiesce, it is more likely to do so before the sanctions are implemented and begin putting a bite on their economy. In studies of implemented sanctions, the overwhelming conclusion is that sanctions fail most of the time. Many of these studies suggest that domestic political considerations within the sender are at the root of sanction failure. That is, the sender country uses the sanctions to "do something" in order to placate its public. As a result, the sanctions are never designed or expected to change the target's policies. Regardless of the explanation for sanction failure, the literature is unable to accurately explain failure.

The next chapter continues with an analysis of the most common, widely used data set in order to show empirically the problems within the effectiveness literature. The results show that while economic pressure does significantly increase success, the model is unable to explain a large portion of the variance. This gap in our ability to explain the effectiveness of economic coercion leads to the question of what conditions lead the president to use this foreign policy tool.

Chapter 3
Evaluating Sanction Effectiveness

Economic coercion that places more costs on the target—especially relative to the sender—is expected to work better since that pressure should drive the target leadership to conceding to the sender's demands. Although there have been multiple empirical studies of various aspects of this claim regarding economic sanction effectiveness, it is valuable to directly and explicitly assess what aspects of the conventional wisdom hold up under simultaneous empirical testing. The results in this chapter show that while many of the extant literature's claims are supported, the overall accuracy of the model is not very high. This poor performance suggests that we must move beyond analyzing effectiveness and seek other answers for why sanctions are used.

I begin by constructing a multivariate model accumulating aspects of the conventional wisdom from Hufbauer et al.'s policy conclusions and recommendations. The multivariate model shows how the different variables interrelate, something impossible to see in Hufbauer et al.'s original bivariate analysis, as well as providing an overall performance evaluation. In addition to Hufbauer et al.'s policy hypotheses, I include three more hypotheses discussed in the sanctions literature. I then operationalize the measures needed to test these relationships using an updated version of Hufbauer et al.'s data. Furthermore, I compare the multivariate results with Hufbauer et al.'s original bivariate findings and policy recommendations and discuss the accuracy and importance of their recommendations.

Hufbauer et al. (1990a) have written the most comprehensive study of economic sanctions in their volume, *Economic Sanctions Reconsidered: History and Current Policy*, for the Institute of International Economics. Their analysis generated the first real empirical study evaluating the effectiveness of economic sanctions, which they use as the basis for making several policy recommendations. It is important that these policy recommendations be accurate because economic sanctions allow nations to exercise coercion without resorting to the use of military force. When used properly, sanctions can assist policy makers to avert war by enforcing their nation's will and still allowing time and room to settle the dispute diplomatically and without bloodshed. Alternatively, when military force is not an acceptable option because the issue is not one of high politics for the sender, sanctions provide a means by which the sender can exert pressure on or signal the target of its displeasure or resolve.

Although Hufbauer et al.'s (1990a) recommendations contribute toward bridging the gap between theory and practice that Alexander George (1993) identifies as an important mission of scholars, the empirical analysis used to develop the recommendations has some rather serious problems that lead to questions about their accuracy. These conclusions are based on a series of bivariate analyses. While the nature of the data is largely categorical, which makes their cross-tabulations not inappropriate, there is a consequence to using this statistical technique: it is virtually impossible to rule out spurious relationships due to a lack of control variables. It is also impossible to know how important their recommendations are or how much weight to give any one of them, because there is no overall model to evaluate.[1] Thus, it is difficult to know how well Hufbauer et al. have explained economic sanctions and how seriously their recommendations should be taken.

Although their work lacks an explicit theory, these recommendations are an implicit series of hypotheses meant to elaborate on the sanction literature's conventional wisdom. It is possible to combine the variables in these hypotheses into an overall model. Below I develop this methodological possibility as a testable model and then use a multivariate, ordered logit analysis to assess how accurate and important or weighty Hufbauer et al.'s bivariate policy recommendations are within the context of a multivariate analysis. In addition, this analysis provides a general test of the conventional wisdom's explanation for sanction effectiveness. I turn now to translating the conventional wisdom into testable hypotheses.

Modeling the Conventional Wisdom

I begin the multivariate analysis with the definition and measurement of economic sanction effectiveness. According to Hufbauer et al. (1990a), economic sanctions are financial or trade restrictions used by a state in order to change another nation's policies in some prespecified manner. This definition sets their focus to be on solely economic coercion as a tool for foreign policy goals. This characterization of sanctions excludes the foreign economic goals that Drezner (2001) has argued should be included, as well as the domestic goals and international symbolism. While these are very valid goals that should be considered, the practice of including them is very problematic.

For example, determining if the international community received and respected the symbolism that a given state attempted to send is virtually impossible. Canadian attempts in the 1970s to enforce non-proliferation with economic coercion certainly were also meant to send a signal to potential future proliferators. While such public sanctions may have sent a clear signal, attempting to determine how much impact it had seems next to impossible. Is the development or attempted development of nuclear weapons by India, Iran, North Korea, Pakistan, and the like a sign of failure or are there other countries that forwent nuclear arms development because of the Canadian efforts?

One would need to know if any state included the potential threat of Canadian sanctions in their decision-making. Hufbauer et al. take a very practical approach to the issue by excluding these non-foreign, nontarget directed issues. While there are certainly drawbacks to this approach, the data are more reliable given these constraints. From a pragmatic perspective, working with somewhat limited or censured data is better than no data or inaccurate, unreliable data. To construct the following model, I follow Hufbauer et al.'s (1990a: 114) discussion of nine policy recommendations (all firmly rooted in the conventional wisdom) and infer eight different hypotheses from them. I add three more hypotheses derived from the sanction literature. Following the discussion of eleven total hypotheses, I also add three controls to the model. Each of the following hypotheses is based on the conventional wisdom's assertion that more economic damage done to the target will beget more successful outcomes. In fact, Hufbauer et al.'s analysis is an attempt to spell out what type of economic damage makes sanctions effective.

Hufbauer, Schott, and Elliott Hypotheses

The first three hypotheses deal directly with the target's economic and political characteristics. First, politically unstable and economically distressed targets tend to succumb to economic coercion more easily than strong targets, according to Hufbauer et al. (1990a). Targeted nations that are weak (unstable/distressed) will have less ability to resist the sender nation because (1) its economy is so weak that the loss created by the sanctions is too much for it to bear and/or (2) the target regime is politically unstable and therefore cannot mitigate or at least isolate and minimize the impact of the sanctions. Countries with strong economies can more easily weather the economic consequences from sanctions.

Given that the target's average annual cost of a sanction is $197 million, it is easy to see how an economy like China's or India's can absorb the loss. Smaller, weaker economies do not have that ability. In the political realm, the effect is similar. A strong regime can take steps to control the economy and mitigate the effects of the economic coercion on the ruling coalition. For example, the Smith government in Rhodesia was able to completely control the tobacco market so that the farmers lost both economically and politically. Since the farmers were likely to lose from the sanctions regardless of what the government did, the white minority regime created policies that transferred political power to the industrial sector, the part of the economy that was gaining rents from the imposition of the sanctions (Rowe 2000, 2001).

Essentially opposite to Hufbauer et al.'s claim, Galtung (1967) argues that sanctions can increase the political integration within the nation, subsequently increasing the stability and strength of the government. However, this scenario is unlikely to take place if the target nation is under rather extreme duress. Eland (1995) argues that for Galtung to be right, the target government must control the communication within the target state. This power, for example, was apparent in Iraq before the second Iraq war, and it gave Hussein the ability to misinform the Iraqi people as to the motives of the international community. Basically, he blamed the sanctions on the United States and UN and not on his own policies and aggression. To have this ability to control information indicates that a regime is not weak or unstable. Therefore, for Galtung's integration to take place the regime would have at least a minimal level of power in the first place. Following these lines of reasoning, I hypothesize that *if the target is under extreme duress, sanctions should be more effective (hypothesis 1)*.

Second, Hufbauer et al. find that the size differential between the sender and the target is unrelated to sanction effectiveness, presumably because the absolute size differential between the sender and target does not tap the trade flows between the two. Morgan and Schweback (1997) find a similar effect when looking at military capabilities. While theirs is a different measure than the GNP ratio Hufbauer et al. use, GNP often represents national power or is a component of national power. Therefore, I *expect no relationship between the GNP ratio and effectiveness (hypothesis 2)*.

The third hypothesis states that *a prior friendly relationship between the sender and the target makes the economic sanctions more effective (hypothesis 3)*. Sanctions aimed at allies or friendly nations are expected to be more successful because there are not only typically close trade ties but also close political ties. These economic and political ties increase the sender's ability to influence the target because the target has more to lose if the dispute is not resolved.[2] As Drezner's (1998, 1999) conflict expectations theory asserts, friendly nations not only have an incentive to comply and thereby avoid the cost of the sanctions, they also do not expect future conflict with the sender. Therefore, there are no reputational costs or concerns of relative gains. Targets that do expect future conflict have an incentive to resist the economic coercion so that they do not appear to give in to their future opponent or enemy. Also, because relative—rather than absolute—gains matter, the target will prefer to deny the sender any potential gains. Even though the relative closeness of trade ties is modeled below, it is nonetheless possible that other aspects of friendly relations, such as political ties and unmeasured economic ties, would make the sanctions more effective.

The next two hypotheses characterize international cooperation on the side of either the target or the sender. Unlike size differential (hypothesis 2), these balance of power relationships are directly tied to the sender and should, therefore, have an important affect on the success of economic coercion. As argued above, the absolute difference between the sender's size and the target's size may have no independent effect on success. On the other hand, if other nations cooperate with the sender, then there are fewer suppliers to sell goods to the target, fewer markets in which the target may sell its goods, and more possible presanction trade ties with the target. Conversely, if another nation or nations act to aid the target, a supplier and possible market have been specifically and exclusively opened for the sanctioned nation.

Following this logic, one would then expect that cooperation with the sender would increase sanction effectiveness. Martin (1992) and Mastanduno (1992) discuss the positive impact cooperation should have on effectiveness, stating that it is obviously true. As Mansfield (1995) asserts, multilateral cooperation increases both the costs to the target and the legitimacy and size of the signal sent by the sanctioning states. This logic, while seemingly valid, is flawed. The more states involved in the sanctioning effort, the more likely they will "spoil the broth" (Hufbauer et al. 1990a: 96; Miers and Morgan 2002). Miers and Morgan argue that this problem is the result of bargaining difficulties that the potential senders face.

Drezner (2000) disagrees that the primary problem is bargaining. Instead, he shows that multilateral sanctions fail because of enforcement issues between the primary and secondary senders (those states that are part of the coalition). "Backsliding" by the secondary senders as a result of incentives to cheat and trade with the target is the primary reason multilateral economic coercion fails more than unilateral sanctions, according to Drezner. These difficulties can be overcome in the presence of international organizations, a point I return to below. Doxey (1971, 1980, 1987) also argues that too many nations involved in the sanctioning effort can ruin any chances for success. Thus, I hypothesize that *the greater the level of cooperation with the sender, the less effective the sanctions will be (hypothesis 4).*

While Hufbauer et al., as well as several other scholars, have found that multilateralism is not a good strategy for economic coercion, they do find a strong negative association between effectiveness and the presence of one or more "black knights," states that consciously seek to counteract the sanctions. Sanctions such as those against Cuba and North Korea during the Cold War certainly suggest that assistance to the target would make success an impossible goal. Although neither Cuba nor North Korea have acquiesced since the fall of their patron, the Soviet empire, the strong bivariate findings, as well as a certain amount of face validity, indicate that *black knights will make sanctions more likely to fail (hypothesis 5).*

Sanction Attributes

The next three hypotheses deal directly with the sanction's attributes. *Hypothesis 6 asserts that the closer the prior trade relationship between the sender and target, the greater the chance for success.* This hypothesis is based on the idea that closer ties with the target increase the sender's ability to visit damage on the target, and according to the conventional wisdom, the greater the damage, the more effective the sanctions will be. Hufbauer et al. (1990a) combine both presanction imports from and exports to the sender country into one measure. However, the effects of imports and exports may be very different. For example, greater imports by the target mean that it is dependent upon the sender for certain goods. Unless these goods are unique to the sender and nondurable, it may be easy for the target to replace them on the world market (Crumm 1995). Of course, it would be easier to replace goods now than in 1950 since the level of world trade is so much larger, not to mention the ubiquitous corporations that operate in multiple countries who can bypass one country's sanctions by selling/shipping their product from another country (Shambaugh 1999).

Still, replacing most products is quite different from the other type of trade sanction—export restrictions. When the sender stops purchasing goods or services from the target, the target must find a new market for its goods or suffer an economic loss. Rhodesia's inability to export tobacco severely cut the country's source of wealth, and while there are plenty of nations that may be willing to sell the target goods lost from the sanctions, opening markets to the target is much more onerous. The difficulty diplomats have in opening markets and limiting tariffs proves this point. Therefore, it is important to examine the characteristics of the trade that connects the sender and target. To accomplish this, I test three versions of hypothesis 6: the greater the (1) total trade (imports plus exports), (2) imports, or (3) exports, respectively, between the sender and target, the more effective the sanctions.

The final two hypotheses represent the core of the conventional wisdom. First and foremost in the literature is the idea that *the more costly the sanctions are to the target, the more effective they should be (hypothesis 7)*. The assumption behind this hypothesis is the economic pressure itself forces the target government to concede. Normally, the economic cost to the target is expected to function as a direct form of pressure, and therefore, the cost is relative to the size of the target's economy. That is, wealthier economies have more capacity to absorb the economic loss and continue to resist the sanctions. A hypothetical example may be helpful. An eight trillion dollar economy similar to the United States' can more easily pay for $100 million a year in losses due to a sanction than a five billion dollar economy similar to Haiti's. In the first case the percentage cost is only 0.001 percent of the total economy while in the second it is 2 percent. However, sanctions have symbolic effects as well as instrumental ones. Even if the losses to a target are small in comparison to their GDP, a large absolute loss may still be perceived as significant pressure—a large dollar amount is symbolic of considerable pressure. As a consequence, it is important to assess the impact that both the relative and absolute costs to the target have on economic sanction effectiveness.

The last hypothesis representing the conventional wisdom asserts that economic coercion that costs the sender dearly is more likely to fail. Schwebach (2000) theorizes that costly sanctions send a more potent signal to the target; that is, if the sender is willing to suffer significant economic loss from the coercion, then it must be serious about its demands and resolve. However, Hufbauer et al. find that sanctions costly to the sender reduce their effectiveness. Morgan and Schwebach (1997) also show that costs to the sender favor the target's resistance to the coercion—high costs to the sender mean the target has a chance to ride out the effort and wait for the sender to give up. Therefore, I hypothesize that *costly sanctions are more likely to fail than those that cost the sender little (hypothesis 8).*

Additional Hypotheses

In addition to the eight hypotheses earlier, I include four more hypotheses that have been discussed throughout the sanctions literature. First, if the sanction issue concerns national security for the sender, then one would expect the sender nation to prosecute the sanctions more seriously. While some of this effect can be seen in the cost the economic coercion imposes on the target (national security issues are significantly associated with higher costs to the target), the sender may be more willing to sanction strategic goods when the issue is one that concerns national security. For example, placing an embargo on oil exports to a large country will significantly cut into the revenues of an OPEC state. Cutting off or reducing the oil supply to a nation truly threatens its lifeblood.[3] It would be much easier for a sender to cut off sales of a less profitable good. The sender pays dearly, too, so such a cost will be easier to bear if the issue has a high salience. Therefore, *in sanctioning cases involving the sender's national security interests, I expect success to increase (hypothesis 9).*

Second, the sanctioning literature has stressed the importance of not only international cooperation but also the involvement of international organizations (Doxey 1971, 1980, 1987; Drury 1998). The primary problem with international cooperation (and the reason Hufbauer et al. give for their finding that cooperation inhibits success) is coordinating the cooperative effort. As discussed above, the coordinating costs can involve determining who will join the effort to coerce the target, what goods will be sanctioned, and keeping the coalition together (Drezner 2000; Miers and Morgan 2002). Most authors agree that international organizations can mitigate or limit the coordination problem, whether these problems concern bargaining or enforcement. In effect, organizations have the ability to act as mediators that provide a forum for bringing together senders and create transparency that permits more effective policing of the coalition and better sanction enforcement. Thus, *involvement of an international organization should decrease the problems associated with cooperation and subsequently increase sanction effectiveness (hypothesis 10)*. Multilateral economic coercion implemented through an organization may not be more effective than unilateral sanctions but the involvement of an institution will limit the negative impact multilateralism has on the effectiveness of economic coercion.

The last additional hypothesis concerns the regime type of the sender. Robert A. Hart (2000) argues that democracies should be better at leveraging economic coercion than autocracies. He bases this argument on the idea that democracies face domestic audience costs that limit their ability to back down from a demand. That is, if a democratic leader publicly demands that another country switch one of its policies, the democratic leader cannot back down from that demand without looking weak to his own constituency. Therefore, democratic leaders must stay the course to preserve their standing and tenure at home. As a result, the economic coercion levied by a democratic sender will more likely be prosecuted fully than non-democracies. The empirical results of democracy's impact on sanction effectiveness are somewhat mixed. Hart does find support for his argument, but Drury (2003) finds the opposite is true—democracies are less effective users of sanctions.[4]

Kaempfer and Lowenberg (1988, 1989) repeatedly point out that all nations face significant pressures from those interest groups that will gain (and lose) from the sanctions. Therefore, leaders face much more than just audience costs, they face imposing real profit losses on some of their country's firms. Further, it is not clear that the public in a democracy pays much or any attention to the use of economic sanctions, and the leadership probably suspects this is the case. If this is true, then the effect of audience costs would certainly be less important than the effect of rent-seeking firms lobbying the leadership prior to its use of sanctions. Further, the rent-seeking that Kaempfer and Lowenberg describe should exist equally in autocracies and democracies.[5]

However, since autocrats and democrats face the same constraints vis-à-vis industries, it seems possible that the audience costs that democrats face do have an effect at the margin. This marginal effect will be enhanced if the target perceives that the audience costs matter to the democrat. That is, if the target thinks that the democracy has tied its hands and will deploy and maintain the sanctions, it will be more willing to concede. A target facing an autocratic sender is unlikely to ever have such a perception since autocratic targets have free reign to engage in cheap talk (Hart 2000: 269–271).

Finally, the dispute between the sender and target may garner public attention even if the sanctions do not. Many more Americans heard about Tiananmen Square than followed the debate of whether to condition China's MFN status. Thus, the leaders may not be concerned that the public pays attention to whether it uses sanctions or not, but those leaders are concerned about their constituency's attention to the issue at hand. Given these arguments, it is reasonable to hypothesize that *democratic senders will be more effective at using economic coercion (hypothesis 11).*

One could also argue that the regime type of the target may affect the success of the sanction episode. For example, command economies should be more able to control their response to sanctions than free markets (Crumm 1995; Bolks and Al-Sowayel 2000), and according to Edward Mansfield et al. (2000), only nondemocracies have command economies. However, the ability to control the response to the sanctions is not simply a matter of whether the economy is liberalized or centralized. The Rhodesian response was quite effective and was not a command economy, although the government certainly exerted considerable control over it as time passed. Further, the flexibility of a liberal economy does offer more options to evade the negative economic impact of the sanctions. The key to understanding the target's ability to respond is more a function of state strength than the type of economy. Strong states should be able to take what measures are needed to mitigate the impact of the economic sanctions. Weaker states, whether a command economy or not, will be less able to take such control. Since the target state's political and economic health are already hypothesized to influence effectiveness (hypothesis 1), I do not make another hypothesis about the target state's regime type.[6]

Control Variables

Finally, there are three control variables that must be introduced. The first assesses the effect of the sender's additional policies, such as covert action or limited use of force, in conjunction with economic sanctions to enhance their effectiveness. It is entirely possible that if this variable was omitted, any relationship between the sanctions and success could be spurious. For example, the success of the sanctions against Allende's regime in Chile may have been impossible if covert actions were not also included. If these policies are not controlled for, then it is impossible to tell if the sanctions or the covert action caused the Chilean regime to fall.

Second, because the world economy has become increasingly interdependent (Keohane and Nye 1977; Gilpin 2001), sanctions may be more or less effective as time progresses. One may expect that as nations became more interdependent, they would be able to visit more damage on each other. However, greater interdependence is a double-edged sword; as the global market grows, more markets may be open from which a targeted country could buy, helping them subvert the sanctions and therefore making the sanctions less effective.

The last variable controls for the United States as the sender. Because the United States accounts for more than two-thirds of the sanctions, they may have a strong effect on the overall results. For example, if the United States is particularly poor at sanctioning relative to the rest of the world, then the results would be biased toward failure. The control variable will account for this possibility as well as determine if the United States is significantly better or worse at sanctioning relative to the rest of the world.

Sanction Effectiveness Data

I now turn to a discussion of the data that I use to test the hypotheses laid out above. Unless otherwise specified, all of the data come from Hufbauer et al. (1990a, 1990b) and are supplemented by several updated cases available from the Institute for International Economics web site (www.iie.com). The unit of analysis is the sanction episode, including all observations of multiple senders, multiple targets, and multiple goals arrayed as a cross-section of each conflict. One effectiveness score is used to represent all the goals, and if multiple senders or targets exist, averages are used to represent variables such as presanction trade. Clearly, there are other ways to array the data. Instead of using the episode as the unit of analysis, a dyadic version could be developed whereby each unit was the sender–target dyad. In this case, an episode would have observations for each sender–target dyad. Although this form of the data would work well for testing when sanctions occur (Cox and Drury 2002), it would be more problematic for assessing effectiveness. Creating multiple observations for each episode would have the effect of (1) creating more variance in some of the independent variables (e.g., size ratio between the sender and target) while duplicating the values of the dependent variable (effectiveness) and some of the independent variables (e.g., presence of a state supporting the target or involvement of an international organization). Another alternative to the sanction episode is creating observations for each goal. Although this would create new values for the effectiveness variable, none of the explanatory variables would change; they would only be duplicated. While Barber (1979), Lindsey (1986), and Hufbauer et al. (1990a) rightly point out that sanctions often have multiple purposes, assessing these independently is unfeasible with this data set.

Measuring Sanction Effectiveness

The first measure to discuss is the outcome of economic coercion. Hufbauer et al. use two four-point scales in combination to measure effectiveness of economic coercion. The first scale taps the policy achievement of the sender. "Policy outcomes are judged against the foreign policy goals of the sender country" (Hufbauer et al. 1990a: 41) and are rated on a four-point scale where one equals failure and four equates success. While Hufbauer et al. do acknowledge the fact that sanctions may have multiple goals that go beyond those aimed at the target (satisfying domestic demands for action, for instance), they limit their data and analysis to the "changes in policies, capabilities, or government of the target country" (Hufbauer et al. 1990a: 41). This admitted limitation is a reasonable one given the difficulties in determining what other goals, in Barber's (1979) terms secondary or tertiary, the sender may have. Lindsey's (1986) assessment of the effectiveness of different sanction goals, while novel and insightful, does suffer from problems of systematically determining at what goals economic coercion is aimed. The second scale measures the contribution the sanction made toward attaining the goal. This four-point scale ranges from one for "no contribution" to four where the sanctions are "solely responsible for the outcome."

Both scales are based on the expert opinions of several scholars regarding each case. While this method does involve "subjective evaluation" by other scholars, Hufbauer et al. recognize this problem. They argue that "by relying on the consensus views of other analysts, we believe we have minimized the bias resulting from our personal views" (Hufbauer et al. 1990a: 41). Given the significant problems with evaluating a sanctioning effort, their use of multiple, outside evaluations provides a solid and probably least problematic solution.

The two scales are multiplied together to create an overall measure of economic sanction effectiveness. By multiplying these two scales, they imply that an interactive relationship determines how much effect the economic sanctions actually had on the outcome. Their success variable can therefore have the following values: 1, 2, 3, 4, 6, 8, 9, 12, and 16. They consider a value of 9 or greater to be successful sanctions. Their logic is that the sanctions must have had at least a modest contribution to an outcome that was at least "a somewhat successful result" (Hufbauer et al. 1990a: 42). A case that has a value higher than 9 is considered a more significant or major success.

Two potential problems arise with the coding of the dependent variable; first, it is not contiguous. That is, the values do not increase by standard increments, implying that there is a greater difference between sanctions that marginally succeeded (a value of 9) or marginally failed (a value of 8) and solidly successful sanctions (a value of 12). Technically speaking, this means that there is only a one point difference between marginal failure and marginal success, while there is a three point difference between marginal success and solid success. It is certainly possible and perhaps justifiable that these differences are valid if the measure of success is an interval measure of success and not an ordinal one. However, the authors do not offer an explanation or justification for these differences.

Further, it is not unreasonable to argue that the difference between success and failure should be larger than between gradations of success. This is not to say that Hufbauer et al. are wrong, but that their scale is problematic. Given this problem, it is difficult to accept that there is a logical argument behind the multiplicative relationship. To identify the extent of the problem, I recoded the scores by removing the gaps and then correlated the original measure with the new, gap-free one.

The two versions of the effectiveness variable are highly correlated (0.97), indicating a high degree of similarity. Thus, it is unlikely that the noncontiguous nature of the variable has any significant effect on analyses based on it.[7]

A second, more serious problem that arises with the dependent variable's composition is the inclusion of the "contribution" the sanctions made to the effort. Since the goal of the analysis is to determine what makes economic coercion succeed, including the contribution of the sanctions as part of the measure of success creates a potential endogeneity problem. That is, determining the factors that make sanctions successful is similar to determining what contribution the sanctions made toward success. Therefore, the contribution of the sanctions is included explicitly in the dependent variable and implicitly in the independent variables. This problem is made worse by the inclusion of an independent variable (specified and discussed below) that indicates the presence of supplemental policies such as covert action or military force. The inclusion of this variable clearly violates the assumption that the dependent variable is exogenous. That is, it is not independent of the explanatory variables or the model itself. The model Hufbauer et al. develop is meant to grasp the effects the sanctions had on securing the goals set out by the sender.

Thus, the analysis is meant to determine the contribution the sanctions made toward the sender's goals. As a control for other foreign policy measures, the variable indicating the presence of these measures should be included. However, the dependent variable should not include a contribution measure because that would be redundant and therefore endogenous. To solve this endogeneity/exogeneity problem, I use as the dependent variable only the policy result scale (1 = failure to 4 = success) as determined by Hufbauer et al. (1990a: 42–44).[8]

Measures of the Independent Variables

I now turn to the measures that tap the independent variables. The first hypothesis (distressed targets are more likely to give in to sanctions) is measured by Hufbauer et al.'s (1990a: 46) assessment of the target's political and economic well being. The ordinal variable is coded such that three equals "strong and stable" nation, two indicates that a nation has "significant problems," and one indicates that "acute economic problems, exemplified by high unemployment and rampant inflation, coupled with political turmoil bordering on chaos" plague the nation.

The second independent variable is the GNP ratio between sender and target; it taps the relative size difference between the two states (or more in the case of multilateral sanctions). Next, a dummy variable taps the prior relations between the sender and target. The measure takes a value of one for friendly relations and a zero for all other relations. The fourth independent variable, the level of cooperation with the sender, is measured by an ordinal scale that indicates a one for no cooperation, two for "meaningful restraints from some but not all important trading partners," three for greater restraints from trading partners, and a four for "major trading partners make major effort to limit trade" (Hufbauer et al. 1990a: 44–45). Next, a dummy variable indicates the presence of a "black knight" or nation that openly aids the target in order to counteract the sender's attempt to coerce the target.

Three measures are used to tap the presanction trade level in hypothesis 6, namely the percent of imports, exports, and total trade accounted for by the sender. Two measures tap hypothesis 7 that states increased costs to the target should increase success. First, the percentage of GNP lost as a result of the sanctions gauges the relative impact of the sanctions on the target. Second, the absolute cost of the economic coercion, measured in millions of dollars, represents the more symbolic effect that a high, absolute cost may have. The last of the conventional wisdom hypotheses concerns the costs to the sender (hypothesis 8). The independent variable in this hypothesis is measured by an ordinal scale in which a one equals a net loss to sender, a two equates a minimal loss to sender, a three equals a minimal gain to sender, and the top score, four, represents a net gain to sender.

Hypothesis 9 asserts that if national security is involved, the sanctions will be more effective. I define national security as any threat to sender's security that includes a military dispute between any of involved nations (senders or targets), nuclear proliferation, threat to an alliance, or threat of communist expansion. In addition to the more obvious "low politics" issues such as human rights, the measure does not include attempts to destabilize the target unless the destabilization campaign is the result of a national security threat as previously defined.

The last two hypotheses concern the presence of an international organization as part of the sanctioning effort and the sender's regime type. To measure international organizations (hypothesis 10), I use a dummy variable that equals one when any international institution was involved in sanctioning effort. This definition includes not only the United Nations and League of Nations but also organizations such as the Arab League, the OAS, and so on. To tap the sender's level of democracy, I use the Polity IV data (Marshall and Jaggers 2000). These data measure a country's level of democracy and autocracy and create an overall measure by subtracting autocracy from democracy. The resulting score ranges from −10 (perfect autocracy) to +10 (perfect democracy).

Finally, the three control variables must be delineated. First, a dummy variable indicates whether the sender uses supplemental policies with the sanctions. These policies may include: covert action, limited use of force, or regular military.[9] The calendar year is included as a measure of time passing and represents the increasing interdependence in the world system. Finally, I use a dummy variable that indicates whether the United States is involved in the sanction effort as a sender.

Now that the hypotheses and data have been delineated, I turn to the assessment of the model. I begin first with a brief methodological discussion and then turn to the models themselves.

Testing the Model

Because the scale for the dependent variable is ordinal and has only four values, an ordered logit must be used to assess the model.[10] An ordered logit analysis estimates the effects of multiple independent variables on an ordinal dependent variable. In the case at hand, where there are four possible sanctioning outcomes (complete failure, limited failure, limited success, and complete success), the ordered logit will generate four different probabilities for each of the outcomes. The coefficients then affect that distribution of probabilities. For example, if the level of trade between the sender and target has a positive effect on effectiveness, then as it increases so will the probability of a limited or complete success.[11]

Ordered logit has another quality to recommend it. It does not assume anything about the numerical values of the dependent variable except that they are ordered from high to low. Therefore, the criticism that a success (a value of four) is more than twice as weighty as a marginal failure (a value of two) is dispatched. The estimator does not distinguish the distance between these values, only that they are independent from each other and sequentially ordered.

To begin the analysis, I assess Hufbauer et al.'s (1990a) bivariate findings that were used to derive the first eight hypotheses. In order to make this assessment, I estimate a multivariate model with only the variables they used in their bivariate analyses. This means I only include one measure for presanction trade just like Hufbauer et al. The results from the ordered logit appear in the first column of table 3.1.[12]

The first thing to note in the estimation is the generally poor performance of the model and few significant variables. These estimates indicate that there may be problems with some of Hufbauer et al.'s conclusions about the impact of their variables. More importantly, they show that the conventional wisdom, in general, cannot accurately explain the outcome of an economic sanction. This inability to explain precisely sanction effectiveness suggests that more attention should be paid to the reasons or conditions that economic coercion is used. Before addressing that issue, I first turn to the model at hand and later attempt to improve it.

Only four variables, political/economic health of the target, presanction trade between the sender and target, dollar cost to the target, and the year the sanctions were applied attain significance (p-value <0.05); one additional variable, international cooperation, approaches significance (p-value $= 0.105$). As the health variable indicates, stronger targets are more likely to successfully resist sanctions, making them ineffective. Just as Hufbauer et al. show, weakened or distressed targets are more likely to acquiesce to the sender's demands. The model in column 1 indicates that a distressed target has a 66 percent probability that the sanctions will be either a partial or total success, while a healthy or strong target has only a 38 percent likelihood of either a partial or total success.[13] Clearly, the impact is quite strong reinforcing Hufbauer et al.'s (1990a: 114) recommendation to "pick on the weak and helpless."

The level of cooperation with the sender approaches a significant and inverse relationship with the effectiveness of the economic coercion. Its substantive impact is considerable and consistent with the conventional wisdom. Unilateral sanctions have a 62 percent probability of being at least partially successful; multilateral sanctions with a large coalition have only 37 percent of that same partial success, thus "more is not necessarily merrier" (Hufbauer et al. 1990a: 95). As expected, presanction trade has a positive impact on the likelihood that sanctions will coerce the target to change its policy. As presanction

Table 3.1   Estimating Sanction Effectiveness, 1914–1992

	Original Hufbauer, Schott, and Elliott Model	Extended Model with Total Trade	Extended Model with Imports	Extended Model with Exports
Distress	−0.587**	−0.569*	−0.579*	−0.570*
	(0.304)	(0.326)	(0.326)	(0.326)
GNP ratio	1.07E-04	8.75E-05	8.81E-05	8.39E-05
	(1.05E-04)	(1.18E-04)	(1.17E-04)	(1.19E-04)
Prior relations	0.196	0.268	0.243	0.334
	(0.405)	(0.434)	(0.442)	(0.426)
Multilateral cooperation	−0.35*	−0.652***	−0.680***	−0.622**
	(0.216)	(0.249)	(0.252)	(0.247)
Black knight	−0.682	−0.591	−0.508	−0.666
	(0.476)	(0.497)	(0.501)	(0.498)
Total trade	0.010**	0.009*		
	(0.005)	(0.005)		
Imports			0.018	
			(0.011)	
Exports				0.015
				(0.009)
Target GNP cost	−0.032	−0.038	−0.038	−0.033
	(0.035)	(0.037)	(0.037)	(0.036)
Cost to target	0.001**	0.001**	0.001**	0.001**
	(0.000)	(0.000)	(0.000)	(0.000)
Cost to sender	−0.038	−0.043	−0.019	−0.059
	(0.290)	(0.314)	(0.315)	(0.313)
Additional policies	0.294	0.846	0.873	0.836
	(0.474)	(0.537)	(0.537)	(0.535)
Start year	−0.024**	−0.026**	−0.026*	−0.027**
	(0.012)	(0.013)	(0.013)	(0.013)
U.S. sender	0.048	−0.702	−0.747	−0.654
	(0.428)	(0.587)	(0.587)	(0.585)
National security issue		−0.769*	−0.780*	−0.787*
		(0.417)	(0.417)	(0.416)
Institutional involvement		0.995**	0.962*	1.021**
		(0.504)	(0.504)	(0.505)
Sender regime type		0.083*	0.086*	0.080*
		(0.047)	(0.047)	(0.047)
Observations	119	114	114	114
Pseudo-R^2	0.078	0.119	0.118	0.118

Notes: Standard errors in parentheses; * significant at 10 percent; ** significant at 5 percent; *** significant at 1 percent

trade increase from its 25th percentile to 75th percentile, the probability of at least a partial success increases from 45 percent to 58 percent. While this impact is not terribly strong, it does show that increased trade relations also increase the likelihood that the sender will prevail.

The last two variables attaining significance are the cost in absolute dollars to the target and the year in which the sanctions were imposed. The significance of the absolute costs and not the cost as a proportion of GNP suggests that the impact is more symbolic than actual economic pain. That is, instead of the target giving up because its economy cannot bear the cost of the sanction, it complies with the sender's demands because the dollar figure is perceived to be too large. The mean cost as a percent of GNP is only 2 percent, and a full 61 percent of the cases involve costs that are less than 1 percent of the target's GNP. Although these costs may be unpleasant, they clearly are not crushing. In absolute dollar terms, however, the mean is $200 million. This figure does drive the target to give in to the sender's demands. According to the model, when absolute costs are at their 25th percentile, partial or better success is 45 percent likely; when those costs reach their 75th percentile, the probability is 58 percent.[14]

The impact the year of initiation has on the outcome is consistent with Hufbauer et al.'s finding that sanctions are becoming less successful with time. Originally, Hufbauer et al. only used a dummy variable for time indicating a pre-1973 period and a post-1973 period. Using the actual year the sanctions were implemented increases the information we can glean from the analysis. That is, sanctions actually have become less effective through time, not just less effective at the approximate half way point in the data. The estimate shows that a two decade shift forward reduces the probability of at least partial success from 55 percent to 43 percent.

None of the other variables attain significance. As expected and found by Hufbauer et al., the size differential between the sender and target is not significant. The presence of a black knight, a country supporting the target, does approach significance (p-value = 0.15) and is in the expected direction. It is rather surprising that such aid to the target would not significantly inhibit the effectiveness of the sanction. Given the strong bivariate findings in Hufbauer et al., it is not wise to discount too heavily the impact of this variable. This is not to say that the null hypothesis should be rejected, but that strong conclusions about the impact of a black knight should not be made based on these results.

This is not true with the other results. First, a friendly relationship between the sender and target does not seem to have any impact on the sanction outcome. This is surprising given that Hufbauer et al. (1990a), Drezner (1998, 1999), and Davidson and Shambaugh (2000) make very clear cases and provide compelling evidence as to why allies make better targets than opponents. Even as the results do not support the previous finding that friendly relations increase sanction effectiveness, they are not contrary to them. That is, the results are not significant and in the direction opposite to expectations. Additionally, supplemental policies are insignificant suggesting that additional measures will not increase the effectiveness of the sanctions.

Also surprising is the insignificance of the cost to the sender. Morgan and Schwebach (1997) argue and provide limited evidence showing that coercive efforts that cost the sender considerably tend to fail more often. As the results in column 1 show, there is no support for this relationship. It is possible that costs to the sender have differential effects depending on the mechanism through which the sanctions work. For sanctions that function by increasing the costs to the target (the conventional wisdom), high costs to the sender may limit its ability to continue to mount such economic harm on the target. For sanctions that function by signaling the target (Schwebach's (2000) "line in the sand" argument), high costs to the sender may increase effectiveness by showing its resolve. Since these effects are ambivalent, they may be canceling each other out. Unfortunately, there is no feasible way in which the sanction mechanism can be determined, a priori. Therefore, separating the effects of sender costs is untenable.

The next step in my analysis expands the model to include the variables representing the three additional hypotheses. I also explore which type of trade with the target (total, imports, or exports) makes sanctions more effective. These results appear in columns 2–4 in table 3.1.

When I reestimate the model appearing in column 1 with three new variables and the three measures of trade, there is little change in the conventional wisdom variables with one exception. The variables that had already attained or nearly attained significance became more robust with lower p-values. The one exception is that the supplemental policies variable approaches significance. The variable shows that as covert action or some form of military threat or action is engaged, the target is more likely to alter its policy to conform to the sender's demand.

The three new variables are all significant, but they do not all support the hypotheses they measure. First, when the sanction issue rises to the level of national security for the sender, economic coercion is less effective; a finding that is contrary to the expectation. Holding other variables at their means (or modes for dichotomous variables) there is only a 47 percent likelihood that economic coercion will yield at least a partial success. This probability drops precipitously to 29 percent if the sender considers the issue to be one of national security. The explanation for this rather unexpected effect may lay in the definition of national security used herein. Since military disputes, nuclear proliferation, and communist expansion would also be considered high political issues for the target as well as the sender, the target will be more willing to resist the sanctions just as the sender is more willing to prosecute them. Future analyses might attempt to measure the salience of the issue for the sender and target separately and test to see if the difference between the importance each state gives to the issue affects the outcome of the economic coercion.

The involvement of international institutions is significant and in the expected, positive direction. To understand its effect, three scenarios must be considered. First, in the case where there is a multilateral coalition deploying the sanctions but no international organization, there is only a 19 percent chance that the sanctions will be effective. This result is not surprising, as Doxey (1971: 90) points out: "Collective action which involves the commitment and diversion of national resources will be easier to organize if the overriding policy goals of a group of nations happen to coincide . . . Much more common are cases when collective action appears to conflict with national goals . . ." The involvement of an international institution such as the UN, IMF, or OAS increases the probability to 40 percent. Clearly, these institutions do much to solve (1) the bargaining problems between the senders as they decide to deploy the economic coercion and (2) the cheating or backsliding within the coalition once the sanctions are in place. These findings suggest that the cooperation costs associated with sanctioning issues may be high, but they can be drastically decreased by international organizations. Thus, institutions provide a forum for settling the disputes that appear when forming a cooperative sanctioning effort.

International organizations do not, however, make for the best type of sanction sender—unilateral economic sanction efforts succeed, at least partially, 63 percent under the same conditions.[15] Thus, the single sender is the best way to get the target to cry uncle. It is worth noting that this is probably the most commonly misunderstood regularity of economic coercion, especially by policy makers. For example,

Vice President Dick Cheney, in explaining why he supported ending the sanctions against Iran while he was CEO of Halliburton at the 2004 Vice Presidential Debate, said that he was for ending sanctions because they were unilateral and thus did not work. Instead, he argued that multilateral sanctions through the UN would be more effective. Each of the other candidates running for the White House said similar things about the importance of multilateral sanctions. As the results show, this is simply wrong.

At first blush, more cooperation among senders certainly would seem to make sanctions more effective since a coalition could put more potential pressure on the targets. However, the coordination and enforcement issues far outweigh any advantage multilateralism may provide. Further evidence for this conclusion is that in a limited number of cases international institutions were employed by a unilateral sender. For example, the United States initiated sanctions in part by utilizing the IMF. It was the only nation acting as a sender, but it used its influence in the IMF to control debt rescheduling and liquidity loans. As a result, it was able to increase the economic impact on the target without having to negotiate a multilateral effort. Additional research may show that authoritative power within a sanction coalition limits the negative impact multilateral sanctions have. Until then, it is rather encouraging to see the positive impact institutions have on sanction effectiveness. As data from the rest of the 1990s and beyond become available, it will be interesting to see if this positive effect continues.

The last hypothesis, that democracies are more effective at using economic coercion, is supported by the analysis. Using the average Polity score in the model (a seven) for the starting point, the model predicts that 47 percent of the cases will be at least partial successes. For an autocracy with a Polity score of -7 (the inverse of the mean score), the likelihood of success is only 22 percent. This finding fits with Hart's (2000) argument that democracies face domestic audience costs that make their signals more credible.

Two points are worth considering before making too many conclusions based on this finding, however. First, the Hufbauer et al. data include a disproportionate number of democratic senders. Therefore, it may be the case that if more representative sanction data were collected, this finding would weaken. As Kaempfer and Lowenberg argue, democracies will be more likely to be affected by domestic demands from rent-seeking firms not to mention the "do something" demands from the public. These factors would tend to make economic coercion less effective because the sanctions would be used not to influence the target but to placate a domestic group.

Second, democracies may be better at using sanctions because their liberal markets provide them with more dynamic economies that can both cause economic harm on the target and sustain the costs required to do so. There is more to causing economic dislocation than simply dollar costs, as mentioned earlier in the example of sanctioning oil over a less profitable good. Democracies, with their liberal economies, may have a greater capacity to hurt the target more effectively than a centrally planned economy common in autocracies. While the outcome (democrats sanction more effectively) is the same, the mechanism is different. In Hart's argument, the democratic nature of the regime causes the sanctions to be more effective; on the other hand, it is the liberal, market- driven economies that cause the sanctions to be more effective.

The last issue to discuss is the effects of the different types of trade: imports, exports, and total trade. As the results in columns 2–4 indicate, there is very little difference between the different measures of trade. The p-values range from 0.09 to 0.11, revealing they are only marginally significant at best. The other explanatory variables are also stable, suggesting that the type of presanction does not matter, although that there *is* presanction trade that does matter.

Does the Conventional Wisdom Matter?

The results of the multivariate analyses indicate that Hufbauer et al.'s (1990a) policy recommendations need to be revisited. Only five of their original eight findings are supported. First, distressed targets tended to succumb to sanctions more often than strong, healthy targets. Their ability to resist, both economically and especially politically, helps determine the outcome of the sanction effort. Second, the size ratio between the sender and target was found to be insignificant. At first blush, this impact may seem surprising, but once one considers that sanctions typically do not cost either the target or the sender much, the lack of a relationship between the size ratio and efficacy makes sense. Third, international cooperation tends to decrease sanction effectiveness, but this relationship was marginally significant at best. Still, coordination and enforcement costs of multilateralism clearly outweigh the increased trade connections and legitimacy that multiple senders may possess. Fourth, presanction trade increases the likelihood of success. Fifth, the absolute dollar cost to the target has a positive, significant effect on success; however, the cost as a portion of GNP is not significant. As a result, target costs function more as signals than actual pressure on the target's economy.

The results of the multivariate analysis undermined two of the conventional wisdom's tenets. First, the presence of a sanction spoiler or black knight does not necessarily have an adverse impact on the effectiveness of the sanctions. The statistical results approach significance, but the fact that they do not attain it does suggest that the policy recommendation concerning black knights is at least overstated. Given the nonintuitive nature of this finding, more analysis is warranted before any policy proclamations are made. For example, black knights may have been important during the Cold War, but not beyond. If this were the case, then senders will not have to concern themselves with these spoiler states. However, this is a question that requires more data and future assessment.

The second policy recommendation to be questioned concerns the suggestion to "attack your allies, not your adversaries" (Hufbauer et al. 1990a: 99). The ordered logit analysis shows no support whatsoever for this variable. This finding is rather surprising since others have argued and found evidence supporting it (Drezner 1998, 1999; Davidson and Shambaugh 2000). Once again, future analyses should examine the extent to which prior relations may influence the outcome of the economic coercion. Until that point, policy recommendations about these two variables should be taken with a shaker of salt, not just the required grain with which all studies should be taken.

While the salience of the issue (national security or not) and the sender's polity cannot feasibly be manipulated by the sender and therefore cannot be translated into policy recommendations, the rather powerful impact international organizations have on the outcome of economic coercion can be. As the results clearly show, the involvement of international institutions can mitigate or limit the damaging effect of multilateral economic coercion. Thus, senders should first avoid multilateral efforts when sanctioning, but if they must join with others, then they should do so through some international organization. Cooperation can be a serious detriment to success without an organization to administer the sanctions and give them legitimacy. That is, an international organization not only acts as an impartial coordinator and enforcement mechanism for the sending nations but also gives legitimacy to the sanctioning effort in the world community.

Overall, Hufbauer et al.'s recommendations hold up rather well. In previous analyses (Drury 1997, 1998), I found that their recommendations did not fair nearly as well. These analyses were based on their original data from their 1990 study. I have added here only a few new cases to the old data, and the bivariate correlations between the old data and updated data are extremely high (all correlation coefficients were above 0.90). I conclude that the updates Hufbauer et al. have made are responsible for the more supportive results found herein. Thus, some of the policy advice they provide should be viewed quite skeptically; however, most of their recommendations should be considered by policy makers as they approach the decision to use economic sanctions. The one major qualification to this inference is the overall poor performance of the models. I address this issue below.

Conclusion

The literature studying economic sanctions is as diverse as the countries which sanction. However, commonalties do exist. The conventional wisdom asserts that (1) leaders use sanctions to affect the target's policies, (2) more severe sanctions are more likely to succeed, and, in general, (3) sanctions fail. Further, this literature tends to address only partly the conditions under which states use economic coercion, normally only alluding to their goals and not to the circumstances in which they are selected. Few have addressed the question of what conditions lead to the use and maintenance of economic sanctions. Instead, most authors are simply concerned with the effectiveness of economic coercion regarding the goal of altering the target's policies.

The repercussions of this deficiency are clear in the reanalysis of Hufbauer et al.'s (1991a) study. Many of their policy recommendations were supported, a result which also leads to the inference that the conventional wisdom is at least partly correct. However, such an optimistic conclusion may not be warranted. The measures-of-fit show that the models are rather poor at accurately explaining the sanction outcome. The pseudo-R^2 never exceeds 0.12, and the predicted probabilities show that the model predicts at most 20 percent of the outcomes correctly.[16] As a result, Hufbauer et al. and the conventional wisdom may not be wrong when they connect the target's cost, cooperation, and so on to effectiveness, but these variables are still unable to provide a very precise explanation of why targets concede. Part of this less-than-perfect ability to determine the outcome must be a function of the diverse means and ends through which sanctions work.

To begin with, sanctions can have a variety of goals, as many scholars have pointed out. It is possible that several of the sanctions in the Hufbauer et al. data are aimed primarily at the sender's public. That is, these sanctions may have been levied to placate the public's demand to "do something." If this is the case, then their success measure is not tapping the real goal and would indicate failure when the sanctions may not have failed.

Further, almost none of the independent variables measure domestic political phenomena. Therefore, virtually by definition the model cannot predict the outcome of domestically driven economic coercion. The one possible exception may be the cost to the target, which would indicate to the sender's public that their government is taking their demands seriously (or at least seriously attempting to placate the public). The same is largely true for sanctions aimed at setting an international precedent or deterring other actors in the world. The Hufbauer et al. measure of success does not include international symbolism (with good reason). So again, the effectiveness of these cases is not properly measured.

The second confounding problem with determining sanction effectiveness is the means through which they operate. As the conventional wisdom asserts, some sanctions work by putting economic pressure on the target. Other sanctions are signals that tell the target how resolved the sender is (Schwebach 2000). Clearly, these two types of economic coercion function very differently. One is direct and instrumental, while the other is based on symbolic phenomena such as the reputation of the sender, the target's relationship with the sender, desires for future relations, and so on. The problem here is twofold. First, while the model contains variables that partly tap the signaling properties economic coercion has, the model does not directly attempt to estimate these features. Second, even if a comprehensive model could be created, one that tapped both instrumental and symbolic aspects of economic coercion, the different ways in which these two types function may be so incongruent that keeping them in the same estimation may not be efficient. Including sanctions, which function so differently by signaling and by causing direct economic harm, may cause variables to be insignificant and measures-of-fit to be very low.

Unfortunately, current data prohibit separating the cases by the process through which they function. Measuring the different goals may very well be impossible. It is also likely that many sanctions have multiple goals and means, a characteristic that further complicates matters. Current data and theories limit our ability to explain the outcomes of economic sanctions with much precision. This inability suggests a different research focus on conditions rather than goals may be profitable. To understand economic sanctions better, we must understand the conditions under which leaders use this form of coercive diplomacy. In the next chapter, I develop a theory of why U.S. presidents decide to use economic coercion. This theory addresses the international and domestic conditions, incentives, and constraints that the president faces, as well as the particular characteristics of the president. Subsequent chapters derive hypotheses and test this theory with quantitative data.

Chapter 4

Why Does the President Sanction? Beyond the Conventional Wisdom

As I attempted to show in chapters 2 and 3, economic sanctions are quite complex. They can have a variety of different goals (improve human rights, stem communism, etc.), leaders may impose them for different reasons (placate the domestic public, punish, etc.), and the process through which they function—instrumental versus symbolic—differs. This complexity makes explaining accurately the outcome of economic coercion very difficult. The results in chapter 3 clearly show that what is generally accepted as the conventional wisdom is partially true at best. Further, even for those variables that are significant, the overall accuracy of the model leaves much to be desired. With a model that explains less than 12 percent of the variance, an outsider might think that economic sanction effectiveness is a random walk; after all, 88 percent of the question is left unexplained. It is not surprising that policy makers tend to make such contradictory and ill-informed comments—such as Vice President Cheney during the 1994 debate—they do not have an accurate, consistent base of knowledge from which to draw.

The main argument in this book is that an important question regarding economic sanctions has been overlooked by the literature: under what conditions do leaders initiate, increase, decrease, or lift economic coercion? In this chapter, I develop an explanation of why the U.S. president initiates and modifies an economic sanction.[1]

I first show that a connection between the decision calculus for the use of force and economic coercion exists. Although the decision to use sanctions has been addressed by a small handful of scholars, much theorizing and analysis has focused on the use of military force. Because both military force and economic sanctions are foreign policy tools aimed at influencing another nation, they are both types of coercive diplomacy. Coercive diplomacy is defined as the effort to use some sort of coercion (be it military, economic, diplomatic, etc.) to compel another nation (Baldwin 1985; George 1991). Since both military and economic sanctions share this characteristic, it seems quite possible that the general theories and models used to explain the use of force by states can also be used to inform a theory of the decision to initiate and modify economic sanctions. For example, when Iraq invaded Kuwait, the first reaction of the international community was to demand the withdrawal of Iraqi troops (best illustrated by President Bush's comment "This will not stand"). On the heels of this demand was a set of comprehensive economic sanctions. When Iraq would still not comply, tensions mounted, and Operation Desert Storm was initiated. Led by the United States, the international community used increasingly more severe forms of coercive diplomacy while trying to remove Iraq from Kuwait.

The connection between these levels of coercive diplomacy goes further than simply the rank ordering of their intensity; there are similarities in the decision process that leads to their use. In the example above, it is important to realize that the decisions to increase the pressure on Iraq are essentially the same. While there are differences between the decisions (highlighted by the direct use of physical violence), each decision is based on the same goal against the same opponent and involves the same issue. During the Iraqi invasion, Bush wanted to remove Hussein from Kuwait. The decisions to increase the pressure all followed a very similar calculus. If this connection between the use of military and economic sanctions exists, then the vast literature focusing on the use of force may inform us of the conditions under which economic sanctions are used. With this connection between military and economic coercion postulated, I use four specific theories below to develop three different models of political rationality that explain the president's decisions on economic coercion.

A soft rational choice or utilitarian approach provides the basis for the first model. Essentially, this model asserts that the relationship between the sender and target determines the conditions that lead the president to use or modify economic sanctions. The diversionary theory of war and the poliheuristic theory of decision-making form the foundation of the second model, which delineates domestic constraints and incentives that condition the president's use of economic coercion. Finally, psychological theories of leadership and the organization of the president's advisory system supply a lens through which the president makes his decision. This last model suggests that greater flexibility in the decision-making process increases the likelihood that economic coercion will be attempted.

I turn next to connecting economic and military coercion. Drawing from this scholarship, I develop three models of the decision to initiate, increase, decrease, or lift economic sanctions,[2] which are three models of political rationality. The chapter ends with a summary of the theory explaining the president's sanction decisions.

Connecting Economic and Military Coercion

In this section, I place both economic sanctions and military action into a common framework: coercive diplomacy. Before turning to the connections between these two forms of coercion share, there are some differences to note. Most obvious is the direct physical violence that economic coercion lacks. An austere sanction policy can have a devastating impact on an economy, subsequently limiting its ability to feed the target's citizens. The sanctions against Iraq in the 1990s drove up infant mortality. However, there is a big difference between bombing an area and killing those in the target area and reducing the welfare of the target country so much that people die as a result. In the case of the military, there is a direct causal link—the bombs actually killed the people. There is not such a clear link in the case of economic sanctions. To continue the example of Iraq's infant mortality, Saddam Hussein's policies were designed to provide as much benefit to his ruling coalition (essentially the Baath Party) as possible. Clearly, this came with a significant cost to the rest of Iraq. Funds from the oil-for-food program were diverted to those in power to ensure the government stayed in power.[3] The rest of the Iraqis suffered. Therefore, one cannot establish a direct causal link between the sanctions and the infant mortality. This same pattern appears in other brutal autocracies such as Haiti and Burma. These points are not meant to demean the deaths caused by the sanctions. Instead, they show that military force and economic coercion differ regarding their level of direct violence.

A second difference applies only to one type of military action: a ground invasion. In the case of the introduction of ground troops with the goal of invading the target, there is no question of fungibility. If successful, the military will physically force the target to comply with its demands. The British and French incursion into Egypt to secure the Suez Canal is a good example. By physically taking the Canal, there was no question whether the military actions are linked to control of the Canal. Had London and Paris attempted economic coercion, they would have been engaging in linkage politics, which would have required that the economic sanctions have a fungible connection to Nasser's decision to nationalize the Suez Canal (Li 1993). The key difference is that ground troops (assuming they are successful) locate the power with the sender—to decide when to take power, relinquish it, destroy the target, and so on. In the case of economic coercion, there is a try-and-see approach (George 1991: 7–9) in which the sender applies the sanctions and must wait for the target to decide what the outcome shall be. The target can decide to concede or resist—which leaves the decision in the hands of the target, not the sender (unless, of course, the sender is willing to escalate the dispute to include ground troops).[4]

This distinction between economic coercion and military invasion only holds for actual invasions. Air campaigns that involve even massive bombing are similar to sanctions in this regard. The sender decides what pressure to put on the target—in this case, bombs—and the target decides when or if to acquiesce. It is always possible that a bomb might kill the leader, but it is highly unlikely and almost historically unprecedented.[5] While there is no doubt that a bombing campaign is different from an economic sanction, they do have many similarities. It is to these similarities that I now turn.

Economic sanctions, like limited military action, are a form of coercive diplomacy, which is best defined as using enough pressure "to demonstrate resolution to protect well-defined interests and also to demonstrate the credibility of one's determination to use more force if necessary . . . The coercive strategy, therefore, has a signaling, bargaining, negotiating character . . ." (George et al. 1971: 18). George et al. only include military force when defining coercive diplomacy, but as the quote above shows, it is not necessary to exclude other forms of foreign policy pressure. According to George et al., coercive diplomacy is the use of the military to signal resolve and the potential for further escalation to the target in order to get them to cease, reverse, or alter a policy. The military action is meant to reinforce verbal demands or threats from the sender, to make them more credible. Instead of actually physically forcing the target to change its policy, military actions or threats are meant to force the target to negotiate with the sender.

When the military is used in this manner, as a signal of preferences and resolve, economic sanctions have the same characteristics, although at a less acute level of hostility. The deployment of sanctions or the threat to do so signals the target of the sender's resolve. For instance, the United States initiated economic coercion in 1976 against Taiwan to pressure it to stop developing fissile material. A verbal demand alone would not have signaled Washington's resolve to Taipei. A stronger signal would have been movement of the Seventh Fleet toward Taiwan, of course, but the sanctions imposed by President Ford are conceptually the same as military coercion. The sanctions sent a signal that the United States was serious about its demand to forgo nuclear reprocessing. They showed Taipei that the United States was willing to bear significant costs to make their point. Military action, such as President Clinton's movement of the Seventh Fleet through the Taiwan Strait in 1996 to signal the People's Republic of China that the United States would intervene in a conflict if Beijing's missile tests and maneuvers turned hostile, functions in the same manner. It sends a signal to the target indicating how displeased and resolved the sender is, or in more rational choice terms, what the sender's preference ordering is.

The idea that economic coercion is a less severe form of coercive diplomacy is not new. David Baldwin (1985) characterizes economic sanctions as part of a larger continuum of foreign policy tools. Baldwin argues that propaganda, diplomacy, economic sanctions, and military sanctions are all forms of increasingly hostile statecraft. While diplomacy and particularly propaganda may be hard to envision as forms of coercion, it is useful to view the wider context of foreign policy options available to states. A propaganda campaign aimed at discrediting the target state in the international arena may push them to negotiate with the sender. The report at the United Nations during the Cuban Missile Crisis clearly helped America's position against the Soviets. Although it was the naval quarantine and the threat of nuclear exchange that turned the Soviet ships around and led them to dismantle their missiles, accounts of the Missile Crisis include the UN report by Adlai Stevenson as key to gaining world support and putting more pressure on Moscow. Like these examples of propaganda and military coercion, economic coercion works in a similar manner. Sanctions signal the target of the sender's intentions, resolve, and so on, and potentially incur costs that the target would prefer to avoid. Thus, they coerce the target to do something it would not otherwise do.

In addition to economic sanctions operating the same as other forms of coercive diplomacy, the decision process that leads to their use is very similar. Increasingly severe disputes lead the disputants to use increasingly hostile forms of coercion. Simply put, hostile disputes are much more likely to involve more hostile forms of coercion, in part by definition. As state leaders face more intransigent targets or policies that are more objectionable, they will want to use more pressure on the target to resolve the situation to their liking. Constraints also play a role in economic sanctioning efforts, just as they do for other forms of statecraft. As witnessed by the considerable anti-sanction lobbying by groups such as the National Association of Manufacturers, sanctions cost the sender state by decreasing economic activity with the target state.

Although the costs of economic sanctions are not the same as the human and financial cost of military action, they are costs that the leader must be willing to expend if coercion is to be applied. It is worthy to note that economic sanctions are not always an acceptable option to the leader because of these costs, just as military coercion is often unacceptable. As Mintz (2003) and others have pointed out, leaders narrow their choices by first selecting those that are politically acceptable. There are obvious examples when military force is not acceptable—environmental issues come to mind. Sanctions can be unacceptable, too. Denying antidrug aid to Mexico has proven to be an unacceptable means to coercing the Mexican government to step up reforms to combat drug trafficking to the United States.

To sum up, economic coercion shares multiple characteristics—including a common decision calculus—with military force. Differences between the two forms of coercive diplomacy are also apparent, perhaps more than their similarities. However, their commonalities suggest that theories seeking to explain the political use of force have the potential to explain the use of economic coercion as well.

Models of Political Rationality

I now turn to three models of political rationality.[6] Each of these models adds increasing detail to the explanation of why the president initiates economic coercion. They are not competing explanations but complementary where each advances our understanding of the conditions that lead the president to use or modify economic sanctions. Collectively, they combine into a multivariable model of the conventional wisdom on the use of military force the same way Hufbauer et al.'s model combines the conventional wisdom on economic sanctions.

Model I: International/Dyadic Conditions

Model I is based broadly on the logic of coercive diplomacy. According to this model, the president makes his decision to enact sanctions based on the recent and expected future relations with the target. It essentially predicts that the president, contemplating only the U.S.–target relations, will use sanctions when the benefit of their use outweighs the cost of their imposition. The president will apply or perhaps increase the level of economic coercion when recent history or future expectations suggest that the target is intransigent toward the president's demands. In the simplest of terms, when the target resists the president's demand, he will apply more pressure in the form of economic sanctions. Because the model considers only the U.S.–target relationship and interactions (the international circumstances, pressures, utilities, etc.), its explanation is limited to sanctions seeking international goals. Therefore, the model assumes that the sanctions are used for either affecting the target's policies or sending a message to the target.[7]

According to the coercive diplomacy literature, the process that should lead the president to consider using economic sanctions begins when a conflict of interest arises between the United States and another country. Snyder and Deising (1977) assert that this conflict or dispute is set in motion by a precipitant. The precipitant "is threatening to the state's external or internal security, it threatens the state's economic viability or affronts its national dignity and prestige" (11). This precipitant or threat, which can be perceived or real, most commonly is the result of actions or policies of the target state. For example, the United States and its allies placed economic sanctions on East Germany in direct response to the building of the Berlin Wall in 1961—a case of the target's actions being offensive and threatening to the United States and its allies. Alternatively, the precipitant can be the result of an internal change within the sender. That is, the sender's preferences or perceptions can change and subsequently a preexisting policy practiced by the target becomes threatening to the sender.

This situation is best clarified by an example. When Jimmy Carter assumed the presidency in 1977, he changed American foreign policy to have a distinct focus on human rights. Several countries, especially those in Latin America, had not changed their human rights policies in the past couple of years, but the change Carter instituted had redefined these countries as perpetrating unacceptable human rights abuses.

The result was the initiation of economic sanctions against several of these countries. Thus, the precipitant was the result of a change in the sender not the target.

The precipitant propels the offended state to challenge the other (Sislin 1994). The challenge is some kind of demand that the target cease the offending behavior. If the target alters its behavior as desired by the offended state, the crisis is averted. However, if the target resists the challenge by either publicly denouncing the sender's demand or by simply ignoring it, confrontation ensues (Snyder and Deising 1977: 13–14). The confrontation is "the core of the crisis" (14) and the point at which the sender decides whether to issue coercive threats or take coercive action. This decision to escalate is determined not only by the severity of the offense or threat but also by the expected reaction of the target. If the sender expects the target to retaliate, then it will be at least somewhat less likely to initiate some coercive action against the target (Sislin 1994). If the sender decides to back down from its initial challenge, then the crisis is again averted. Assuming that the sender decides not to back down, however, it will initiate some form of coercive diplomacy or at least threaten to do so. If the crisis continues to escalate, open hostilities or war may result. The level of tension and its rate of change are the primary determinants of how the crisis will be resolved.

What should be clear is the role an economic sanction plays as one form of coercion available to the sender. When the president contemplates using economic coercion, the United States and a target have already entered into a crisis or dispute—the target has taken some offensive action (the precipitant) resulting in a demand from the president (the challenge); the target resists the challenge, a move that increases the U.S.–target tension level and begins the confrontation. If the tension is sufficient, the president will decide to levy economic sanctions in an attempt to force the target to capitulate to his demands.

For example, the United States and Peru were engaged in expropriation proceedings beginning in 1963. The precipitant was the initial Peruvian decision to expropriate U.S. assets. The president threatened Peru that he would cut off aid to Peru by enacting the Hickenlooper Bill if Peru did not make progress in the proceedings.[8] The president had thereby issued the challenge, and Peru was negotiating to avoid losing aid. In October 1968, the Peruvian military deposed President Belaunde and proceeded to expropriate the International Petroleum Company's assets in Peru. This action not only constituted resistance to the United States but also drove up the tensions between the two nations. As a direct result, President Johnson sanctioned Peru by reducing aid. Peru subsequently invited the United States to appeal the expropriation, and the two nations reached an agreement averting further conflict.[9]

T. Clifton Morgan's (1990, 1994) spatial model of crisis bargaining casts economic sanctions in a similar light. Morgan's primary findings concern the role a nation's resolve has in crisis resolution. He finds that nations with greater resolve are more likely to attain a favorable outcome, but that war is also more likely. In addition to resolve, Morgan (1990: 282; 1994: 49) asserts that when two nations are bargaining over some issue, one or both may use economic sanctions as a way of increasing the costs to the opponent for not conceding, a move meant to bring the opponent closer to the challenging nation's demands. Thus, during the crisis or dispute (after which the target has decided to resist the sender's demands), both nations have an incentive to increase the costs on the opponent for not conceding. Morgan's analysis of his formal model shows that the nation most able to increase the bargaining costs is more likely to attain a favorable outcome in the dispute. This finding suggests that when the target resists the president's demands, the president has a rational reason to impose costs on the target. In the Peruvian case, the president imposed economic sanctions in an attempt to force the Peruvians to restart the expropriation proceedings. In that case, the U.S. ability to impose sanctions on Peru led to the outcome favored by the United States.

Economic sanctions also provide the sender with a signal of resolve. While James Blessing's study of suspension of international aid is rather pessimistic about its ability to coerce the target, he notes that sanctions "symbolize American dismay over recipient behavior" (1981: 535). Zachary Seldon (1999: 7) concurs by arguing that following the Soviet invasion of Afghanistan, "[s]anctions were imposed as a means of demonstrating the United States' resolve." Thus, the use of economic coercion as both pressure and signal fits directly into the process through which a crisis escalates. Taking this argument a step further, Peter van Bergeijk (1994) suggests that economic coercion is replacing military coercion as an acceptable form of statecraft in the post–Cold War era. Seldon agrees, asserting that "[b]ecause economic rather than military strength is increasingly seen by many as the prime determinant of international power, sanctions may begin to assume an even more prominent role" (1999: 3).

Empirical analyses support the picture presented thus far. Goldstein and Freeman (1991) analyze great power relations to determine if their actions toward each other are a result of prior relations or bureaucratic momentum. Unlike Snyder and Deising's (1977) and Morgan's (1990, 1994) emphasis on modeling, Goldstein and Freeman take a quantitative approach. They show that U.S.–Soviet–Sino relations are a result of bureaucratic momentum, reactions to the other state (U.S. actions toward the Soviets result from prior Soviet actions toward the United States), and reactions to the third state (U.S.–Sino relations are conditioned by U.S.–Soviet relations as well as prior relations with China). Important for the coercive diplomacy model, Goldstein and Freeman (1991) find that prior hostile actions by one nation lead to hostile actions by the target. As the tensions between two (or three in their analysis) nations increase, each side is more likely to respond in kind. Thus, the president is then more likely to use economic sanctions when the tensions between the United States and the target increase.

Studying how nations act in crisis situations, Russell Leng (1993: 69–73) argues that crisis processes are characterized by two concepts. First, the magnitude or level of the tension between the disputants and the rate at which that tension increases. These two concepts gauge the hostility of the crisis and are essential to determining how the crisis will unfold and what its outcome will be. The second characteristic important to crisis behavior is the level of reciprocity between the two nations. Combining escalation and the level at which each state mirrors its opponent's moves as separate variables, Leng derives four crisis behavior types: (1) fight, when there is a high level of reciprocity between the two states and both are willing to escalate hostility of the crisis, (2) standoff, when there is high reciprocity but a lack of willingness to escalate the dispute, (3) resistance, when one state is unwilling to respond to hostile escalatory actions by its opponent, and (4) put-down, when there is both low reciprocity and low escalation within the crisis dyad. Leng confirms Snyder and Deising's assertion that high rates of escalation are most likely to end in war.

These findings relate directly to the Model I's explanation of the use of economic coercion. As Leng's measure of escalation (which includes both magnitude and rate of change) increased, so did the probability that the crisis would end in war. While economic sanctions are not war, economic sanctions are simply one measure in a larger set of coercive acts. Thus, as nations become embroiled in a dispute, and the tensions between them rise, they should be more likely to use economic sanctions.

Daniel Drezner's explanation of sanctions use and effectiveness is based on a similar theory. He asserts that—in addition to the immediate political and economic costs associated with an economic sanction—both the sender and target consider the consequences of the sanctions for the future. As two nations engaged in some dispute expect future conflict with each other, the likelihood that each will attempt to coerce and resist the other increases. "Adversaries will expect more zero-sum conflict in the future, and so will care more about the material and reputational repercussions of existing conflicts" (Drezner 1998: 710). Drezner makes two important points here.

First, adversarial states are concerned more with relative gains. As such, the sender will be more likely to initiate sanctions quickly so as to begin causing economic harm to the target. This harm should both (1) weaken the target vis-à-vis the sender and (2) end any gains from trade the target was enjoying. Thus, the sanctions should provide the sender with a gain relative to the target, or at least they will end a loss relative to the target. Second, a target that expects future conflict with the sender will be more likely to resist economic coercion because giving in to the sender's demands at the present time may signal weakness and a willingness to concede to the sender in the future. The combined incentive for the sender to attempt coercion and the incentive to the target to resist create a more rapidly escalating dispute.

Drezner assesses his conflict expectation theory by looking at past relations between the sender and target. If the relations were adversarial, then he concludes that the dyad expected future conflict. While using past relations to determine future expectations may not be optimal, there are no valid measures of how states view the future and the best proxy is the past. Even decision-makers rely heavily on prior actions of other states to determine what they may do in the future. For example, the main arguments to invade Iraq and depose Saddam Hussein were based on his past use of chemical weapons on the Kurds and documents that showed he had been developing weapons of mass destruction. Thus, recent prior relations with the target can be expected to influence the president's decision to use economic coercion.

To complete this model of the president's decision, the actual effects of the magnitude of the conflict, its escalation, and prior relations must be synthesized. To accomplish this, I draw on Alexander George's work on the conditions that affect the decision-maker's choice of coercive diplomacy tools and implementation. George (1991) lays out eight conditions that affect the leader's decisions concerning coercive diplomacy. Of these eight conditions, three pertain directly to the use of economic coercion: (1) the conflict's magnitude, (2) the urgency with which the United States wants resolve the conflict, and (3) the type of provocation by the target (George 1991: 69–71; see also Leng 1993: 71). As these variables increase, so do the pressures on the president to levy additional pressure against the target, and the costs of not acting become more apparent—the target is not likely to acquiesce to the president's demand, at least not without additional pressure.

Magnitude is understood as the level of tension between the United States and the target state. More hostile interactions between the two nations indicate a higher magnitude of tension. Cooperation between the United States and target are indicative of low magnitude levels. The magnitude of the dispute is the basis for understanding the pressures or conditions facing the president. In some ways, there is a simple cost–benefit analysis the president performs: as tensions (magnitude) rise, so do the costs of inaction as well as the benefits of action.[10] The costs here are the target's continued resistance to the president's demands. The benefit is target concession. The dispute or crisis tension must rise to a certain level before the president will consider using economic sanctions. Assuming Baldwin's (1985) characterization of foreign policy levels (propaganda, diplomatic, economic, and military) is accurate, the tension level should be less than what would bring the United States to use force and greater than what would bring the United States to use diplomacy or propaganda.

The second of George's conditions is the time pressure facing the president. There are several reasons a dispute may become urgent, for example, "concern that international or domestic support of the policy may decline . . . fear that one's ability to manage the crisis is breaking down" or anxiety that waiting will permit the target to take steps that mitigate the ability of the sanctions to cause any harm such as securing alternative sources or markets for the potentially sanctioned goods (Seeler 1982; George 1991: 70). These concerns are driven by the speed at which the crisis is becoming more hostile. If the dispute is escalating at a rate faster than the president wants, he will be more likely to use economic sanctions because he either expects the dispute to become very hostile soon, that there are concerns about maintaining support, controlling the crisis, or making the sanctions more effective. Thus, the president may use sanctions before the tension level reaches the typical level at which sanctions are used because he expects the situation to escalate to that level in the very near future or must act before other conditions have made sanctions untenable.

The third and final condition is the provocation perpetrated by the target. Provocative acts that are more hostile and more definitive in their purpose are harder to reverse. Therefore, such hostile provocations could be expected to pressure the president into using economic coercion more quickly. In essence, the president must act because the target was so provocative that it circumvented the need for tensions to rise, simply because the target has acted in a manner which requires an immediate response.

While this position is certainly logical, there is an alternative expectation. An extremely provocative, bellicose target state not only raises the absolute tension level of the dispute and does so rapidly but also sends a signal to the United States that it is unlikely to back down in the face of coercion. For example, the Soviet invasion of Afghanistan sent a clear signal that it was likely to resist pressures to withdraw. While this signal may not have been intentional, the fact that a superpower was willing to invade another state clearly indicates that it did not take the situation lightly. Therefore, U.S. decision-makers must have realized that it was very likely that economic coercion was destined to fail. This is especially true for economic coercion, which does not bring to bear the same pressure that military coercion does. If the target is likely to resist coercive pressures by the sender, then it is even more likely to resist economic pressures than military ones. Thus, I expect that highly belligerent provocations by the target will decrease the president's penchant for initiating economic sanctions.[11]

Briefly summarizing, the president considers the relationship when deciding to initiation or alter economic coercion against the target. While these considerations are the primary driving force behind the White House's decisions, other factors also enter into the calculus. I address these factors below.

Model II: Domestic Political Factors

The pressures and the condition of the relationship with the target certainly plays a big role in the president's decision to use economic coercion. The president does not, however, make the decisions in a vacuum that isolates him from domestic conditions. Model II adds to the explanation of the president's decision by incorporating the impact domestic political factors have on that decision. The model shows that the president may use economic sanctions as a way to placate public demands for action or simply to appear as a more active president in general. Based primarily on the diversionary theory of war and the work done on presidential approval and war, Model II widens the goals that sanctions may have by including domestic objectives in addition to the international ones modeled in the coercive diplomacy model.

There are two basic arguments as to why domestic politics will affect the president's decision to use or alter economic sanctions against another country. First, domestic groups that will gain rents from sanctions will pressure the president to enact sanctions so as to benefit them. As discussed before, Kaempfer and Lowenberg make a compelling argument with their public choice theory of economic coercion. Because economic sanctions have protectionist externalities, domestic firms will be very interested in seeing those sanctions enacted in such a way that optimizes that benefit. Kaempfer and Lowenberg argue that this type of sanction is most likely to be levied by the Congress and not by the president, but certainly such effects could still be present in White House decision-making.

This connection between domestic groups and presidential decision-making is true first because democracies, especially the United States, avow liberal trade. Therefore, protectionist policies should be antithetical to American foreign policy. This preference for free trade is enhanced by the WTO and the trade court that now seeks to enforce liberal trade. However, economic sanctions provide a cover or at least proverbial "fig leaf" for the White House to employ protectionism. Second, although the president may not try to please domestic groups with sanctions, he will certainly attempt not to anger important groups that would be hurt by them. Protectionism benefits exporting groups, but it hurts importers. Therefore, while sanctions may generate some winners, they also create losers. The president may well consider not who benefits from the sanctions as Kaempfer and Lowenberg argue but who loses.

This second reason, avoiding the political costs that come from the economic harm done to certain industries, raises the questions of whether economic coercion is always a politically acceptable option to the president. The costs sanctions place on the sender are relatively small compared to military action, but relative to other forms of diplomacy, they are quite costly. Further, the costs can be specific and acute for a given industry.[12] Therefore, sanctions cannot always be an acceptable option to the president. Poliheuristic theory sheds valuable light on this decision process. In spelling out the theory, Alexander Mintz (2003) contends that the leader first rules out politically unacceptable options for dealing with another state and then maximizes the utility of those remaining options. The theory specifies that the first gate keeping stage will be driven largely by domestic political concerns, although international factors may also play a role.

In addition to ruling out the obviously objectionable options such as massive military strikes to contend with less acute precipitants, unacceptable sanctions must also be ruled out. That is, some sanctions would be so costly that imposing them would be politically unacceptable at home. For example, the threatened sanctions against China following the Tiananmen Square violence would have cost the United States billions in lost trade (Chan 2000; Li and Drury 2004). Such costs were so high as to make such total trade sanctions (revoking Most Favored Nation status) a nonviable option. It seems quite likely, then, that the president considers domestic political costs before embarking on an economic sanction.

Costs are not the only factor the president considers, however. Returning to the Tiananmen case, the White House did initiate a set of economic sanctions against China following the June 4, 1989 crackdown. President Bush (the former) banned the sale of several military and military-related products (Hufbauer et al. 1990a: 269). However, he rather rapidly lifted the sanctions as different firms requested exemptions from them (Li and Drury 2004). For example, Boeing was not permitted to sell airplanes under the sanctions. As soon as they were ready to deliver on a contract with Beijing, however, Bush exempted them from the sanctions a mere month after the crackdown.[13] It seems very likely that Bush's sanctions against China were more a response to domestic demands for action than Beijing's actions. Referred throughout the literature as the "do something" hypothesis, it suggests that the president initiates sanctions because the public is outraged by the actions of the target and demands some kind of response. The president has little interest in actually taking significant action against the target and so chooses to sanction the target as a low-cost means of satisfying the public's demand to "do something."

Thus, there are several reasons domestic political concerns will affect the president's decision to use economic coercion. Rent seeking firms and public calls for action spur the president on, while domestic costs constrain his options. I now turn to developing this model more completely.

Diversionary Theory

The diversionary theory of war argues that when a leader is losing domestic support because of internal ills, then the leader will try to divert the public's attention from those ills and point it toward problems in the world arena. The theory originates from a large body of anecdotal evidence, and it asserts that the leader will be more likely to take adventuresome foreign policy actions when there are problems at home (Levy 1989). In the case of the U.S. president, these domestic factors are typically conceptualized as public approval, inflation, and unemployment (Morgan and Bickers 1992).

Similarly, the literature on presidential popularity asserts that the president wishes to be effective and powerful during both election and nonelection years, and high levels of public approval make the president more effective and powerful (Neustadt 1980; Light 1991). Thus, the president will act to ensure higher public approval. Further, John Mueller (1973: 209) and Richard Brody (1991: 47) have shown that when the United States is involved in a specific, dramatic, international event, the president's approval increases as the public rallies in support. This literature, especially that surrounding diversionary theory, is still quite contentious on what effect, if any, domestic variables have on the president's decision to use military force. In particular, there are inconsistencies between the findings and the theory.

One of the first and certainly best known studies of the connection between domestic politics and foreign policy is Charles Ostrom and Brian Job's work on the president's political use of force. The authors develop a cybernetic model of presidential decision-making exploring the presidential decision to use military force. The cybernetic model is similar to bounded rationality and asserts that the president cannot process all of the available information and will, therefore, use shortcuts to help make decisions (Ostrom and Job 1986: 543–544). Within the model, they delineate three environments. The first focuses on international factors, looking specifically at the level of international tension, strategic balance-of-power, and extent of involvement in an ongoing war. The second is the domestic environment. It concentrates on the public's attitude toward international tension and balance, war aversion, and the domestic economy. The last environment is political. It emphasizes public support and political success of the president, as well as electoral proximity (545–546).

Combined into a cybernetic model, variables from these environments explain 75 percent of the cases correctly (555). Interestingly, the results show that the most important variable explaining the use of force is the president's approval rating, which is actually positive, contrary to the theoretical expectations. Thus, Ostrom and Job find that the president is more likely to use force when his approval is high, not low. They explain this reversed finding by arguing that the president prefers to have a positive balance of political capital at home before engaging in military hostilities. Essentially, the president wants to be rather popular so that he can implement the military action as he sees fit without having to bargain with Congress and sell the idea to the public. High approval ratings permit the president to act more autonomously, something desired and perhaps needed to effectively engage in coercive diplomacy. This finding is the first sign of empirical incongruity with the diversionary theory of war.

In a later refinement of Ostrom and Job, Patrick James and John Oneal (1991) add three new variables to the original analysis. They begin by creating two new dependent variables. The first is an interval level variable that measures the level of force used instead of the dichotomous force–no force variable in Ostrom and Job. This variable is designed to get at the interval nature of the decision, that is, the level of military force the president is willing to use. The second is a dichotomous variable similar to Ostrom and Job's, except that it indicates when the president used force during a crisis situation. Because crisis situations typically restrict the time needed to make decisions as well as highlight an international hazard to the United States, the president can be expected to weigh his decision to use force almost entirely on international factors. Thus, this crisis variable poses a tough test for diversionary theory because the decision should favor international or realist factors and not domestic ones; if the domestic variables are still important, there is strong support for diversionary theory. The third variable they add is an independent variable that taps the severity of the international situation confronting the United States. During the period the president must decide whether or not to use force, this index gauging "the systemic instability inherent in a situation" increases the model's sensitivity to the effects that the international situation has on the president's decision-making (James and Oneal 1991: 318).

Their results confirm Ostrom and Job's conclusions that while the international level variables, especially their measure of severity, affect the president's decision, the domestic and political variables are the most influential in each of the equations testing their three dependent variables (dichotomous use of force; level of force; crisis use of force). Further, they find that presidential approval is positively associated with the use of force in each of the equations, including the crisis use of force; a finding that confirms the idea that political capital better explains reality better than diversionary theory (325–326).

Interestingly, the one constant finding in all of the above authors is that the president's approval was positively related to the decision to use force. Diversionary theory informs us that the opposite should be true; the president's approval should be inversely related to the decision to use force. T. Clifton Morgan and Kenneth Bickers (1992) offer an interesting solution to this contradiction between the theory and empirical findings. They improve the tests performed on diversionary theory by separating the support the leader receives into those within his ruling coalition and those outside of it. This improvement follows the theory's assertion that a leader will only use a more adventuresome foreign policy when threatened by a loss of support within his ruling coalition, not if groups unimportant to the leader's rule do not support the leader. They use two dependent variables to test their hypothesis. First, similar to Ostrom and Job (1986), they use a variable coded 1 for each quarter the president used force, and 0 for those quarters he did not. The second dependent variable is the number of days between the last presidential approval poll and the next use of force. The findings from both dependent variables support their theory, showing that decreasing support from the ruling coalition (in their study, presidential partisan support) is associated with an increased probability of military action and a shorter period between the last poll and the use of force.

Most importantly, they find that overall support (presidential approval) is positively associated with the use of the military and inversely associated with the length of time between the last poll and the use of force. They explain the previous contradiction between the diversionary proposition and the findings by arguing that the president prefers aggregate support when taking military action but has an incentive to take action only when his partisan approval is low. Thus, the diversion is aimed at the president's party, the U.S. equivalent to a ruling coalition. The president has an incentive to use force to prove his active leadership to his party and deter any potential challengers from within it. This incentive to act is conditioned by a preference for strong support from the general public. Thus, the president prefers overall support, but he only has an incentive to act when his party support is failing.

Karl DeRouen (1995) concurs with Morgan and Bickers by showing that when general public sentiment is against the use of force, the White House is less likely to deploy troops. DeRouen argues further that, while elections do not affect the president, the constant need to maintain his approval rating pushes the president toward forceful alternatives when dealing with other states. Nincic (1997) similarly argues that the president will use force to protect himself from a declining job approval rating. A prospect theory argument, Nincic asserts that people put more value on those things they already have rather than those things they have yet to obtain (Levy 1992; McDermott 1992, 1998; Tversky and Kahneman 1992). Therefore, presidents facing a sliding rating seek to stop such slides with the diversionary use of force.

Agreeing with this pro-diversionary theory position but taking a different approach, Christopher Gelpi contends that the empirical findings do not support diversionary theory "because they focus too narrowly on the incentives state leaders have to use external force as a diversionary tactic without considering alternative solutions to quieting domestic unrest" (1997: 256). He points out that leaders can satisfy domestic demands, engage in repression or initiate diversionary military action. Autocracies tend to repress, but democracies tend to favor diversionary actions when faced with domestic unrest short of rebellion. Thus, Gelpi argues that domestic conditions do affect democratic leaders when they decide to deploy the military.

Still, several scholars are not convinced that there is any support for diversionary theory. James Meernik (1994) refines Ostrom and Job's analysis. Like James and Oneal, he uses the number of troops deployed to capture the political use of force instead of the dichotomous decision to use force. In addition to the troop level, Meernik (122–124) looks to all possible opportunities to use force, which Ostrom and Job (1986) suggest in their conclusion. These are conceptualized as anti-American threats and operationalized below.

Meernik's results derived from a Tobit estimation show that, contrary to the previous studies, there are only two domestic variables that reach statistical significance. The first is a variable indicating those opportunities to use force that included anti-American threats or violence. Meernik hypothesizes that these threats or violence will lead the president to be more likely to engage in military efforts to defend U.S. prestige or satisfy the public's demand for action (1994: 130–131). The results indicate that this variable, confirming the hypothesis, is positively related to the presidential decision to use force. The second variable indicates those opportunities when the United States was already engaged in military conflict with a different nation. The hypothesis predicts that the president will be less likely to use force when the United States is already committed overseas. Confirming the hypothesis, this variable is inversely related to the use of force.

It should be noted that neither of these variables is exclusively domestic. Both are based on international factors: international violence against Americans and U.S. involvement in a foreign war. While public approval of the president is clearly based on many phenomena, both foreign and domestic, Meernik's two variables do not tap the public's opinion of the international arena, but the arena itself. Therefore, these variables must be considered international, and consequently, none of the domestic variables are significant. These findings draw into question both the validity of Ostrom and Job's (1986) findings and their political capital argument, as well as the diversionary theory of war that suggests presidential decision-making is influenced by domestic factors. Two possible conclusions can be drawn from the contradictions these findings present.

First, Meernik (1994) is correct, and the realist principle that international factors determine when military force is used does not need reexamination as Ostrom and Job suggest. Instead, the principle accurately characterizes the decision to use force, and domestic factors do not influence that decision. The other conclusion is that Meernik used a different independent variable that led to the differences between his and Ostrom and Job's results and that independent variable was invalid. By including the provocations when the president could have used force, Meernik includes an additional component to the international environment's tension/conflict.

The five provocations that Meernik used to identify opportunities to use force are: (1) threat to U.S. territorial security or the security of its allies, (2) danger to U.S. personnel, civilians, or assets, (3) advances by communist or leftist groups or nations, (4) loss of U.S. influence in region, and (5) consequential military conflict between nations (Meernik 1994: 123). Each of these five conditions characterizes the level of tension or conflict in the world directed specifically at the United States. Thus, Meernik contends that international factors play the critical role in when the president sends troops into action, not domestic considerations.

Countering DeRouen's (1995) argument, James Meernik and Peter Waterman (1996) go as far as to refer to the theory as applied to the president as a "myth." They argue that the empirical results showing the domestic–military use connection are faulty because they rely on quarterly aggregations that assume the president views these averages when deciding to deploy the military. Why would the president view these averages and not current polls or economic figures? He does not, they conclude. The problem with this critique is the president may not explicitly consider the averages, but he certainly considers the general state of the economy and his approval rating. While American domestic politics may be measured on a daily basis, something that supports Meernik and Waterman's argument, some lagged moving average of those domestic factors important to the president is also likely to affect the decisions to use force. Thus, Meernik and Waterman may very well be right, but with the condition that the White House does look at recent trends in addition to recent absolute polls and economic figures.

A second criticism Meernik and Waterman raise is that international crises "are not all equally compelling enough to provide a president with the necessary justification for embarking on a military operation of sufficient size and impact to capture public attention" (1996: 576). If the public thinks that the president is trying to divert their attention from a domestic situation, then the attempt may backfire. Following President Clinton's cruise missile attack on Afghanistan and the Sudan, many news stations raised the question of whether Clinton was making up the conflict to divert attention from Monica Lewinski's second testimony—the one that led to his later impeachment. Whether this was the president's plan or not, the media raised that specter and may have limited the diversionary impact the attacks had. The authors conclude that while domestic politics may affect the president's decision, the evidence does not support this connection. Instead, security interests, the world arena, and the context of the crisis best explain when the president uses force.

Presidential Approval and Crises

Overall, this literature still exhibits considerable controversy. It is probably safe to conclude that domestic politics play some role in the use of military force (Miller 1995; Dassel 1998; Dassel and Reinhardt 1999). What role that is, however, is not clear. Diversionary theory does not stand up to empirical testing without significant conditions and sometimes not even then. Given this controversy, an alternative view would be beneficial. This different angle of approach is available thanks to those scholars studying presidential approval. Mueller's (1973) study of the public's approval of the president finds that there is a "rally 'round the flag" effect that boosts the president's approval anytime the United States is involved in a specific, dramatic, international event such as the use of military force. Brody (1991) finds cases which fit Mueller's profile but do not show a rally effect. Instead, he finds that if opinion leaders (the president, high officials, well known media types, and prominent figures) supported the action, then the public would as well. However, if there was dissention among the opinion leaders, the public would not support the president. The president has an incentive to involve the United States in some international event to boost his public approval, but he must be selective regarding the international event.

Disturbed by the implication that the president may risk American lives to boost his popularity, Lian and Oneal (1993) study the president's approval following the use of military force. Contrary to Mueller's and Brody's findings, they show that when the president uses force, his average boost in the polls ranges from zero to three percentage points. This finding initially questions the validity of the assertion that the president's foreign policy decisions are affected by domestic approval, and in fact, they conclude that the president does not use the military to try to increase his standing in the polls (293–295). However, the authors argue that it is still possible that the president perceives that using the military will increase his approval.

Two points need to be made concerning their argument. First, Lian and Oneal argue that the media also hold the belief that the president uses the military to increase his approval. Among others, they cite a 1991 political cartoon with President Bush pondering sending troops to fight either Gadhafi or Saddam Hussein and a little figure saying "What do you mean 'or'?" (278). Further, several months before the 1996 election, one of President Clinton's campaign advisors said that they wanted the President to issue a new policy each day before the November election. Thus, if the nonacademic (particularly including the media) conventional wisdom holds that the president can increase his approval through foreign policy actions, then the empirical fact that using force had little effect on approval may be unimportant to the decision-making process. That is, the president may continue to use coercive foreign policy as a way to increase his approval even in the face of Lian and Oneal's findings.

Second, Lian and Oneal only study the use of force, and they suggest that other nonmilitary foreign policy actions or focused international events may account for the increase in approval that is found by other studies. In this category, James and Hristoulas (1994) show that the president is influenced by domestic factors when deciding to enter into an international crisis situation. Thus, there are valid theoretical reasons and empirical precedents to believe that presidents will tend to use coercive foreign policy actions when their approval is low and/or when they want to be seen as active.[14]

Domestic Politics and Economic Sanctions

It is clear that the president is influenced by domestic politics when making foreign policy decisions; even those scholars opposing diversionary theory do not dispute that assertion. What is less clear is how domestic politics affects the president's decision to initiate or modify an economic sanction. Since the evidence shows that presidents tend to prefer a higher approval rating before engaging in coercive diplomacy, I expect that approval will be positively associated with the use and increase of economic coercion. The greater the president's political capital, the more he will be able to absorb criticisms that the sanctions are ineffective and costly to the American public.

When considering the impact of elections, however, the opposite will be true. While the president prefers to look active in the time prior to an election, few want to be seen by voters as placing foreign policy ahead of the domestic economy. While few voters may pay much attention to such policies as economic sanctions, voter knowledge increases during campaigns and every president can count on his opponent to help educate the public as to possible deficiencies in the administration's policies (Aldrich et al. 1989). Thus, the president should be less likely to initiate or modify economic sanctions in the months leading up to an election.[15]

The impact of the U.S. economy will be similar to that of elections (with one exception)—it will constrain the president's use of economic coercion. Like elections, no president will want to be seen as placing foreign policy above U.S. domestic economic needs, especially when the American economy is suffering from either inflation or unemployment. Again, one can argue that few pay much attention to when sanctions are imposed, and I certainly do not argue that these domestic considerations are the most influential in the president's decision. However, it is reasonable to expect that a suffering economy will draw the president's attention away from foreign affairs to domestic issues. Consider the media attention that a president would get during a recession if he spent most of his time discussing a dispute with another country. Critics would obviously point out that the president had wrongly prioritized his agenda and should spend more time concerned with the average American.

No president wants that kind of coverage or criticism and therefore, will hesitate to enact a sanction regime while the economy suffers. The one exception to the constraining effect of the economy is the trade balance between the United States and target. If there is a trade deficit that favors the target, the president may use the dispute as an excuse to deploy sanctions that have a strong protectionist effect and would, therefore, begin to offset the trade deficit (Mastanduno 1998; Reinhardt 1999, 2000; Zeng 2004). Thus, a trade deficit with the target provides the president an incentive, not a constraint, to using economic sanctions.

In sum, the domestic political arena both places constraints upon and provides incentives to the president when an international dispute occurs. The international or dyadic factors in Model I will have a greater impact on the occupant of the White House, but the president's approval, the economic situation generally, and the U.S. economic relationship with the target will affect how sanctions are used and modified.

Model III: Cognitive Constraints

In the first two models, there is an underlying assumption of objective or substantive rationality (Simon 1985). That is, in each model, the president is reacting to outside stimuli and making a decision to maximize his benefits and minimize his costs. For instance, the coercive diplomacy model (model I) predicts the president will enact economic sanctions when the tension between the target nation and the United States has risen—when the costs of not acting become greater than the costs of acting. The stress model II places on domestic imperatives predicts that the president will be more likely to take action when there is a trade deficit with the target and when his approval is high; again the president seeks to maximize benefits and minimize costs. That these models have underlying assumptions derived from rational choice theory should not be surprising as they are both generally based on previous literatures (e.g., coercive diplomacy and diversionary theory, respectively), and those literatures derive their expectations from mostly rational choice assumptions.

The first two models are quite reasonable in assuming that the president reacts to outside stimuli, but to stop the analysis there is shortsighted. As Stephen Walker and Mark Schafer point out "leaders matter in the explanation of foreign policy decision by action on their definition of the situation in the domain of world politics" (2003: 2; see also Snyder et al. 1962). More specifically, the president has severe constraints on his time and as such, may not always make decisions as a rational maximizer. That is, the president is under such serious time pressures that he only has minimal resources to allocate to making a decision (Neustadt 1980). Therefore, the president will make decisions without considering all the information and alternatives. Separately but related, the president's beliefs about the world around him affect how he processes and interprets the available information. The decision to use economic sanctions—as with any foreign policy decision—becomes bounded, and therefore, at least one model must rest on the assumptions of bounded rationality. The last model does just that.

Model III is based on two different but complementary concepts. First, the impact of the leader's cognitive characteristics will influence the sanction decision by affecting how the president interprets the international and domestic situation. Second, the president's choice of advisory system type will determine the quantity and quality of the information getting into the Oval Office. This control over information will affect what foreign policy options the president considers. I begin with a discussion of cognitive effects on the decision to use economic coercion and then turn to the impact of different advisory systems.

Herbert Simon argues that there are effectively three different ways in which cognition may affect decisions. The first is what he refers to as "radical irrationality" which is when the individual makes his or her decision based on impulses unmediated by cognitive processes (1985: 301–302). This passionate decision-making responds to the environment and stimuli as a result of the individual's emotions and nothing else. This type of decision-making is clearly quite rare. Radical irrationality is be hampered considerably by democratic institutions. Given that the president must persuade his cabinet and administration to carryout his orders, decisions without deliberation and cognitive efforts are unlikely to be implemented.

Simon's second type is substantive rationality. Effectively the opposite of radical irrationality, substantive rationality is defined as decisions based solely on the environment. In this case, beliefs simply "mirror" what is going on in the real world (Walker and Schafer 2003).[16] Models I and II follow this logic—the president uses sanctions because of actions taken by the target and in view of domestic political conditions.[17] This logic is used widely to explain the actions of nation-states in studies that do not consider the individual level of analysis. For example, some of the democratic peace arguments explain the low incidence of conflict between democracies as a function of rational choices of those states. Leaders in democracies are less likely to go to war because it jeopardizes their tenure, while autocrats may increase their job security by engaging in war (e.g., Bueno De Mesquita and Siverson 1995; Chan 1997). This argument does not depend upon individual characteristics. Instead, all leaders are assumed to want to stay in office and will therefore act in a manner that increases that likelihood.

While substantive rationality has much to recommend it, there are important limits to its ability to explain decisions. First, in many situations, leaders may face multiple rational options, yet substantive rationality cannot determine which of those rational choices the leader will select. One can easily imagine a situation in which a relatively hostile dispute has erupted between the United States and some country. The president could initiate economic sanctions, use a limited air strike, attempt to coerce the state diplomatically, and so on. Each of these options may be a rational choice, but which one does the president choose? Eisenhower could have blockaded Cuba immediately after Castro's takeover and planned for subsequent military action before the Soviets got involved, but instead he imposed a sugar quota that grew into a comprehensive set of economic sanctions. Certainly, one could make a strong argument for the rationality of military action against Castro since a watered down version of such a policy was attempted with the Bay of Pigs.

To explain presidential decision-making when multiple rational options exist—which they often will in interstate disputes—beliefs must be considered. The limit to substantive rationality means that humans must interpret the world in which they live, and that interpretation will vary from individual to individual. It is safe to assume that leaders seek to maximize their benefits while minimizing their costs, but how each leader interprets their environment will affect how they seek to maximize their utility.

Simon's third type of rationality is bounded rationality, in which "actions are meditated by thought processes that contain a mixture of beliefs inferred from previous experiences (old information) and current perceptions of stimuli in the present environment (new information)" (Walker and Schafer 2003: 4). Simply put, the president's beliefs influence how he interprets events, and those events affect his beliefs. This implies a learning or feedback loop in which the president starts out with a set of beliefs about a situation, and as information comes in, he updates those beliefs and makes decisions accordingly.

Thus, beliefs act as a dynamic lens through which the president sees the world, and the world updates and modifies the lens itself.

The process of bounded rationality is particularly important for understanding the decision to use economic coercion. Most disputes in which sanctions are applied sit between those that can obviously be resolved through diplomacy and those that require a strong military response. For example, explaining Roosevelt's response to the bombing of Pearl Harbor need not involve his beliefs. The attack was an act of war, and the only possible response was war. On the other end of the spectrum, when the U.S. honor guard at the 1992 World Series displayed the Canadian flag upside-down there was little that Ottawa would do other than demand an apology—diplomacy was the only rational answer. Disputes that are tense enough to warrant economic sanctions occupy the grey area between these two, and as such, psychological attributes of the president will be much more likely to influence the decision-making.

Bounded rationality is represented by the president's operational code. Originating with Nathan Leites' work on Bolshevik ideology and refined by George (1969), an operational code is the political belief system that both diagnoses (interprets) the situation and helps form a strategy for action. The diagnostic element is the leader's philosophical beliefs about the nature of the political world. How conflictual or cooperative does the leader perceive the world to be? "What is the fundamental character of one's political opponents?" (201). By answering these questions, we can estimate how the president will interpret stimuli from the world. Thus, a president who views the political universe to be highly conflictual will be more likely to diagnose actions by the target state as hostile and provocative while a president who views the world as rather harmonious will interpret the same actions more benevolently. The leader's instrumental beliefs suggest action not interpretation. The question here is "What is the best approach for selecting goals or objectives for political action?" (205). Presidents who tend to believe that the target will only respond to coercion rather than engagement will be more likely to initiate economic coercion. Conversely, those holding the opposite position will wait longer before applying coercion.

Both philosophical and instrumental beliefs are assumed to be flexible. As discussed above, a feedback or learning process occurs so that inputs from the dispute with the target will inform the president's beliefs both toward diagnosing and acting upon a move by the target. For example, President Carter's views and actions of the world changed throughout his administration, especially with the Soviet invasion of Afghanistan when Carter shifted from a Liberal to more Realist approach to foreign policy (Walker et al. 1998). Thus, the operational code of the president is not a constant, but a variable that will affect his decisions to use economic sanctions.

Apart from the operational code but consistent with the argument of Simon's bounded rationality, the advisory system the president develops also affects his decisions by filtering information and prescribing actions (M. Hermann and C. Hermann 1989). George (1980) and Margaret Hermann and Charles Hermann (1989) also suggest that the president's information preferences will affect the decision. George (1980), building on Johnson (1974), identifies a tripartite typology of presidential advisory systems: competitive, collegial (also known as informal), and formal. While only FDR used the competitive system, the other two have been used more often to shape the way the president receives information. The informal advisory system puts a premium on discussion among the advisors, stressing decisions that are both optimal and doable (George 1980: 149 and 165). The discussions typically involve the president and make him the hub of the information flow, thereby increasing considerably the amount of information he receives.

More information is not always better, however. The president in an informal system must spend a great deal of time sitting in meetings discussing the issues involved with his advisors. This process forces the president to sort through and analyze all of the information discussed. These two aspects of the informal system, discussion and analyses, significantly reduce the president's time to deliberate on the decision. That is, the president can spend too much time learning about a situation and not have enough time to consider the pros and cons of potential solutions. In the worst of all worlds, the president can be left with information overload and consequently be unable to make good decisions.

Conversely, the formal system sets up an orderly hierarchy that controls the information flow to the president. This system stresses each advisor's separate point of view and releases the president from the time-consuming meetings an informal advisory system requires. The president receives briefs with different positions from the appropriate staff members and then makes the decision with these information/ advisory summaries. The formal system does not allow the different advisors to discuss their points of view with each other; it only allows them to present their opinions to the president. As a result, there is no exchange of information or discussion of views. Further, this system often has one or more gatekeepers who limit and control what information/advice gets to the president.

While George's (1980: 164–165) analysis points out that each of these systems has costs and benefits, which can affect decisions for either better or worse, M. Hermann and C. Hermann show specifically how the amount of information affects the decision. They show that decision groups that are closed to external information tend to make more extreme foreign policy decisions, decisions that often lead to acute hostilities. M. Hermann and C. Hermann (1989: 363–373) develop the notion of an ultimate decision unit of which they define three types: the predominant leader, the single group, and multiple autonomous actors. The predominant leader decision unit most closely resembles George's presidential advisory systems. Each of these decision units are characterized as either open or closed to outside information. The closed units are theorized to have more extreme foreign policies and to be more conflictual in nature ". . . because they are less constrained by the complexities and nuances of the specific setting" (373). Open decision units tend to ". . . engage in more moderate, provisional behavior" and take "the incremental approach to action" because they are open to the complexities and ambiguities of the situation (375–376).

The logic of Hermann and Hermann's analysis can be applied to George's formal and informal advisory systems in the form of the following expectation. Presidents with formal advisory systems will tend to adopt more extreme foreign policy measures than presidents with informal advisory systems, because the information flow to the president is more constrained and less open for communicating complexities and nuances.

Are economic sanctions "more extreme"? When discussing the more extreme policies of closed decision units, Hermann and Hermann point out that they will ". . . use economic and military instruments of statecraft in addition to or in place of diplomatic channels" (373). At first blush, this quote implies that formal advisory systems are more likely to use economic sanctions than informal systems. However, they also assert that informal systems will take incremental steps toward action. Recalling Baldwin's (1985: 13–14) portrayal of economic sanctions being one step toward military force and one after diplomatic sanctions, it seems that informal systems may be more likely to use economic sanctions as one of a series of steps. Another factor suggesting that informal advisory systems would be more prone to generate decisions to use economic sanctions is that they tend to be more innovative than formal systems. Considering Renwick's (1981) characterization of sanctions as being the president's way of "doing something," one would expect the more innovative decision-maker to apply sanctions in contrast to a leader in a formal system "[agreeing] to attempt a diplomatic solution—at least at the outset of a problem—avoiding more costly and, perhaps, more controversial instruments" (M. Hermann and C. Hermann 1989: 383).

To answer the question of whether sanctions are more or less severe, and thus, which advisory system type will be more likely to use them, one must know what options were available or were being considered by the White House. While there is no doubt that sanctions are more severe than diplomacy, there is also no doubt that they are significantly less severe than militarized conflict. For example, the economic sanctions that were imposed against Iraq after its invasion of Kuwait in 1990 were certainly less severe than the subsequent Desert Storm military operations. Had President Bush stopped with the sanctions, the logical interpretation would be that he chose the less severe option. However, if the United States was attempting to coerce Japan to change its policy on whaling and the president initiated a set of economic sanctions against Tokyo, then the sanctions would have been interpreted as the more severe option since it is unthinkable that the United States would attack Japan over the whaling issue. Thus, to understand the severity of economic coercion as a policy option, one must know where it sits relative to other options.[18]

Given the propensities of the two advisory systems, I argue that when sanctions are the less extreme option available, the informal advisory system, with its more innovative and less extreme decision-making, will tend to use sanctions more often. Conversely, when economic coercion is the more intense option available, the formal advisory system will be quicker to pull the trigger on a set of economic sanctions.

Summary

The coercive diplomacy, domestic approval, and information processing models address progressively deeper levels of analysis and bring more detail to explain the president's decision to use economic sanctions. They offer a more complete view of the incentives, imperatives, and contexts that lead the president to initiate, increase, decrease, and lift economic sanctions.

To test these models, two different stages of assessment must be followed. Conceptually, the president cannot decide to increase, decrease, or lift economic sanctions before he decides to use them in the first place. Thus, the first stage of analysis must determine the conditions under which the president decides to use economic sanctions. This level is the most basic, and asks the question: When does the president decide to use economic sanctions (or force)? That decision is best portrayed with binary variable indicating whether or not sanctions are initiated against the target at a given time. Once the president puts sanctions in place against a target nation, the second stage of the analysis can assess the model's ability to determine the conditions under which the president lifts, decreases, or increases economic sanctions. Using the models specified above, I generate seven hypotheses and develop their measures in the next chapter.

Chapter 5

When Does the President Sanction? An Empirical Analysis

This chapter begins the empirical testing of the president's use and modification of international economic sanctions. There are two specific decisions that the executive must make with regard to the use of economic coercion. First, sanctions must be initiated against a target. Second, once sanctions are in place, the president must decide whether to lift, decrease, maintain, or increase them. It is in this chapter that I test the decision to initiate the economic coercion. I begin by developing hypotheses that represent three models of political rationality. They represent my theoretical explanation of the conditions that lead the president to use economic sanctions. Ten hypotheses represent the international conditions, domestic political factors, and cognitive constraints in the three models; three control variables are also included. Because some of the data sources cover different periods, two different data sets are compiled. One begins in January 1966 and ends in December 1992. The other begins in January 1991 and ends in December 2000.

While a split data set is not optimal, the division does occur at the Cold War/post–Cold War juncture, and therefore, there is a theoretical (albeit inadvertent) justification. The shift in the balance of power structure from a bipolar to unipolar or multipolar world, as well as the end of the confrontation between the Western and Eastern Blocs, created changes in how the United States used economic coercion. The general acknowledgement that more sanctions were used in the 1990s than in previous decades suggests that important differences exist between the Cold War and post–Cold War periods. As a result, the bifurcated data permit an examination of how these differences affect the president's decision calculus.

The results of the tests support several of the hypotheses but many are also left lacking in empirical evidence. Generally, they show that the president tends to deploy sanctions for international/foreign policy reasons, rather than domestic ones. However, domestic factors play a stronger role in sanctions geared toward foreign economic goals, namely the Section 301 sanctions. Further, the results suggest that the president's belief system affects the decision, supporting bounded rationality or the idea that decisions are based on a combination of external stimuli and cognitive constraints. The chapter ends with a discussion of how the results inform our understanding of economic coercion.

Hypotheses

Nine hypotheses and two controls compose the model used to test the president's decision to initiate sanctions.

Model I: International/Dyadic Conditions

Beginning with the international factors (model I), I first tap the idea that the tension between the sender and the target is positively associated with the use of sanctions. Probably the most basic aspect of the theory, this hypothesis suggests that more intense disputes are more likely to experience the onset of the sanctions. Specifically, *the president is more likely to initiate an economic sanction against a target when the dyadic tension between the United States and that target increases (hypothesis 5.1).*

The second hypothesis concerns the rate of escalation of the dispute between the United States and the target. As discussed in chapter 4, the president is likely to react to a rapidly escalating dispute by imposing economic coercion. Instead of waiting for the tension level to reach some threshold common to the use of sanctions, the president will prospectively view a highly escalatory dispute as one that will quickly reach a high tension level and initiate the sanction. Thus, *hypothesis 5.2 states that the greater the rate of increase in the tension level over time (denoting increased escalation), the more the more likely the president will be to enact economic sanctions.*

The third and last hypothesis for model I taps the effect provocative actions by the target have on the president's decision to use economic coercion. While one might expect a provocative, belligerent target to increase the incentive for the president to use coercion, it also sends a very clear signal that the target is going to resist the sender even if it means suffering considerable economic cost. Consequently, it seems likely that if sanctions are imposed against a belligerent target, the sanctions will be protracted. Since the United States would also suffer considerable costs in such a protracted sanction episode, there is an incentive for the president to forego the economic coercion for some other policy, be it engagement, containment, or some other, more intense form of coercive diplomacy.[1] Therefore, *if the target acts in a provocative, bellicose manner toward the U.S., the president will be less inclined to initiate economic sanctions (hypothesis 5.3).* It is possible that the negative effect provocation has on the likelihood of sanction initiation may also apply to escalation. That is, instead of viewing escalation as a sign that the dispute between the United States and target is spiraling upward, the president may interpret it as a signal that the target will go to great lengths and bear great costs to resist the sanction effort. Therefore, it also seems possible that high escalation will mimic intense provocations and decrease the probability of the use of economic coercion.

Model II: Domestic Political Factors

Four hypotheses represent the domestic political factors that are theorized to have an impact on the president's decision to sanction. Because the president seeks to maintain his job approval rating since it is a source of political capital, I expect that lower polling results provide an incentive for the president to take action. In the case of a dispute with another nation, the president will be more aggressive so that he appears more presidential or as a strong leader at home. Therefore, *the lower a president's public job approval rating, the more likely he is to enact economic sanctions (hypothesis 5.4).*

In addition to job approval, the president must concern himself with reelection and the election of the House and Senate during the midterm. Clearly his reelection is important, but the midterm elections also affect the president directly. Most tangibly, changes in the House and Senate determine the composition of the legislature with which the president must govern. How well or poorly the president's party does in the midterm election is considered a referendum on the president's performance. Popular presidents presiding over a strong economy do better in the midterm than weak presidents with shaky economies. Given the desire to do well in these elections, the president will be more active in foreign affairs as well as domestic ones. Thus, *as the proximity of an election increases, the president will be more likely to initiate economic coercion (hypothesis 5.5)*.

The president is concerned with not only his approval and election chances but also with the economy. In the literature on the diversionary theory of war, it is hypothesized that the president will be more likely to engage in adventurous foreign policy when economic conditions are poor. Simply stated, the president is expected to attempt to divert the public's attention from the faltering economy by attacking another country. This, however, does not translate well to economic sanctions because of the nature of the coercion. Military actions draw the public's attention, and although they are expensive, costs are not the first issue raised when the military is deployed. For that reason, when the military is used, it can distract the public's attention from economic woes. Economic sanctions, however, cost the economy and make a worse distraction from it. As argued in chapter 4, no president wants to be seen as putting costs on an economy that is already suffering. Therefore, *as inflation and unemployment increase, the president is more constrained and less likely to use economic coercion (hypothesis 5.6)*.

Not all economic conditions have the same effect, however, and the trade balance between the United States and target provides the president with an additional reason to economically coerce a target. Sanctions have protectionist effects that could potentially affect the trade balance with the target. Therefore, the president has an incentive to initiate a sanction against the target as cover for a protectionist policy. *A trade surplus (deficit), then, will decrease (increase) the probability that the president will commence an economic sanction (hypothesis 5.7)*.

Model III: Cognitive Constraints

The final three hypotheses tap the last model, cognitive constraints. First, the advisory system that the president uses to control the information flow should influence the decision to coerce another nation. Greater levels of information that occur in informal or collegial advisory systems should increase the number and variety of options made available to the president. As a consequence, the president will be more likely to select more innovative and incremental policies, such as an economic sanction, rather than revert to military action right away. Formal advisory systems, alternatively, will be quicker to pull the trigger on more acute forms of coercion. Consequently, *informal systems should make the president more likely to enact economic sanctions than presidents with formal advisory systems (hypothesis 5.8)*.

Additionally, the president's belief system will have an effect on the likelihood that sanctions are deployed. While economic coercion may be a more incremental policy relative to military coercion, it is still a hostile action. If a president's belief system is more cooperative, then he will hesitate before using sanctions than a president with a more hostile world vision. Specifically, *presidents (1) who have a more friendly view of the political universe and (2) approach goals more cooperatively will be less likely to initiate an economic sanction (hypothesis 5.9 and hypothesis 5.10)*.

Controls and Summary

In addition to the ten hypotheses, there are three controls that must be added. First, several scholars have argued that democratic dyads will be less likely to sanction one another (Cox and Drury 2002; Lektzian and Souva 2003), and if they do, the sanctions will be shorter (Bolks and Al-Sowayel 2000) and then return to presanction trade levels faster (Lektzian and Souva 2001). To control for this effect, I include the target's regime score in the model.[2] Second, the target's GDP per capita must be added to the model to control for the potential tendency to select weaker targets. Olson (1979a) argues that an asymmetric balance of power favoring the sender increases the likelihood that sanctions will be used and be more effective when used. Therefore, the wealth of the target must be added to control for such a potential bias. Finally, I include the total trade between the United States and the target/country to control for the possibility that the president will be more likely to use economic sanctions against a state with which the United States has trade. Basically, I must control for the potential tendency to sanction countries that the United States can sanction—those with whom there is significant trade.

These ten hypotheses and three controls compose the following equation representing the depiction of the president's decision to use economic sanctions:

Equation 5.1: Sanction Initiation = Tension + Escalation − Provocation − Approval + Election Proximity − Inflation − Unemployment + Trade Surplus + Informal Advisory System − Image of Others − Tactic Preference

Data

I now turn to a description and discussion of the data that I use to assess the model laid out above. The data are separated into two sets, one that runs from 1966 to 1992 and the other from 1991 to 2000. They are arrayed as a time series cross-section (TSCS) where the time period is the month and the cross-section is the target/country.[3] Also known as a pooled time series, the method stacks or pools each unit's (in this case the target/country) time series on top of the others. The result is a larger data set that includes both cross-section and time series elements. The benefits to compiling the data this way are multiple. First, because time is included in the analysis, trends and processes can be discerned from the data. These characteristics, particularly the processes, provide leverage toward inferring causation. Second, thanks to the inclusion of the cross-section, the data allow me to test the theoretical models across both time and space (target/country) for greater generalization. That is, I am testing the relationship with not one country over a 35-year period but 50 countries. Thus, the results can help infer causation and be generalized more readily to the rest of the world.[4]

Since I am interested in explaining the conditions that lead the president to initiate sanctions against another country, I include all of the states that were targeted for economic sanctions by the United States. However, including only those countries that were economically coerced is, in effect, selecting on the dependent variable. That is, the cases would have been selected because they were sanctioned, not because they represent the population of states. Hence, a set of non-sanctioned countries must be included in the analysis. These cases act as a null set or control group that permits the hypotheses to be falsified.

King and Zeng (1999a, 1999b; see also Bueno de Mesquita and Lalman 1992: 282–283) show that a sample of null countries (in this case, those not sanctioned) can be used in place of the population. The interesting thing about economic sanctions is that the United States has sanctioned a very large number of countries if only for a single month.

For example, in a previous analysis that used data ending in 1978 (Drury 1997), Israel appeared as a control country. However, in the updated sanction data, I found President Reagan held up the sale of some F-16s for one month, in effect, sanctioning Israel. Thus, to consider only those countries, which have never been sanctioned, as the only way to falsify the tests is inaccurate. Instead, the many countries that were only sanctioned for brief periods can also falsify the tests during the long periods (years) they were never sanctioned. Going even further, since most states were not being constantly sanctioned during the entire period, they too offer an opportunity to falsify the model.

For example, the United States sanctioned Peru from August, 1967 to February, 1974, from August, 1975 to October, 1977, and from August, 1985 to September, 1985. Thus, in the 240 months between 1966 and 1985, Peru was under U.S. economic coercion for 108 months, less than half of the time. Therefore, the model could theoretically be falsified on the Peruvian case alone. While such a research design strategy would be far from optimal, the point is that the current strategy of including null cases provides ample opportunity to reject the hypotheses.

Ultimately, the use of both time series and cross-sections allows the hypotheses to be falsified through both time and space. During the first period (1966–1992), the White House sanctioned 28 countries at least one time during the 27-year period. An additional 22 randomly selected countries were added to the data as a control group of unsanctioned states.[5] When these 50 sanctioned and non-sanctioned states are combined, the result is a data set with 16,200 data points.[6] For the second period (1991–2000), there were ten years during which the United States sanctioned 26 countries. An additional 20 randomly selected countries were added to the as the control group. As a result, there are 5,520 data points in the second period.

Two issues with these data exist. First, four of the countries that were not sanctioned for political reasons were subject to Section 301 sanctions.[7] This means that when Section 301 sanctions are included in the dependent variable, there are four fewer null/control group cases. As discussed above however, this should not pose a problem given that there is plenty of opportunity for the model to be rejected. Further, these four states only lose their sanction-free status when the Section 301 sanctions are included.

The second issue is the overlap of the data in 1991 and 1992. While the data could be bifurcated such that no overlap existed by simply cutting out these two years in one of the data sets, reducing observations comes at a cost of lost information. In particular, these years cover the later half of President Bush's (the former) term in office. Removing these years from either data set reduces the variation for that administration. Further, tests revealed that no substantive effects occur from removing portions of the data from either period. Therefore, I keep all the data for each period.

Dependent Variable: The Decision to Initiate Economic Coercion

The dependent variable is the president's decision to initiate economic sanctions against another nation. A presidential decision to initiate is defined as a statement or act by the president, spokesperson, or secretary-level member of the administration that (1) immediately imposes economic sanctions against another country, or (2) imposes a sanction that will come into effect in the near future. It does not include threats that sanctions may be deployed; instead, the economic coercion must be implemented or in the implementation process. Some cases involved Congressional action in the form of legislation that either created an economic sanction or required the president to impose a sanction. Unless the president took direct positive action toward the legislative bill, the case was dropped. Direct positive action is defined as signing a bill into law, issuing a supportive statement, or any supportive executive action on a Congressional initiative. For example, Congress passed sanctions against South Africa over President Reagan's veto in 1985. These Congressional sanctions are not included as a presidential decision.[8] In 1996, President Clinton signed the Helms-Burton sanctions against Cuba. This case meets the definition of a Congressional sanction on which the president took direct positive action. Therefore, it is included as a presidential decision in the data.

While Congressional sanctions are important, I am interested in explaining what conditions lead the president to use economic coercion. If I included sanctions that were completely imposed by Congressional action, then my model would not apply because it is a model of presidential action not Congressional action. As Kaempfer and Lowenberg (1989) have pointed out, sanctions imposed by legislatures are more likely to be driven by domestic groups lobbying for protectionist rent as compared with executive sanctions that will be driven more by foreign policy goals. Therefore, the conditions that lead Congress to enact sanctions are potentially much different from the conditions that lead to presidential sanctions. Consequently, any purely Congressional actions are not considered as part of the data.

In this chapter so far, I have discussed sanctions as a general term, mentioning only briefly the Section 301 sanctions. As discussed in chapter 2, the difference between sanctions aimed at foreign policy goals and those aimed at foreign economic goals (e.g., sanctions that seek to increase trade openness) may be quite important. Several scholars do not include foreign economic sanctions in their definition of economic coercion because they are not expressly political. As I concluded in chapter 2 however, there are good reasons to maintain a broader definition of what economic coercion is, particularly because we can learn more about the president's use of economic instruments to coerce other nations—the main point of this book. The data sources for these two sanction decisions are different. I address first the data that measures the foreign policy oriented sanctions and then turn to the foreign economic policy sanction data.

The data measuring the president's decision to initiate economic sanctions seeking foreign policy goals were gathered from a variety of sources. First, the Hufbauer et al. (1990a, 1990b) volumes provided the foundation for the cases of U.S. sanctions. Many of the Hufbauer et al. cases are extended episodes of economic sanctions during which several decisions were made. For example, President Carter chose to sanction Nicaragua seven times during his term in office. In April and June, 1977, Carter cut aid to Managua because of human rights violations. In July that year, he banned the sale of police equipment. Finally in September, 1977, Carter cut economic credits. In February and September of 1978, Carter suspended military aid and sales, and during his last month in office, the President cut aid to Nicaragua. Each of these decisions is a distinct use of economic coercion. While they represent an escalating pattern of economic pressure placed on the target as President Carter attempted to get Managua to reform its human rights policies, each of the decisions was a new sanction on the target. Therefore, each decision was coded as a separate datum.

Several other sources were used to supplement Hufbauer et al. (1990a, 1990b). For sanctions that started after the 1990 Hufbauer et al. volume was published, I used a list of the all the economic sanction cases from their forthcoming third edition.[9] The case list lacked the actual month and day that the sanctions were initiated. These data were acquired through searches of the LexisNexis database of newspaper and government documents. Thus, the case list provided the information about the existence of the sanction and the issue over which the United States and target were in dispute, and papers like the *New York Times*, *Wall Street Journal*, and *Washington Post* provided exact dates of the decisions. Additionally, some of the updated cases from the Institute for International Economics (the publisher and employer of Hufbauer et al.) are available in complete form on their website (www.iie.com). These cases were also used to build the decision data.

To supplement the Hufbauer et al. case histories, the news digest/archive Facts on File (1966–2000) was searched for all instances of economic sanctions and subsequently added to the data. This search yielded only a small handful of decisions that were not already in the data. To check for sanctions that did not make any of these lists, all U.S. sanctions listed in the World Event Interaction Survey (1966–1992) and Integrated Data for Events Analysis (1991–2000) were identified and checked against the data. Again, only a very small handful of decisions were added to the data.

Turning to the foreign economic policy, I reiterate the definition of these sanctions as the implementation of an economic sanction under Section 301 auspices. The data for the decision to deploy a Section 301 sanction comes from four interrelated sources. First, Thomas Bayard and Kimberly Elliott's (1994) *Reciprocity and Retaliation in U.S. Trade Policy* and Elliott and Richardson (1997) provide a case list and history of most of the Section 301 sanctions. Additionally, Ka Zeng (2004) and Erick Duchesne (1997) supplemented the original Bayard et al. data.[10]

Other measures of the decision to sanction were considered. Originally, I coded the data as interval data, increasing by one each time the president initiated an economic sanction or decreasing by one for each permanent decrease in the sanction level. This coding scheme could be viewed as having two different qualities. First, the data could be interpreted as event counts; that is, the number of sanctions levied by the president against a given target. This interpretation would not be inaccurate, but there would be little value to knowing how many times the president had sanctioned a country. For example, if the United States was engaged in militarily coercing another state, the number of times it dropped bombs on the target would not be as interesting a fact as what caused the onset of the coercive action. Understanding decisions to initiate are more interesting than understanding how many sanctions are in place.

The second interpretation might be that a count of the sanction decisions could act as a proxy for the severity of the economic pressure. If each decision put in place an equally acute sanction, then this interpretation would be correct and very interesting. Knowing what factors caused the different levels of economic coercion would help us understand how and why states escalated disputes. However, each decision is not equally acute in the economic pressure it brings to bear on the target. The initial sanction against Cuba was a sugar quota. While sugar was an important element to the Cuban economy, the subsequent decisions to completely embargo the island were more severe. Similarly, more recent decisions that affect the amount of money that can be sent to relatives in Cuba are certainly not as harsh as the original sugar quota. Thus, each decision is different in what it accomplishes. Counting up the number of decisions does not provide any information about the level of the economic pressure on the target.[11]

For these reasons and others, which become more apparent below, I have dichotomized the decision variable. A value of one indicates that the president decided to initiate some kind of sanction (foreign policy or Section 301) against the target state. The decision to use sanctions is quite rare. Only 1 percent of the target/country months include sanction decisions. The remaining 99 percent of the data are zeros—no sanction deployment decisions made by the White House.

I now turn to the data that measure the independent variables in the three models: international/dyadic conditions (model I), domestic political factors (model II), and cognitive constraints (model III).

Independent Variables

The data needed to represent the first hypothesis—that more tense disputes lead to economic coercion—is a gauge of the tension between the United States and the target. To measure the magnitude of tension between the United States and the target, I use data from the World Event Interaction Survey (WEIS) and Integrated Data for Event Analysis (IDEA). The WEIS data are nominal events coded primarily from the *New York Times* concerning the interactions between nations for the years 1966–1992. For example, if two states sign an arms control treaty, the event is given a specific code. As nominal data, however, little more than the frequency of their occurrence can be analyzed. The Conflict and Peace Data Bank (COPDAB) has a conflict–cooperation scale that overcomes this problem. The COPDAB scale measures the conflict and cooperation between two nations using a 15 point scale, 15 being total war and 1 equaling a peaceful merger of two nation-states (Azar 1980: 148). Joshua Goldstein (1992) created a weighting scheme that converts the nominal WEIS codes to a COPDAB-like cooperation–conflict scale. The scale ranges from 8.3, which is defined as extending military assistance, to −10, which is a military attack, clash, or assault. For purposes of analysis and interpretation, I transformed the data so that extending military assistance equals a zero and military attack equals 18.3. Thus, as the tension variable increases, the tension level between the United States and target also increases.[12]

For the post-1992 data, I use IDEA. Like WEIS, IDEA codes events between states as reported in the news media, in this case, Reuters Newswires.[13] These data are different from WEIS in that they are machine coded, that is, the coding was done by a computer rather than a human being. However, the nominal codes that are generated match closely with the WEIS codes, and therefore, the Goldstein weights for WEIS can be appropriately applied to the IDEA data (Bond et al. 2001). The result is a similar tension variable for each target/country for the 1991–2000 period.

One issue with the IDEA data is worth noting. During research unrelated to this book that used daily data, some strange anomalies in the IDEA data were found. On seven different occasions, IDEA reported that the People's Republic of China had used chemical weapons on Taiwan, and on two occasions, Taiwan had used chemical weapons on the PRC.[14] A chemical weapons use, not surprisingly, gets the top hostile tension score of 18.3.[15] Clearly, this is a mistake. The data do report that it was not the government or military that engaged in this warfare, but the event code is very clear—chemical weapons use. Although Gary King and Will Lowe (2003) argue (and provide evidence) that the machine coding is equivalent to human coding, this argument, generally speaking, is based on the number of events that a computer can code relative to a human in the same period of time.[16] Because computers can code hundreds or thousands more observations in the same time that human coders can code only a handful of events, any mistakes the computer makes should be randomly distributed and cancel each other out once the data are aggregated by some measure of time (i.e., month, quarter, or year). This argument assumes that the researcher is aggregating the data. If they are not, then there could be significant problems with the analysis such as explaining open war between China and Taiwan on certain days but not others. The point here is to realize that these data, like all data, are not perfect. However, the monthly aggregation used herein should dispel these potential errors.

Because I need a measure of the tension between the United States and the target/country, I create a proxy for dyadic tension, where high levels of conflictual behavior are synonymous with high tension levels. To do this, I take the average of the United States to target and target to U.S. tension scores. That is, WEIS and IDEA code actions by one state toward another. Therefore, I must include not only actions by the United States aimed at the target but also actions by the target directed at the United States. Thus, the average of these two scores produces a measure of overall dyadic tension. Since the unit of analysis is the target/country month, these data are generated for all of the targets/countries and then aggregated into months.[17] All missing values were coded as missing, since it would be wrong to assume that no interactions between the two countries could be interpolated into some other meaningful tension score. That is, a lack of interaction between the United States and another country does not provide any information about the status of that relationship. It could mean that the tension level is stable since the last datum, or that it is adjusting itself in a function similar to a moving average, or it could mean simply that the two states are not interacting. Therefore, missing values are left as just that, missing.

The WEIS and IDEA data also include sanction initiations as part of their measure of interstate relations. Sanction initiations coded by WEIS and IDEA would potentially contaminate the analysis. So that economic sanctions imposed by the United States do not appear as both the dependent variable and as part of the independent variables derived from WEIS and IDEA, I removed all uses of economic sanctions from the WEIS and IDEA tension measures. Thus, the WEIS and IDEA derived measures do not include any economic sanctions initiated by the United States and therefore do not contaminate the analysis.

Hypothesis 5.2, that an escalating dispute will lead the president to initiation economic coercion, is measured by the percentage change from one month to another in the tension between the United States and the target/county. Thus, the variable simply measures the growth or contraction of tension. Missing values were recoded to zero, since a lack of tension to determine what the escalation rate was can also be regarded as a zero change in the U.S.–target/country relationship.

To measure the provocation from hypothesis 5.3, I use the difference in the United States and target/country tension scores to determine how much more hostile or less cooperative the target/country is being toward the United States, relative to the U.S. tension directed at the target/country. To derive this variable, I subtract the U.S. WEIS/IDEA score directed at the target/country from the target's WEIS/IDEA score directed at the United States. Since I am only interested in provocation by the target/country toward the United States, I recode all negative scores (times when the United States was acting as the provocateur) to zero. All missing values are also coded as zero since a lack of data can be regarded as a lack of provocation. That is, if the target was provocative, I expect it to appear in the data. If nothing appears, then it should be safe to assume that no provocation occurred. In the end, the variable is zero for all observations when the United States was acting provocatively or where there was no provocation either way, and therefore, it indicates only how provocative the target is toward the United States with higher scores indicating more provocative actions.

Turning to the domestic political variables, I begin with the measure of the president's job approval rating as laid out in hypothesis 5.4. I use the standard measure of presidential approval rating from the Gallup Poll question: "Do you approve or disapprove of the way (president's name) is handling his job as president?"[18] Normally these data are reported monthly, but when more than one survey was taken in a single month, an average was computed. During the Truman, Eisenhower, and Kennedy presidencies, there were a few months in which surveys were not taken. In these cases, I used an average or moving average to supplement the data.[19]

I tap the president's electoral concerns (hypothesis 5.5) with a count variable. I measure the proximity to the next midterm or presidential election by counting the number of months left until the next election.[20] This variable ranges in value from 23 to zero.

America's economic health is also hypothesized to affect the president's decision to initiate an economic sanction (hypothesis 5.6). The economic conditions are characterized by the inflation and unemployment rates as reported by the U.S. government. The inflation rate is annualized to a one-month percentage. The unemployment rate is simply the monthly percent of unemployed workers. To best capture the effect these variables have on the decision to initiation economic coercion, I add them together to create the misery index.

In addition to the domestic economic health of the United States, I hypothesize that the president will be more likely to be economically coercive when there is a trade deficit with the target/country and less so when there is a trade surplus (hypothesis 5.7). I calculate the trade surplus between the United States and each target/country by simply subtracting the U.S. exports from the target/country imports. In order to standardize the variable, I divide the difference by the total U.S. trade. This process creates a variable that measures the trade surplus with the target as a percent of overall U.S. trade.[21]

Hypothesis 5.8 asserts that the president's advisory system will have an impact on his decision to use economic coercion. To measure the president's different advisory systems, I use Hermann and Preston's (1994: 78, 88–92) data to create a dichotomous variable that indicates whether a president has a formal (0) or informal (1) advisory system.[22] Nixon and Reagan both had formal advisory systems, while Johnson, Ford, Carter, Bush, and Clinton had informal or collegial systems.

The final two hypotheses (5.9 and 5.10) suggest that the president's belief system will have influence on his decision to use economic sanctions. To tap these hypotheses, I use two different measures of the operational code, one that represents the philosophical beliefs and one that represents instrumental beliefs (Walker et al. 1998, 2003). First, I used the measure of the president's outlook on the political universe, also referred to as his image of others in the political realm. Identified as P1, this measure gauges how conflict prone or cooperative the president thinks the world is, generally speaking. P1 ranges from $+1.0$ (the world is a friendly place) to -1.0 (the world is a hostile place). Second, I1 taps the president's approach to goals or direction of strategy. Essentially, this variable measures what kind of strategy or tactic (cooperative or conflictual) the president prefers with interacting with other leaders. I1 ranges from $+1.0$ (highly cooperative tactics are preferred) to -1.0 (high preference for conflict/coercive tactics).

The data for both of these variables were generated from speeches of all of the presidents using the Verbs in Context (VICS) coding scheme and the *Profiler+* (version 5.1) text parser (Walker et al. 1998, 2003). Multiple speeches from each presidency from Johnson through Clinton provided an average of 350 verbs-in-context per president. These were used to generate both the P1 and I1 variables. While the speeches provided plenty of data to calculate the operational code, there were not enough speeches to generate longitudinal data for each president. Therefore, P1 and I1 scores are generated for each president and remain constant throughout their tenure in office. Clearly, this is not as optimal as a monthly, quarterly, or even yearly average; however, these data are not currently available. Further, the scores themselves do accurately reflect each administration's outlook on the world and approach to goals.

Control Variables

I now turn to the final variables, the controls for the model. First, democracies tend not to sanction one another. To control for this potential effect, I include the target's regime score as determined by the Polity IV data set. The Polity IV data independently measures a country's level of democracy and autocracy; it then subtracts the autocracy score from the democracy score to create an overall measure of regime type (Marshall and Jaggers 2000). The resulting variable ranges from -10 to 10. Second, to control for the potential preference to use economic coercion on weaker states because there is a greater possibility that they will not be able to withstand the economic pressure and they therefore make soft and attractive targets, I include the target's GDP per capita from the Penn World Tables. Finally, to control for the potential bias to sanction those countries with which the United States has significant trade, I include the total trade with the target. This variable is measured by adding U.S. imports and exports with the target and logging the values.[23]

The Decision to Use Economic Sanctions

Now that the hypotheses, variables, and data have all been delineated, I turn to the analysis.

Results, 1966–1992

I report the following analysis in stages so that the differences between political sanctions and those seeking foreign economic goals can be compared independently as well as assessed together. Further, the impact of the information processing variables is analyzed separately due to issues of multicolinearity. Specifically, the operational code variables P1, I1, and the president's advisory system are all highly collinear.[24] Therefore, they are separated into different equations. Thus, six equations appear each in tables 5.1 through 5.4 later: two for

Table 5.1   Foreign Policy Sanction Decisions, 1966–1992

	Foreign Policy Sanctions	
Tension	0.214***	0.230***
	(0.039)	(0.037)
Escalation	−0.225	−0.267
	(0.252)	(0.249)
Provocation	−0.131***	−0.141***
	(0.033)	(0.033)
Presidential approval	0.011	0.017*
	(0.009)	(0.010)
Number of months before election	0.013	0.018
	(0.017)	(0.016)
Misery index	−0.075**	−0.087**
	(0.036)	(0.043)
U.S. trade surplus as % of total trade	51.316**	34.265*
	(25.298)	(20.335)
Operational Code I1	−6.513***	
	(2.205)	
Presidential advisory system		0.191
		(0.252)
Polity score	−0.025	−0.028
	(0.020)	(0.020)
Target GDP per capita	−0.000***	−0.000***
	(0.000)	(0.000)
Logged total U.S. trade with target	0.145***	0.159***
	(0.046)	(0.046)
Time since last decision	−0.070***	−0.069***
	(0.014)	(0.015)
Spline 1	−0.000***	−0.000***
	(0.000)	(0.000)
Spline 2	0.000***	0.000***
	(0.000)	(0.000)
Spline 3	−0.000**	−0.000**
	(0.000)	(0.000)
Constant	−0.337	−5.078***
	(1.744)	(0.807)
Observations	5,785	5,785
Pseudo-R^2	0.172	0.163

Notes: Robust standard errors in parentheses; * $p < 0.1$; ** $p < 0.05$; *** $p < 0.01$

the foreign policy sanctions, two for the foreign economic sanctions, and two for the combination of the two.[25] I also discuss the 1966–1992 period first as it contains the most data. Once I have discussed these results, I compare them to the 1991–2000 period as well as discuss those results independently.[26]

Foreign Policy Sanctions

I begin with the basic, common definition of sanctions—those seeking a foreign policy goal. The first two models estimating the conditions that lead the president to initiate foreign policy sanctions fit the data reasonably, although not very well. The pseudo-R^2 for the two models is 0.17 and 0.16, respectively. Four of the nine hypotheses received support from the models, while the results contradicted two of the hypotheses. Further, two of the three control variables acted as expected.

As hypothesized, increased tension between the United States and the target/country increases the likelihood that the president will initiate an economic sanction (hypothesis 5.1). With the exception of the temporal dependence variables, the tension level has the strongest impact of any variable by more than four fold. Holding all other variables constant, as the tension increases by one standard deviation, the probability that the White House will initiate economic coercion rises from 28 percent to 42 percent, at a two standard deviation increase, the probability rises to 58 percent.[27] Two aspects of this finding are worth discussing.

First, the relative power of the tension variable on the decision to use sanctions suggests that the president weighs international factors much more heavily than domestic political ones. That is, if the president were using sanctions primarily to assuage domestic political demands or concerns, then the international variables from model I would not have such a powerful impact. Instead, we would expect that approval, elections, and the economy would be the driving force behind his decision. As the results indicate, this is simply not the case. It seems clear from the influence that tension has that the president must have an opportunity to sanction before he can initiate the coercion. That is, a sanction-worthy dispute must exist before the president can attempt using economic coercion.

While this may seem obvious at first blush, the consequence is that the use of sanctions for domestic political purposes is difficult, if not impossible. Even if the president wishes to divert public attention away from domestic problems, it is exceedingly difficult for him to do so unless the United States is engaged in a dispute with some other country. Of course, the United States is engaged with almost every nation in the world, so the likelihood that there may be some dispute is certainly higher than for smaller states. However, the point that the White House cannot, at least without difficulty, manufacture a reason to engage in economic coercion should not be lost. The consequence is that sanctions are more foreign policy tools than they are tools to divert or satisfy the American public.

The second point about this result that needs highlighting is the idea that sanctions are a logical part of a state's foreign policy tools. As David Baldwin (1985) and others have argued, economic coercion is a normal part of state relations, and, I contend, should be considered along side of military action. That the president uses sanctions as a dispute increases in hostility suggests that sanctions will be followed by military coercion, if the situation is hostile enough. Thus, these forms of coercion do share a common foundation.

Turning to the impact escalation has on the president; the data show no support for that hypothesis (5.2). The variable does not approach significance, and thus, has no effect on the decision process. The idea that the president may be forward looking during a dispute and initiate sanctions with the expectation that the relationship with the other state has gone sour is falsified. This result does suggest that sanctions are not used preemptively. This may help explain the poor success rate economic coercion is concluded to have. That is, if the sender only deploys sanctions at a point in the dispute that the target would expect such an action, then the target will have taken steps to mitigate the impact of that coercive effort. For example, Pakistan must have realized that the United States was likely to hit it with sanctions if Islamabad detonated a nuclear device. Given such an expectation, the Pakistani government probably explored ways to limit the economic damage from the inevitable sanctions. If the president did engage in preemptive economic coercion, the sanctions might be more successful. In essence, apply the pressure and agree to lift it only after the target has conceded. This tactic is, of course, quite aggressive and therefore may have other consequences that would dampen its effectiveness, such as causing even more political integration in the target a la Galtung.[28]

The hypothesis that a provocative, bellicose target can deter the president from taking action is supported by the findings (hypothesis 5.3). With the other variables held constant, a one standard deviation shift upward in target provocation lowers the probably of sanctions from 28 percent to 19 percent. In the example above, when tension rises by two standard deviations leading to a 58 percent probability that the president will sanction, a provocative target can drive that probability down to 44 percent. Thus, targets seem to be able use belligerency as a sign of resolve and deter the president from using economic coercion, leaving him to use an alternative, less intense approach to the crisis (George 1991: 77). It is also possible that the president bypasses the sanctions in the face of a provocative target and chooses military action, but the data do not support this possibility (Drury 1997).

Although the provocation variable's substantive impact is considerably smaller than the tension level, provocation is a moderately strong variable, again, aside from the temporal variables. This finding reinforces the argument that sanctions are primarily driven by interstate relations rather than domestic politics. It also suggests that targets should signal their resolve as much as possible to deter the sender from following through with the sanctions. Particularly since the United States does not seem to engage in preemptive sanctions, acting aggressively toward Washington may pay off.

The change in U.S. foreign policy since September 11 may negate this conclusion. The invasion of Iraq may be evidence that the White House will exert its power prior to overt and imminent threats. Baghdad's refusal to permit the weapon inspectors unfettered access created a festering dispute between Iraq and the United States and UN, not a credible deterrent. While there is no available data measuring the tension between the United States and Iraq prior to the invasion, it seems likely that it was quite high. Therefore, in the model herein, the action was not preemptive in nature.

To be clear, I am not taking a side for or against the war, or even taking a position on whether the invasion was a preemptive action, generally speaking. The point is that the model herein defines preemptive as taking action prior to a relatively hostile dispute emerging. The president acts, according to the hypothesis, because he expects the dispute to become hostile. The dispute prior to the Iraq War was already quite hostile and therefore, does not fit the model's definition. As a consequence, the change in U.S. policy since September 11 will probably not change the noneffect escalation has on the president's decision. In other words, economic coercion is not likely to be used as a preemptive form of coercion in the war on terror.

The evidence for domestic influences on the president's decision to use sanctions is mixed, at best. Presidential job approval (hypothesis 5.4) reaches significance in only the second equation (of the foreign policy sanctions), and then it is relatively marginal (p-value = 0.071). Further, it is in the opposite direction originally hypothesized. Of the significant variables of interest, the president's approval has the smallest overall substantive impact. A one standard deviation increase in the president's approval rating (an 11 point increase in the percent of

Americans approving of his job performance) leads to a mere 2.5 point increase in the likelihood that the president will use sanctions. For example, in the month that he was elected, President Reagan had an approval rating of 51 percent, the mean for all presidents. One year after his reelection, his approval had climbed to 63 percent. Comparing these two points in his presidency, Reagan would have been slightly more likely to pull the trigger on economic coercion in 1985 than immediately following his inauguration in 1981. In terms of the tension level, Reagan would have initiated sanctions with a tension level 5 percent lower when his approval was at 63 percent compared to 51 percent.

Clearly, 5 percent is not much of a substantive difference. Given that sanctions do not command the public's attention, it is not too surprising that the decision to initiate a sanction is only slightly influenced by the public opinion of the president. This lack of public attention may also explain the insignificance of the election proximity (hypothesis 5.5).[29] Economic coercion is not a common issue in a presidential or midterm election.[30] However, it is interesting to see that increased approval may make the president more willing to use economic coercion. The idea of political capital seems appropriate here (Ostrom and Job 1986). The president prefers to sanction when he is more popular with the public so that he has a stronger position when facing different interest groups that will be inversely affected by the sanctions. Still, this variable's significance is not beyond reproach and any conclusions based on it should be taken with a couple grains of salt.

Once again, the domestic political factors directly related to the president (approval and elections) indicate that if a conflict exists between the United States and a target, the president's approval will slightly influence the decision to sanction, but it does not indicate that the president will fabricate conflicts with other countries just so he can levy economic sanctions against them when his approval is low. International factors trump all other concerns.

In addition to the direct domestic political factors, the domestic economy was hypothesized to influence the president's decision (hypothesis 5.6). The data provide some support for the hypothesis that poor economic conditions will influence the conditions under which the White House considers economic coercion. The misery index is significant (p-values of 0.038 and 0.040, respectively) and has a moderate impact compared to the other variables. As inflation increases by one standard deviation (a 4 percent point increase), the likelihood that Washington will employ a sanction falls from 28 percent to 23 percent.

During high inflation periods (those one standard deviation higher than the mean, 16 percent), the dispute must become more hostile by more than 10 percent before the president will use economic coercion compared to periods experiencing the mean misery index level. This impact is larger than the approval variable for two possible reasons. First and as argued above, the public does not pay much attention to the use of economic coercion. Therefore, a president with a low approval rating will perceive that there is no benefit (to his approval rating) to be gained by hitting some nation with sanctions.

Second, a high misery index does catch the public's eye and is discussed regularly in the media. If the Federal Reserve raises rates (to battle inflation) or the jobless numbers are released for a given month, it is very likely that the nightly news will cover these events. This situation potentially puts the president on the defensive. While sanctioning a country is unlikely to affect the U.S. economy on a macro level and is thus mostly unrelated to the inflation and unemployment rates, few presidents would prefer to be seen by the public as more concerned with international affairs, particularly ones that have a foreign economic flavor to them, when the American economy is suffering. James Carville's campaign motto makes the point nicely: "It's the economy stupid!" President G. H. W. Bush spent much of his time campaigning on the success of the Persian Gulf War, the end of the Cold War, and foreign affairs in general. The Clinton campaign was able to portray him to the public as out of touch with the economic plight of the American people. The strategy worked, of course, and President Bush was defeated in 1992. Thus, a high misery index provides a disincentive for the president to focus on foreign affairs, at least those that concern issues that are not salient to the public.

The final economic condition influencing the likelihood that the president will use economic sanctions is the U.S. trade surplus with the target as a portion of total U.S. trade (hypothesis 5.7). The trade surplus, hypothesized to have a negative impact on the decision to sanction, is the second strongest variable of interest in the model, but it contradicts the hypothesis—a greater surplus leads to a higher probability that sanctions will be employed. Thus, the more favorable the trade balance between the United States and the target/country, the more likely that sanctions will be used. As the trade surplus variable increases by one standard deviation, the probability that the president will use economic coercion rises from 28 percent to 41 percent, a rather strong effect. In terms of the tension level, a significant trade surplus means that White House will pull the trigger on sanctions when the tension level is 20 percent lower than when there is no surplus.

Explaining why the United States prefers to sanction those countries with which it has a favorable trade balance is not easy. Clearly, the White House is not using economic coercion as a form of trade protection as Kaempfer and Lowenberg and others suggest. Instead, it seems that the United States prefers to sanction those states that are more dependent upon it for products rather than profits (from sales to the United States). While a state that is dependent upon the U.S. market for the sale of its goods may seem like it would be more beholden to the United States and thus more susceptible to economic coercion, this assertion is problematic. If the United States were to cut off its market to a state, export focused firms within the target will be hurt. This economic pain should provide an incentive to those firms to pressure the target government to concede to Washington's demands. However, the economic dislocation caused by the sanction is not likely to be immediate or immediately acute. Unless the firms have only the U.S. market, they will still earn some revenue from domestic sales and sales to countries not engaged in the sanction effort. For example, Cuba enjoys significant tourism business from Canada and Latin America, as well as Europe. Therefore, the loss of U.S. tourism is still a serious cost but not one that will shut down its economy. Even in cases where exports are critical to the target state's domestic economy, the target government can use its reserves to help temporarily mitigate the economic impact of the sanction. The Rhodesian case is an excellent example of this. As David Rowe (2000) details, the Smith government was able to take actions that limited the initial damage to the tobacco farmers, although they eventually were ruined by the sanctions and the government's policies. Thus, dependence on the sender for market access may matter but only in the long run.

Access to goods produced in the United States will have a reverse effect with a greater negative impact on the target in the short run but decreasing in the long run. While it should be easier to find sellers that will replace the sanctioned goods rather than buyers in a replacement market, it will take time to transition to the new sellers. The target's regime and/or market—depending on the economic system—must find and choose alternative products, if they are even available.[31] Some products may require proprietary parts that are much more difficult to secure. These transition costs act like a friction on the market and make alleviating the impact of the sanctions more difficult in the short run. For example, the United States denied spare parts shipments to Chile during its anti-Allende campaign. This sanction made it difficult for the Chilean economy to function as much of the industrial equipment was U.S.-made.

The White House may perceive that it can do more damage to an economy that is more dependent upon American exports. The administration probably sees the short term costs that it can impose upon the target and is more hopeful that the sanctions will have a more immediate bite and therefore, political effect. If this situation is in fact the case, then it makes sense that a trade surplus would increase the likelihood that sanctions will be used. It is not because the president wants to affect the trade balance with the target but because he thinks that the sanctions may be more effective.

I now turn to the cognitive constraints model (model III). There is limited support for the assertion that the president's cognitive beliefs (hypotheses 5.9 and 5.10) and information access (hypothesis 5.8) influence his decision to sanction. Neither the president's image of the political universe nor his advisory system type has any effect on the initial use of economic coercion. With p-values equaling 0.42 and 0.45, respectively, these variables do not even approach significance.[32] The president's strategy or approach to goals does have a significant, moderately substantive impact on the decision, and the effect is in the hypothesized direction. As the president's preference for more cooperative tactics increases by one standard deviation, the probability that sanctions will be used drops from 28 percent to 21 percent. In terms of the hostility level of the dispute, a more cooperative oriented president will wait for the tension level to rise 14 percent higher before initiating an economic sanction. For example, President Reagan has a 0.643 score for his instrumental beliefs, while his predecessor, President Carter had a more conflict prone score of 0.569. While Carter would initiate sanction at a tension score of 10.4, Reagan would wait until the hostility level reached 12.6. While these numbers seem arbitrary, they show that Reagan would hesitate significantly longer before using economic coercion, waiting until the tension level was 19 percent higher than his predecessor. The belief in and preference for more cooperative tactics clearly translates into more cooperative foreign policy strategies.

Finally, two of the three control variables are significant and in the expected direction. The United States to prefer sanctioning less wealthy countries. As the GDP per capita rises, the likelihood that the president will sanction the target decreases from 28 percent to 17 percent for each standard deviation shift. Clearly, there is a very strong preference for using economic coercion against less developed countries. This preference could be the result of core–periphery coercion as Olson (1979a) suggests, but it is more likely caused by greater ability to coerce weaker targets. Poorer targets are less able to withstand the economic pressure that the United States can bring to bear, and therefore, they make more appealing targets. Further, sanctioning a wealthy target is more likely to be costly to U.S. business. A textile firm can more easily replace the supply of cheap labor from one less developed country with another than the computer industry can replace the supply of memory chips from Taiwan. Thus, poor countries make attractive targets, while wealthy ones are unattractive.

The total U.S.–target/country trade also has a significant and relatively profound impact on the president's decision. For a one standard deviation shift, the probability of sanctions increases from 28 percent to 38 percent. In terms of the tension level, sanctions will occur when the hostility is 21 percent lower if there is considerable trade between the two states. If the president can sanction a country, he will do so much earlier in the dispute than if the trade link is weak. These findings are linked to the effect of the trade surplus and tell a common story. All three variables seem to indicate that Washington attempts to use sanctions against states that it can influence economically. The short run impact of a trade surplus, the poorer economy of a less developed country, and the overall level of trade between the two states increases the perception that the sanctions will succeed. This perception seems clearly to be held by the Oval Office when deciding which states to pressure with economic coercion.

The one control variable that does not reach significance is the regime type of the target/country. This is rather surprising given that others have found democracies tend not to sanction one another (Cox and Drury 2002; Drury 2003; Lektzian and Souva 2003). While this may be true at the international level, it is not true for the United States. The president is equally likely to use economic coercion against another democracy. Cox and Drury (2002) and Drury (2003) find similar evidence at the world level. That is, non-U.S. democracies tend not to sanction one another, but the United States will use economic coercion against democracies. This effect may be caused by the U.S. role as superpower. Needing to maintain its bloc and world order in general, the United States may resort to economic coercion against other democracies.

The temporal variables indicate that the longer the period since the last sanction initiation, the less likely the president is to use economic coercion. Economic peace breeds more economic peace, so to speak.

Conversely, if one sanction is put in place, more are more likely to follow. This effect is quite strong, in part because the probability of a sanction is so rare. That is, there are a tremendous number of months in which no sanctions were initiated, increasing the explanatory power of the temporal variables.[33]

There are two possible confounding factors not included in the model as control variables that are worth discussing. First, the president's party may have an influence on the decision to sanction. It is possible that Democratic presidents are more active internationally and therefore more likely to use economic coercion. Conversely, Republican, although stereotypically thought to be more hawkish, use force less often on average. They may, thus, use sanctions more as a substitute for military force. However, this did not prove to be the case. I ruled out this possibility by reestimating the models with a dummy variable for political party. The president's political party was insignificant (p-values exceeding 0.5) and did not affect any of the other variables. Clearly, once in the Oval Office and faced with a foreign policy dispute, the president leaves his party affiliation aside and is conditioned by the role of chief executive.

The second possible factor is that an individual president may be more likely to use sanctions. When President Carter came to office, he initiated a large batch of sanctions for human rights violations, something he had promised during his campaign. President Carter did use sanctions more than any other president, initiating 42 during his four years in office. President Bush comes in second with 21 in during his term, and President Reagan with 40 over his eight-year tenure in the White House.[34] Interestingly enough, including dummy variables for the presidents does not have an effect on the results.[35] Even including only a variable for Carter yielded no significant change in the equations. Thus, the factors that led Carter to use economic coercion more than his colleagues are already accounted for in the model.

Foreign Economic Policy Sanctions: The Section 301 Cases

I now turn to the second version of the dependent variable, the decision to initiate a Section 301 economic sanction. As defined previously, Section 301 sanctions are aimed at coercing the target to make its trade policy more "fair" or open. The idea is that countries whose trade barriers exceed the U.S. barriers should be made to trade fairly.

The sanctions are essentially aimed at forcing trade reciprocity with the target. These sanctions must be analyzed separately, at least to begin with, because their goal is so different from that of the other sanctions and consequently, the decision calculus that leads to their deployment may be quite different.

There are two significant differences in the analysis of the Section 301 cases as compared to the foreign policy sanctions. First, Section 301 did not come into effect until 1974. Therefore, the data must be truncated to the 1974–1992 period. Including the pre-1974 years would make no theoretical sense—one cannot model the president's decision to enact a policy if the policy does not yet exist. The second difference is the temporal dependence. Unlike the foreign policy sanctions, which were clearly time dependent, diagnostic tests revealed that the Section 301 decisions are not subject to an autoregressive process. Subsequently, I do not include the temporal variables in the analysis. The results appear in table 5.2.

The differences between the conditions that lead the president to use foreign policy and foreign economic policy sanctions are striking. Only two similarities exist between the two types of sanctions, and one of those only approaches significance. The first similarity is the accuracy of the models. Not unlike the decision to use foreign policy sanctions, the Section 301 decision models fit the data reasonable well (pseudo-R^2's of 0.16 and 0.17, respectively). The second similarity is the effect the tension level has on the decision to initiate a Section 301 sanction, although this variable only approaches significance. The tension variable, with p-values of 0.144 and 0.132, does suggest that the president may be influenced by the relations with the target/country when deciding to sanction. Even if one were to overlook the lack of significance, its effect is very small. A one standard deviation shift increases the probability by only three percentage points. Thus, while there is a similarity between the foreign policy and foreign economic sanctions, no real weight can be given to it.

Another variable also approaches, but does not attain significance. The president's advisory system has a p-value of 0.179. The variable suggests that informal systems are slightly more likely to initiate Section 301 sanctions. To examine whether this effect may actually be significant, I tested the difference between the average number of sanctions for each advisory system. The results showed that there was no significant difference, not even one that approached significance (p-value = 0.587). Further, a χ^2 test of a cross-tabulation confirmed the insignificant difference between the two advisory systems. Therefore,

Table 5.2   Foreign Economic Policy Sanction Decisions, 1966–1992

	Foreign Economic Sanctions (Section 301)	
Tension	0.136	0.141
	(0.093)	(0.093)
Escalation	−0.125	−0.135
	(0.715)	(0.685)
Provocation	−0.030	−0.029
	(0.065)	(0.068)
Presidential approval	0.012	0.011
	(0.025)	(0.022)
Number of months before election	0.002	0.003
	(0.036)	(0.036)
Misery index	0.025	−0.038
	(0.090)	(0.086)
U.S. trade surplus as % of total trade	−28.178**	−33.520***
	(11.506)	(12.193)
Operational code I1	0.275	
	(7.779)	
Presidential advisory system		0.837
		(0.623)
Polity score	0.062	0.059
	(0.053)	(0.054)
Target GDP per capita	0.000	0.000
	(0.000)	(0.000)
Logged total U.S. trade with target	0.449	0.434
	(0.436)	(0.411)
Constant	−10.883	−10.420***
	(7.844)	(3.736)
Observations	3,799	3,799
Pseudo-R^2	0.157	0.165

Notes: Robust standard errors in parentheses; ** $p < 0.05$; *** $p < 0.01$

I conclude that the president's advisory system does not affect his decision to initiate Section 301 sanctions.

The only variable that reached significance is the trade surplus the United States has with the target/country. This variable was both significant and confirmed the hypothesis that as the trade balance moved toward a surplus (deficit), the president would be less (more) likely to initiate a Section 301 sanction. The trade surplus variable has a moderate substantive impact, but only at the extreme levels. For example, a one standard deviation shift down (an increasing deficit) changes the likelihood from 3 percent to 4 percent. However, if the trade balance drops to its lowest level (a very high trade deficit), then the probability of a sanction jumps to 43 percent. This result indicates that only in cases where the trade balance is particularly skewed against the United States is the president much more likely to initiate Section 301 sanctions. When the trade balance does not hold an extreme value, then the sanctions are quite unlikely, at least according to the model.

What then is causing the president to initiate these sanctions? Three factors need to be discussed. First, there are a considerable number of observations of Section 301 sanctions lost due to missing data in the tension variable. This loss of sanction observations is slightly more than half the total. While this could simply be ignored, such a loss of data could have a significant impact on the results, and therefore, should not be disregarded. There are several ways to explore these missing data. The mean value for the tension variable for each target/country could be used in place of the missing values. However, since the tension variable is an important predictor in the foreign policy sanctions, it seems unwise to simply fill missing observations with the mean value.

The mean value would not reflect a dispute that the United States and target/country may have engaged in for only a brief period of time. If the relationship with that target/country is normally very collegial, then the mean tension score would reflect cooperative relations. However, the sanctions may have been the result of a specific, relatively short-lived dispute. If that was the case, then the mean score would dampen the impact the tension variable has or even reverse its estimated effect. While the dampening would simply make it more difficult to attain statistical significance, the model could wrongly estimate that friendly relations with the target/country make Section 301 sanctions more likely. Therefore, substituting the mean for the missing values is not an acceptable way to proceed.

The remaining option is simply to drop the tension variable from the model. While this does not come without a cost since the tension variable approaches significance, it is the missing data from this variable that is causing the problem. That is, if more tension data were available, it might become significant. It is not the case that some other variable with missing data are causing the tension variable to be insignificant. Therefore, I reestimated the model without the tension variable. The results are comparable to the full model. The trade balance variable is still very significant (p-value = 0.004) and has the same substantive impact.

There are only two other changes in the results as compared to the full model. First, the target/country GDP per capita becomes significant (p-value = 0.07). The variable indicates that the wealthier the target/country, the less likely the United States will be to sanction it.[36] Like the foreign policy sanctions, this finding suggests that the United States tends to select targets that it can more effectively coerce because they are weaker and less able to resist the economic pressure. The second change in the result is the significance level of the trade link between the United States and target/country. The variable becomes significant (p-value = 0.006) and is positively related to the initiation of economic coercion indicating that greater levels of trade make Section 301 sanctions more probable. This result is not too surprising since it basically says that increased trade increases the opportunities for sanctioning. It is possible that this result also supports the idea that increased trade breeds conflict. However, because the conflict herein concerns trade within the dyad and not some other issue, these Section 301 results cannot be extended to noneconomic conflict.

The second explanation for why the president uses foreign economic policy sanction is that the trade balance does matter. Even though the model predicts that it has a noticeable, substantive effect only when it holds extreme values, the variable is robust, significant, and theoretically consistent. Section 301 sanctions are aimed at opening the target's market because the United States has deemed that the target's trade barriers considerably exceed those of the United States. The sanctions are meant to force the target to engage in reciprocal or "fair" trade with the United States. Clearly, if the United States has a trade surplus with the target/country, it should have much less incentive to engage in economic coercion based on a lack of reciprocal trade agreements. It is important to note, however, that this does occur. In six of the 37 Section 301 sanction cases, the target had a trade surplus with the United States. Because Section 301 cases are based on specific goods, the U.S. Trade Representative can argue, for example, that even though the United States has a trade surplus with Argentina, Buenos Aires was engaged in "unfair" trade practices concerning marine insurance in 1979, leather in 1981, air couriers in 1983, and soybean oil and meal in 1986.[37] Thus, the trade surplus is an important condition in the president's decision to initiate a sanction, but it is not a necessary one.

Third, the decision to use a Section 301 sanction is driven partially by a different process. Like foreign policy sanctions, the president can control the process from start to finish. In this case, the president, through the U.S. Trade Representative's office, can initiate a Section 301 investigation and decided to use sanctions independent of other actors. This action is often done on behalf of some industry, but representatives of that industry can be completely left out of the decision process.[38] More often, however, private corporations or industrial groups file Section 301 complaints with the U.S. Trade Representative's office.[39] These complaints are investigated and then the executive branch makes a decision. In this case, the impetus comes from outside the White House. Thus, the president does not completely control the Section 301 sanction process. Certainly, the White House controls whether or not the sanctions are imposed, but the process is often initiated by outside groups. These sanctions are more likely to be driven much more by domestic factors than their foreign policy counterparts.

Unfortunately, these domestic factors—the presence of an industrial association or firm—is not easy to measure. In every Section 301 case there is an industry that will directly benefit from the sanctions. This is true with non–Section 301 sanctions as well. Any disruption or limitation of trade will create winners and losers. Thus, measuring the impact these groups have on the president's decision calculus is difficult at best.

The inability to capture these influences as well as the different decision process more generally may help explain why there is no impact from the international variables. Because the decision process is apparently so domestically driven, there is little reason that the foreign relations with the target/country would have an impact on the president's decision. If the president determines whether or not to sanction based on either (1) the merits of the case ("unfair" trade) or (2) domestic political pressures (or both), then the relationship with the target is largely inconsequential. It seems as though the president may be more likely to apply the Section 301 sanctions if the relationship with the target is sour. However, using Section 301 to address both a trade issue and some other political dispute may muddy the waters so to speak. There will be now way for the target to know if the Section 301 sanction is aimed at its trade policy or at some political dispute it has with the United States If the target state cannot determine what the sanction is meant to do, then it is unlikely to respond.

In sum, the decision to use foreign economic policy sanctions is quite different from that of more traditionally defined foreign policy sanctions. The relationship between the target and the United States, the president's concerns for his political capital and the domestic economy, and the president's cognitive constraints have no discernable impact on the president's decision. Even though the differences between the decisions leading to these two types of sanctions are quite striking, it is still valuable to combine the decisions into one analysis to highlight the differences further. If combining both foreign policy and Section 301 sanction decisions weakens the model, then there is more evidence that the two types of sanctions are truly different and incompatible. I turn to the assessment of the combined decision next.

All Economic Sanctions

I now turn to the last iteration of the analysis before turning to the post–Cold War era. In this stage, I combine the decisions to initiate foreign policy sanctions with the decisions to initiate Section 301 or foreign economic policy sanctions.[40] The results appear in table 5.3. Not surprisingly, the model estimating all sanctions looks like the foreign policy sanction model with two exceptions. First, the trade surplus shows that the higher the surplus (deficit), the less (more) likely the president will be to initiate economic coercion. This strong effect from the Section 301 cases has transferred to the overall sanction model. These results could indicate that estimating these decisions is not an incompatible enterprise. However, that is not the case. The second difference in the models is their performance. At the most basic level, the pseudo-R^2 for the two estimations is 0.14, somewhat smaller than the model estimating foreign policy sanctions (pseudo-R^2s of 0.17 and 0.16). Further, every measure of fit for the two models indicated that the estimation of the decision to use foreign policy sanctions was more accurate.

While these differences are not great, they suggest that applying the same decision model to both types of sanctions is inappropriate. The decision to use economic coercion for political reasons is based on a variety of factors, but it is most influenced by the relations with the target/country. In the case of Section 301 sanctions, the decision is clearly driven by factors internal to the United States. This means that the president uses the sanctions for difference reasons. Consequently, these decisions and policies must be evaluated separately.

Results, 1991–2000

I now turn to the assessment of the post–Cold War era. The only difference in the data from the earlier analysis is the tension variable.

Table 5.3   Sanction Decisions, 1966–1992

	All Sanctions	
Tension	0.198***	0.211***
	(0.037)	(0.035)
Escalation	−0.186	−0.215
	(0.240)	(0.238)
Provocation	−0.118***	−0.126***
	(0.030)	(0.030)
Presidential approval	0.011	0.015
	(0.009)	(0.009)
Number of months before election	0.015	0.019
	(0.015)	(0.015)
Misery index	−0.089**	−0.103**
	(0.035)	(0.040)
U.S. trade surplus as % of total trade	−14.463*	−15.735**
	(8.116)	(7.801)
Operational code I1	−4.574**	
	(2.151)	
Presidential advisory system		0.282
		(0.236)
Polity score	−0.021	−0.025
	(0.019)	(0.019)
Target GDP per capita	−0.000***	−0.000***
	(0.000)	(0.000)
Logged total U.S. trade with target	0.124***	0.141***
	(0.043)	(0.042)
Time since last decision	−0.061***	−0.058***
	(0.015)	(0.016)
Spline 1	−0.000**	−0.000**
	(0.000)	(0.000)
Spline 2	0.000**	0.000**
	(0.000)	(0.000)
Spline 3	0.000	0.000
	(0.000)	(0.000)
Constant	−1.423	−4.813***
	(1.756)	(0.777)
Observations	5,785	5,785
Pseudo-R^2	0.141	0.137

Notes: Robust standard errors in parentheses; * $p < 0.1$; ** $p < 0.05$; *** $p < 0.01$

Instead of WEIS, these data are drawn from the Integrated Data for Event Analysis (IDEA). The values for the tension, escalation, and provocation variable are similar, although the data themselves are drawn from a different source using a different method. In addition to this change in data sources, the operational code and advisory system variables cannot be included because of a lack of variation. In the operational code case, there would only be two different values, one for President Bush and one for President Clinton. Instead of measuring their respective views of the political world, it would simply have the effect of identifying the two different presidents. As for the advisory system type, both presidents used the collegial or informal system, so there is no variation between the two. I now turn to the results.[41]

Foreign Policy Sanctions

In estimating the decision to use a foreign policy sanction, diagnostic tests indicated that there was a significant autoregressive process in the dependent variable. Like the analysis of the first period, I use Beck et al.'s (1998) correction for the temporal dependency. The results appear in the first column of table 5.4.

Although there are important similarities, to which I turn first, the results are quite different from the 1966–1992 era. The model has a reasonable fit with a pseudo-R^2 of 0.18. Like the first period, the results support hypothesis 5.1. The tension level is significant (p-value = 0.003) and has the biggest overall substantive impact on the president's decision to use economic coercion. A one standard deviation increase in the hostility level increases the probability that the president will deploy an economic sanction from 23 percent to 29 percent; a two standard deviation increase drives the probability up to 37 percent. While other factors are important, the tension level is the strongest influence on the president's decision calculus. This finding should not be surprising. There is nothing about the end of the Cold War that would affect how the hostility of a dispute affects the president's decision-making. Although Cold War politics could constrain the president from using military action if the potential target was in the Soviet Union's sphere of influence, economic coercion was not so restricted. As the multiple and lasting sanctions against the Soviet Bloc attest, Soviet influence did not dissuade the president from acting (see chapter 7). Thus, the consistent effect of the tension between the United States and target/country proves the hypothesis to be quite robust.

The second similarity between the two eras is the misery index. Although it does not pass the 10 percent threshold, the misery index variable approaches significance with a p-value of 0.11. Like the previous period, its effect is negative, which suggests that the president prefers not to emphasize foreign policy when the domestic economy is suffering. When the misery index climes by one standard deviation,

Table 5.4   Sanction Decisions, 1991–2000

	Political Sanctions	Foreign Economic Sanctions (Section 301)	All Sanctions
Tension	0.187***	0.030	0.163***
	(0.064)	(0.169)	(0.052)
Escalation	−0.582	−0.343	−0.539
	(0.564)	(0.841)	(0.425)
Provocation	−0.066	0.013	−0.060
	(0.053)	(0.091)	(0.045)
Presidential approval	−0.037*	0.042*	−0.017
	(0.019)	(0.025)	(0.015)
Number of months before election	0.001	−0.046	−0.020
	(0.022)	(0.037)	(0.019)
Misery index	−0.196	0.180	−0.091
	(0.123)	(0.154)	(0.096)
U.S. trade surplus as % of total trade	3.079	−11.584	−21.730*
	(21.845)	(17.990)	(11.779)
Polity score	−0.062**	0.061	−0.040*
	(0.030)	(0.072)	(0.023)
Target GDP per capita	−0.000***	0.000	0.000
	(0.000)	(0.000)	(0.000)
Logged total U.S. trade with target	−0.011	0.607***	0.001
	(0.062)	(0.160)	(0.052)
Time since last decision	−0.063*	−0.001	−0.031
	(0.038)	(0.063)	(0.039)
Spline 1	0.000	0.000	0.000
	(0.000)	(0.000)	(0.000)
Spline 2	0.000	0.000	0.000
	(0.000)	(0.000)	(0.000)
Spline 3	0.000	0.000	0.000
	(0.000)	(0.000)	(0.000)
Constant	−0.010	−15.009***	−2.473
	(2.102)	(2.794)	(1.655)
Observations	4,137	4,137	4,137
Pseudo-R^2	0.183	0.155	0.078

Notes: Robust standard errors in parentheses; * $p < 0.1$; ** $p < 0.05$; *** $p < 0.01$

the probability that sanctions will be deployed drops from 23 percent to 18 percent. Considering the hostility level of the dispute, the tension level must be 12 percent higher when the economy is suffering before the president will use economic sanctions. While its significance is tenuous and should be interpreted with some suspicion, its substantive impact is rather strong.

The last similarity between the two eras is the impact of the target's GDP per capita. Consistent with the previous period, the White House tends to economically coerce poorer countries rather than richer ones. The target's wealth has a huge impact with a one standard deviation change dropping the likelihood of sanction initiation by 16 percentage points, from 23 percent to 7 percent. Once again, stable across periods, the United States tends to select those targets that are less able to withstand the economic pressure of the sanctions.

There are five significant differences across the two periods. First, the provocation variable does not attain significance (p-value $= 0.21$). This finding suggests that in the current era, targets will be less able to deter the United States from using economic sanctions. It is possible that provocation is becoming less significant because of the new issues over which sanctions are used. Intrastate conflict, particularly ethnic conflict, and democratization have become bigger issues in the post–Cold War period, and ones that often result in the use of economic coercion. Since these sanctions are driven by what is going on within the target state, outward actions by the target should have little impact on the sender.

For example, just because Milosevic was particularly hostile toward the NATO powers did not diminish the moral outrage that drove first British Prime Minister Blair and later President Clinton to push for intervention. Post–Cold War sanctions may be more driven by a concern for what goes on inside the target than what the target says or does. Further, the post–Cold War period has seen an increase in the number of sanctions mandated or at least approved by the UN. Such multilateral, institutionalized sanctions may be more resistant to hostile actions by the target because once set in motion, the bureaucratic momentum of the sanctions is difficult to stop. This characteristic would not make the sanctions more successful, but it would explain why the United States is no longer impressed by a provocative target.

The second difference is the significance and negative effect of the president's approval. Unlike the Cold War era, the White House seems to be significantly more likely to use sanctions when the president's job approval rating is low, rather than higher. A one standard deviation drop in the approval rating increases the probability that sanctions will be used from 23 percent to 30 percent. This means that a president will sanction more quickly when suffering in the opinion polls at home. For example, President Clinton had an approval rating of 55 percent in April, 1993. Less than two years later (March, 1995), his approval had dropped to 45 percent. Comparing these two points in his presidency, President Clinton was slightly more likely to initiate sanctions in 1995. In terms of the tension level, Clinton would have pulled the trigger on sanctions with a tension level 14 percent lower when his approval rating had fallen. That difference in tension level is significantly more than the 1966–1992 period and in the opposite direction. In the first period, a standard deviation drop in approval meant that the dispute with the target needed to be 5 percent more hostile before the president would initiate sanctions. In the post–Cold War period, the model predicts that the tension score would be 14 percent lower.

Explaining why the impact of approval shifted after the Cold War is not a clear task. It is possible that economic coercion became more legitimate and publicized in the 1990s. The use of sanctions as a means to improve human rights abuses, end ethnic cleansing, or stem aggression may have made them more popular tools with the public.[42] As a result, the White House may have seen sanctions as an opportunity to look more active or presidential when the polls said the president was less popular than he wished. Because the data for the post–Cold War era are more limited by the shorter time period, only time will tell if this trend continues.

The third and fourth differences are the insignificant effects of (1) the trade balance and (2) the trade linkage between the United States and the target/country. Neither of these variables have an impact on the president's decision to initiate an economic sanction. Instead of seeking out targets that may be more easily coerced because of their trade connection to the United States, sanctions again seem to be driven by other factors in the post–Cold War period. The moral justification for using economic coercion against ethnic cleansers, for instance, is not easily overridden by the argument that the sanctions may not have much of a bite on the target's economy.

Fifth and finally, the target's regime type becomes a significant factor in the president's decision to target that country with economic coercion. There is a moderately strong tendency in the post–Cold War period to avoid sanctioning other democracies. Moving the target's polity score one standard deviation up (from a weak democracy to a perfect democracy) results in a drop in the likelihood that the president will use sanctions from 23 percent to 17 percent. The tension level would have to rise by 14 percent before the president would initiate sanctions against another democracy. This democratic peace effect has been shown to affect economic coercion, so this effect should not be surprising (Cox and Drury 2002; Lektzian and Souva 2003). Why is this effect not present in the Cold War era? Two complementary factors help answer this question.

First, the United States had much greater security concerns during the Cold War leading it to follow a much more Realist approach to its foreign policy. The Soviet empire posed a real and tangible threat to the United States that trumped other, nonsecurity concerns such as democratization. The bipolar system meant that if a democratic state strayed toward the Soviet bloc, the United States would seek to punish it. The sanctions against Iran in 1951, and Chile in 1973, exemplify this point. In both cases, democratic regimes were sanctioned in large part because of their anti-American bloc policies (Forsythe 1992; James and Mitchell 1995). Thus, there was no American democratic peace for economic sanctions during the Cold War. With the fall of the Soviet empire, however, security concerns were less critical, and therefore, the United States was not under the same pressure to maintain its bloc. As a result, the president became less likely to sanction other democratic states.

Second, there is the increase in the number of democracies in the post–Cold War era. During the Cold War period covered by the data, 54 percent of the targets/counties are nondemocratic; in the post–Cold War era, only 31 percent are nondemocratic. This dramatic increase in the number of democratic states provides a larger group of states that the president is less likely to sanction—given that security is less important after the end of the Cold War. Consequently, the regime type of the target/country begins to have a significant impact on the president's decision to use economic sanctions.

Foreign Economic Policy Sanctions: The Section 301 Cases

I now turn to the Section 301 sanction cases in the post–Cold War period. Like the foreign policy sanctions, there are several differences in this period compared with 1966–1992. First and foremost, the trade surplus is not significant (p-value = 0.52). This change may be explained by the fact that there were bigger trade deficits in the post–Cold War period and considerably more variation in the trade balance. It is possible that the growing U.S. economy during the 1990s fueled more spending on imports, which, in turn, shifted the average trade balance toward larger deficits. This shift could have occurred not because of trade barriers—which would increase the incentives for

Section 301 sanctions—but because of greater consumer spending. However, the trade balance variable is significant when analyzing all sanctions (see discussion below), so too much stock should not be investing in this finding. That is, the time period is shorter and there is little about the change following the end of the Cold War that would indicate that the conditions leading the president to initiate Section 301 sanctions should be any different.[43]

The total trade with the target/country and the president's approval rating also attain significance. The approval rating variable barely reaches significant (p-value = 0.092). The variable suggests that the president prefers to initiate foreign economic policy sanctions when his approval is higher rather than lower. Given this marginal significance, conclusions about this impact should be modest.

The trade linkage variable is quite strong and significant (p-value = 0.000). Recall that the trade linkage was significant in the first period when the tension variable was dropped because of the missing data problem. The trade connection consistently shows that greater levels of trade make Section 301 sanctions more probable. Again, this result is not overly surprising since it says that increased trade increases the opportunities for sanctioning. However, the positive relationship between trade and disputes opens questions about trade and conflict. I discuss this in greater detail in chapter 9.

All Economic Sanctions

The last analysis tests the model on all types of economic sanctions in the post–Cold War period. The results show that, like the Cold War period, the tension between the United States and target/country is the biggest explanatory factor in the president's decision to use economic coercion. The trade surplus has a significant and inverse effect on the probability of sanctions as does the regime type of the target. There are no other changes in the significance of the variables. The differences between the two periods are clear, significant, and relatively stable across the different dependent variables.

Conclusion

The tests above lead to several conclusions about the conditions under which the president uses economic sanctions. First and foremost, the importance of the magnitude of the dispute between the United States and the target must be highlighted. In all of the analyses that included foreign policy sanctions, the tension between the United States and target had a significant and positive effect on the president's decision to use, maintain, or increase economic sanctions. This finding should not be surprising, as we would expect and even hope that the president's decision to initiate a program of coercive diplomacy would be influenced by international factors and especially the relations with the target. That is, this finding shows that the president is acting "rationally"; that his actions are based primarily on his interaction with the target and not domestic or personal factors.

The analyses above also found that the level of provocation had a strong, inverse effect on the president's decision to use sanctions. The best, most probable interpretation for this constant influence is deterrence at work. Smith (1996) shows that the president does take the probability of success into account when deciding to use sanctions. Further, Galtung (1967, 1983) shows that sanctions often can cause political integration within the target instead of the intended disintegration. The resulting integration leads to sanction failure. If the target is acting provocatively or belligerently, then one would expect it to resist the sanctions and be more likely to experience political integration.

Galtung's concept of political integration was based on the idea that the target's public would rally behind the government because the sanctions would be seen as foreign meddling. A target that acted belligerently in the dispute would suggest to its public that it was fighting foreign meddling and thus, be more likely to garner the public's support. Therefore, the president would perceive a belligerent target as one on which sanctions would not work and be successfully deterred from using sanctions in the first place, or be more likely to lift the sanctions if already in place.

While the strongest influences on the president's decision are international in nature, some U.S. domestic factors do play a part in the president's decision. These findings are not supportive of diversionary theory, however. Diversionary theory rests on the idea that the president will use more adventuresome foreign policy to boost his domestic approval. As the conventional wisdom suggests, the best way for a president to boost his approval is to use the military. This assertion is based on the idea that the public will rally behind the president and the troops.

However, this reasoning does not apply to economic sanctions. Typically, they do not grab the headlines like the use of military force does, nor do they involve American lives. The results show that only after the Cold War does approval affect the sanction decision and this effect is very small. However, the misery index is quite robust and shows that a weak economy constrains the president; it does not drive him to attempt diversionary tactics.

Similarly, the trade surplus findings suggest that the president selects targets against which the sanctions may have a more immediate economic impact rather than selected sanctions to alter the trade balance with the country/target. That is, the president is not driven by domestic political concerns, but by a desire to influence the country/target.

As discussed above, this difference between using the military to divert and being constrained from using sanctions is probably caused partly by the riskier nature of economic sanctions when compared to the conventional wisdom's "sure thing" approval boost derived from the use of military force. Unlike the use of military force, economic sanctions do not involve the possible death of Americans. Because American lives are not at stake, it is less likely that the public will pay much attention to the use of economic sanctions (Jentleson 1992: 51–52). Thus, during nonelection years the president can use sanctions as part of a strategy to look more active to the public. It is unlikely that the sanctions will hold the public's attention for more than a few days, and thus, the president can successfully look like he is doing his job without creating an issue that would create weeks of controversy.

Finally, the president's advisory system does not have an impact on the decision, but his strategy preferences do. As hypothesized, presidents who prefer more hostile or coercive tactics use economic sanctions more readily. This finding indicates that sanctions are not a cooperative version of military force—they are noncooperative and coercive.

Three conclusions can be made concerning the Section 301 sanctions. First, these foreign economic policy sanctions are driven by a different decision process than the more purely political sanctions. Instead of an overpowering influence from the tension between the United States and the country/target, the president is affected only by domestic economic concerns. As discussed above, the process through which Section 301 sanctions occur best explains these results. The majority of complaints are filed by private firms or industrial groups. These firms and groups seek private rents not political policy change in the target. Therefore, America's relationship with the target has little to do with the initiation of these disputes.

Second, the different process and its domestic nature make assessing these sanctions and the foreign policy sanctions untenable.

The combined analyses show that the different results from the two types of sanctions either cancel each other out or override one or the other. Finally, although these differences are irreconcilable, assessing the effectiveness of foreign policy and foreign economic policy sanctions is still valid. As Drezner (2001) argues, both forms of economic sanction are attempting to coerce the target to change a policy. What that policy is may differ, but the mechanism is the same.

Overall, the models perform quite well. They have both statistical and theoretical significance, and their accuracy, while not perfect, is rather impressive. The next steps in the analysis are to test for a target selection bias, then focus the decision to modify the sanction policy, and finally to assess the choice of the type of sanction.

Chapter 6
Is There a Target Selection Bias?

The three theoretical models of the presidential decision-making in chapter 5 capture key theoretical elements of the president's decision to initiate economic coercion. Diagnostic tests also showed that the models were consistent across individual targets/countries. However, it is still possible that the president is systematically more likely to sanction a type of country. There are three types of countries/targets that have the potential to influence the president's decision. First, during the Cold War, the United States directed more hostile policies toward communist nations, relative to noncommunist regimes, even if the former were not part of the Sino-Soviet bloc. Second, after the Cold War, the United States regularly pressured autocratic regimes to reform to a liberal political system. Third, the Monroe Doctrine increased U.S. involvement throughout Latin America compared with other regions of the world. All three of these examples could cause the president to act differently toward these types of states.

The possibility that a systematic bias toward different types of countries was present in the president's sanction decisions raises two questions. First, does such a bias exist that is not already controlled for in the earlier analyses? Second, does the United States sanction different types of states for different reasons? For example, were communist states sanctioned primarily for international dyadic reasons, while post–Cold War democracies were sanctioned for domestic reasons? In this chapter, I attempt to answer these questions. I begin with a discussion of the differences between individual versus group target/country effects. I then turn to an analysis of the decision to initiate economic coercion during the 1966–1992 period. Finally, I turn to the post–Cold War period and assess the impact of different target/country types have on the president's decision and then conclude.[1]

Individual versus Group Effects

As discussed in chapter 5, time series cross-section data can have individual or unit-specific effects. In terms of the sanction data, this potential characteristic would mean that each target/country would have a unique effect on the president's decision to sanction. If this characteristic was present, it would bias the model by inflating the error with a systematic disturbance. The problem is easily solved with a fixed-effects model that controls for the unit-specific effects. To diagnose whether this problem exists, a Hausman specification test compares the coefficients from a fixed-effects model and a random-effects model. The diagnostic tests run in chapter 5 showed that no individual effects were present in the data. Therefore, it is safe to conclude that any considerations about individual countries that the president may have had when initiating sanctions do not affect the overall model. This conclusion does not mean, however, that the president is not biased by *types* of countries when sanctioning, only that he is not influenced by the attributes of specific countries.

There are three target/country types that could bias the decision to use economic coercion. First, it seems entirely possible that the president would be more likely to use sanctions against communist countries during the Cold War era. In addition to the more hostile relations the United States has with communist countries that the model already addresses, I expect that the White House will treat communist regimes with more suspicion and distrust, making economic sanctions more likely. Even controlling for the significantly higher tension level that exists between the United States and communist nations, it is quite possible that the White House will initiate economic coercion sooner against a communist state.[2] The president will not give the benefit of the doubt when facing a Marxist regime during the Cold War. I identify those nations that were openly communist, coding them as 1 and all other nations as 0.[3] While any nations with a leftist orientation may be more likely to be targeted with economic sanctions by the president, this relationship should be captured by the hostility of the U.S.–target/country relationship. Thus, I am not assessing whether a leftist nation is more likely to be sanctioned. Instead, I am testing if the president is, in the face of the other variables measuring the relations between the United States and target, still more likely to use sanctions on a communist target/country.

The second classification concerns Latin American countries. The Monroe Doctrine and the U.S. historical interest and involvement in the Western Hemisphere that it represents should make the president more likely to sanction America's southern neighbors. Because the United States has a higher level of influence and closer relations with Latin American nations relative to the rest of the world, the president should be more likely to use economic sanctions against the former. To identify these nations, I created a dummy variable that equals 1 for all Latin American or Caribbean nations and 0 for all other nations.[4]

The third type of country that could influence the president's decision outside the theoretical models is defined by the regime type. As discussed previously, the increase in the number of democratic states after the Cold War as well as the push to democratize more states may influence the president's decision to use economic coercion. The results in table 5.4 already show that democratic nations are less likely to be sanctioned by the United States. To further tap this possibility, I dichotomize the dependent variable so that all nondemocracies are coded 0 and all democratic states are coded 1.[5]

I assess the impact of these three types of targets/countries on the president's decision to initiate economic coercion in two steps. First, I include the communist and Latin American dummy variables in the 1966–1992 model and the democratic and Latin American dummy variables in the 1991–2000 model.[6] Second, I bifurcate the data by the significant dummy variable and rerun the original model. That is, I select a subset of the data using the dummy variables and run the model only on that subset and then repeat that estimation on the remaining data. These results will permit me to judge whether the theoretical models are consistent across the different types of targets/counties.

Finally, the analyses below only consider the president's decision to initiate foreign policy economic sanctions. I also do not include Section 301 sanctions because the analyses thus far have shown that the decision to use this type of sanction is driven by different factors than those driving the more politically oriented sanctions.

Results, 1966–1991

The results appear in table 6.1.[7] Column 1 shows the communist and Latin American dummy variables, while columns 2 and 3 report the estimation of the Latin American and non–Latin American subsets of the data.

Table 6.1   Sanction Decisions by Target/Country Type, 1966–1992

	All States	Latin American States	Non–Latin American States
Tension	0.199***	0.116**	0.319***
	(0.039)	(0.057)	(0.052)
Escalation	−0.202	−0.313	−0.034
	(0.223)	(0.385)	(0.268)
Provocation	−0.128***	−0.061	−0.236***
	(0.032)	(0.042)	(0.046)
Presidential approval	0.009	0.001	0.021
	(0.009)	(0.012)	(0.013)
Number of months before election	0.012	0.019	0.010
	(0.017)	(0.025)	(0.024)
Misery index	−0.072**	−0.034	−0.134**
	(0.036)	(0.048)	(0.056)
U.S. trade surplus as % of total trade	24.367	15.628	26.266
	(24.905)	(65.624)	(28.961)
Operational code I1	−6.136***	−7.531**	−5.290*
	(2.282)	(3.759)	(2.907)
Polity score	−0.029	−0.042	−0.002
	(0.021)	(0.035)	(0.032)
Target GDP per capita	−0.000***	−0.000***	−0.000**
	(0.000)	(0.000)	(0.000)
Logged total U.S. trade with target	0.106*	0.163***	0.083
	(0.055)	(0.063)	(0.064)
Communist target/country	−0.146		
	(0.310)		
Latin American target/country	0.830***		
	(0.245)		
Time since last decision	−0.067***	−0.055***	−0.086***
	(0.014)	(0.019)	(0.021)
Spline 1	−0.000***	−0.000**	−0.000***
	(0.000)	(0.000)	(0.000)
Spline 2	0.000***	0.000**	0.000**
	(0.000)	(0.000)	(0.000)
Spline 3	−0.000**	−0.000*	−0.000*
	(0.000)	(0.000)	(0.000)
Constant	−0.428	1.759	−1.576
	(1.802)	(2.758)	(2.275)
Observations	5,785	1,288	4,497
Pseudo-R^2	0.186	0.138	0.209

Notes: Robust standard errors in parentheses; * $p < 0.1$; ** $p < 0.05$; *** $p < 0.01$

Communist and Latin American States

Of the two potential biases, only one is confirmed. The communist variable is not significant (p-value $= 0.64$) indicating that there is no bias toward sanctioning communist states. Instead, the fact that communist states have had more sanctions applied to them can be explained by the higher levels of tension.[8] The Latin American variable is significant, however, and shows that the White House is significantly more likely to use sanctions against Latin American countries compared to other states. Note that these findings control for the relations between the United States and the different targets/countries. An example may be helpful. Holding other variables constant, the president will sanction a Latin American country when the tension level between it and the United States is 28 percent lower than for non–Latin American states. Thus, the president is much quicker to deploy economic sanctions against a Latin American state.

These findings fit well with the historic involvement the United States has throughout Latin America. Attempts to pressure its southern neighbors include cases of expropriation, drug production and trafficking, human rights, and ties with the Soviets. While all of these issues have also elicited action from the United States toward non–Latin American states, the United States tends to take offense to these issues more quickly when the dispute is with a Latin American country. The U.S. sphere of influence throughout the Western Hemisphere is clear during the Cold War era.

Decision Calculus by Type of State

While the type of target/country does affect the probability of a presidential decision to apply sanctions, it may also affect why the president chooses to sanction. That is, while the analysis above shows that the president is more likely to sanction Latin American states, he may also sanction those states for different reasons. For example, the president may sanction Latin American countries for primarily international reasons and not domestic ones. To assess whether the president sanctions different types of nations for different reasons, I use create two subsets of the data, one including Latin American nations and the other including all other countries. These estimations appear in columns 2 and 3 of table 6.1 and show that there are some differences in the factors that influenced the president's decision to initiate economic sanctions.

Although the tension level is still significant for the Latin American subset of data, it does not have as strong an impact on the president compared to the impact it has on non–Latin American states. Instead of dominating the equation, its shares the most powerful substantive effect with the GDP per capita of the target/country. Thus, the White House is still more likely to sanction Latin American states when the tension increases, but richer Latin American states are significantly less likely to be sanctioned. For example, if the GDP per capita rises by one standard deviation in Latin America, the tension must be 38 percent higher before the president will initiate economic coercion. Wealthy countries to the south of the United States are much safer from the threat of economic sanctions than states with average or below average wealth. This finding does not suggest that rich states are immune from U.S. economic pressure. It simply means they are less likely to be targeted by the White House.

Another change in the results is the lack of significance for the provocation variable. Unlike other states, Latin American countries are unable to deter the president from using economic sanctions by acting belligerently toward the United States. The traditional heavy involvement of the United States throughout Latin America suggests that even strong signals of resistance from the target do not influence the president's decision. Since withdrawal from politics in the Americas is inconceivable to U.S. policy makers, bellicose neighbors are ignored or perhaps even expected.

An alternative explanation may lie in the fact that provocation levels in Latin America are significantly lower than for other states. The U.S. neighbors may prefer not to react too angrily to demands from the White House. The strong economic ties with the United States and the omnipresent shadow of the U.S. military may make these states somewhat more timid in their reactions. Whether the United States is less likely to be affected by a belligerent target or the Latin American states are less likely to act in a hostile nature, it is clear that deterrence against U.S. sanctions in Latin America does not work.

The last two changes in the model of Latin American targets/countries are the lack of a U.S. domestic economic constraint and the increased power of the president's belief system.[9] The lack of significance for the misery index indicates that the president does not consider any domestic economic factors when deciding to deploy economic pressure on a Latin American regime. The influence of the president's belief system, however, is much stronger. For example, President Ford has the least hostile strategy orientation, while Presidents Bush and

Carter have the most hostile strategy preferences. President Ford would wait to use economic coercion until the hostility of the dispute was more than twice as high compared to Presidents Bush and Carter. This effect is much less for non–Latin American states. In the same comparison, President Ford would initiate sanctions when the tension level was slightly more than a third higher.

These findings paint a different picture of the decision calculus that leads to sanctions against a Latin American country. Domestic influences are nonexistent, the dispute is still important, but less so, and the president's beliefs have a much stronger impact on the decision. These effects are best explained by the nature of U.S. politics in the Western Hemisphere. The legacy of the Monroe Doctrine seems to have made politics with Latin American nations more international and not a policy that is played out in the U.S. domestic arena. The desire, especially during the Cold War, to keep regimes hostile to Washington out of Latin America tends to negate any domestic constraints the president feels toward sanctioning these countries. The greater leeway the president has in Latin America also explains why his beliefs would have a greater impact on the decision calculus. The fewer constraints mean that the president has more options, and more options available to the president mean that any predispositions he has will be more likely to affect the decision. Thus, the president's operational code beliefs have a more potent impact.[10]

Results, 1991–2000

I no turn to the post–Cold War results. I include both the Latin American variable and one that identifies democratic regimes. I do not include the communist dummy variable because the end of the Cold War removes the reason for including it. Although communist regimes still existed, they were no longer perceived as a special threat by the United States. Therefore, there should be no bias toward this type of state.

Democratic and Latin American States
The end of the Cold War brings several changes to the model. Like the results appearing in table 5.2, the first column in table 6.2 shows that most powerful explanatory variable is the tension level between the United States and the target/country. Also consistent with the previous period, the misery index and the target's GDP per capita are significant.

Table 6.2   Sanction Decisions by Target/Country Type, 1991–2000

	All States	Democratic States	Nondemocratic States
Tension	0.189***	0.163	0.208***
	(0.064)	(0.147)	(0.079)
Escalation	−0.573	−0.956	−0.529
	(0.558)	(1.068)	(0.643)
Provocation	−0.069	−0.093	−0.059
	(0.053)	(0.101)	(0.064)
Presidential approval	−0.037*	−0.103***	−0.019
	(0.020)	(0.035)	(0.019)
Number of months before election	0.002	0.045	−0.022
	(0.022)	(0.036)	(0.027)
Misery index	−0.214*	−1.029***	0.046
	(0.116)	(0.327)	(0.123)
U.S. trade surplus as % of total trade	−0.740	−89.993	−2.658
	(20.384)	(64.184)	(23.922)
Target GDP per capita	−0.000***	−0.000**	−0.000*
	(0.000)	(0.000)	(0.000)
Logged total U.S. trade with target	−0.032	0.062	−0.023
	(0.056)	(0.224)	(0.053)
Democratic target/country	−0.847**		
	(0.396)		
Latin American target/country	0.053		
	(0.392)		
Time since last decision	−0.063*	−0.062	0.005
	(0.038)	(0.073)	(0.053)
Spline 1	0.000	0.000	0.000
	(0.000)	(0.000)	(0.000)
Spline 2	0.000	0.000	−0.004
	(0.000)	(0.000)	(0.002)
Spline 3	0.000	0.000	0.007
	(0.000)	(0.000)	(0.004)
Constant	0.724	9.221**	−3.208
	(1.942)	(4.402)	(2.106)
Observations	4,137	2,956	1,181
Pseudo-R^2	0.183	0.294	0.104

Notes: Robust standard errors in parentheses; * $p < 0.1$; ** $p < 0.05$; *** $p < 0.01$

However, the similarities end there. Neither provocation nor the trade balance has an impact on the Oval Office, but the president's approval does, suggesting that as the president's approval declines, the probability of sanctions increases. Although this effect is substantively small, it shows that the president has a preference for action when suffering criticism at home, at least at the margin. Cognitive and advisory system constraints are omitted from the model because they do not vary enough or at all for the two U.S. presidents in this period.

The Latin American variable is insignificant and indicates that the White House is no more or less likely to use economic coercion against a Latin American state than any other. With the end of the Cold War, the concerns for communist states inside the U.S. sphere of influence declined significantly. In the first period, 50 percent of the sanctions levied were against Latin American nations, while in the post–Cold War era only 22 percent of sanctions were against Latin American states. Two-thirds of these Cold War sanctions against Latin American nations were initiated by the Carter and Reagan administrations. President Carter's push for a more human rights oriented foreign policy led him to apply economic coercion to the many Latin American regimes with miserable human rights conditions. President Reagan shifted the reason for sanctioning, but not the geographical area. He applied a number of sanctions against communist regimes as he escalated the Cold War with the Soviet empire.

While the human rights issue has become a more important reason for sanctioning in the post–Cold War era, most of the targets of this type of coercion are now outside Latin America. Combined with the end of the Cold War and perceived threat of communism, there is no reason for a bias toward sanctioning Latin American states to exist.

The democracy dummy variable is significant and shows that the United States is less likely to use economic coercion against democracies. The importance given to the democratic process and the reduced security concerns following the collapse of the Soviet Union provided the White House with ample reason to avoid coercing other democracies. The data show that more democracies were sanctioned in the post–Cold War period (26 percent of post–Cold War sanctions were aimed at democracies compared to 18 percent in the first period), but this is the result of there being more democracies. Thus, the conditional probability of sanctioning a democracy increased significantly.[11] However, the powerful incentives that drove the White House to ignore the regime type of the target/county during the Cold War no longer exist. Therefore, the president now tends to hesitate before sanctioning a democratic regime.[12]

Decision Calculus by Type of State

The most interesting findings appear when the model is estimated on democratic and nondemocratic regimes separately. Appearing in columns 2 and 3 of table 6.2, the results show that the conditions that lead the president to use economic coercion against these two types of regimes are quite different. For democratic targets/countries, the only significant variables are the president's job approval rating, the misery index, and the control variable for the GDP per capita. These findings suggest that when sanctioning democratic states, the president is much less likely to consider the actual hostility level of the dispute with the target and more his own domestic standing. Low approval ratings mean the White House will be more likely to initiate a sanction against the target. This preference for action supports the diversionary theory assertion that criticism at home will lead to more adventuresome actions abroad. However, the misery index has an equally powerful effect that constrains rather than encourages the use of economic coercion. Diversionary theory would expect that high values on the misery index would increase the incentives to act out in foreign policy. As I have argued, however, economic sanctions are different from military force in that they have less diverting ability and may make the president look as though he prefers to concentrate on foreign affairs rather than the economic troubles at home.

In the end, it appears that Presidents Bush and Clinton preferred an active stance in foreign policy when they had lower approval ratings. This preference was tempered by a poor economy, which caused the president to reconsider using economic coercion. The larger point here is the power of the domestic conditions to influence the president's decision. Instead of the dominant impact that the tension level has in other cases, domestic politics seem to drive the decisions to sanction.[13]

Nondemocratic states are sanctioned for very different reasons in the post–Cold War era. Apart from the significance of the GDP per capita control variable, only the tension level between the United States and target/country attains significance. These findings indicate that the president's decision is driven almost solely by the level of hostility with the target. Domestic considerations that were important when coercing democracies have no impact here. This result may be explained by how disputes vary across regime types. In addition to not engaging in open conflict with each other, democracies are known to have less hostile interactions. This may decrease the overall tension level making it less of an issue to the president when deciding whether or not to attempt coercing the target state. With nondemocracies, the tension level will tend to be much higher, making it more difficult for the president to consider domestic political factors in the midst of a dispute. Thus, in disputes with nondemocracies, the president can only consider international factors because of greater tension with the target.

Conclusion

In this chapter, I show that the U.S. president's sanction decisions vary by the type of nation he is sanctioning. First, the United States tends to sanction Latin American nations more often and democracies less often. Second, the type of nation (Latin American and democratic) also influence the decision calculus itself. That is, the president sanctions these types of countries for different reasons.

Specifically, the hostility of the dispute alone conditions the president's decision to use sanctions against Latin American countries. Unlike other states, Latin American regimes are unable to deter the White House from using economic coercion. The United States perceives Latin America as part of its sphere of influence and something from which it cannot withdraw. Consequently, a bellicose target may signal that it will resist the economic pressure, but the United States will be undeterred since it refuses to pull out of the region.

The general acceptance that the United States will remain more active in Latin America because of the historical record and security concerns during the Cold War has another effect as well. The president's belief system has a strong influence on the decision to initiate economic coercion. Since domestic political factors do not influence the decision and signaling resolve is ineffective, the president is left with more options and fewer constraints. As a result, his personal preferences for tactics have a direct impact on the decision to use economic coercion.

In the post–Cold War period, the Latin American bias disappears. The end of the U.S.–Soviet competition for influence around the world made Latin America a less strategic region. As a result, the White House was no longer more prone to use economic coercion on Latin American nations as it was for other states. The end of the Cold War also shifted the importance of democracy and created a new sanctioning bias: the president tends to sanction democracies less and for primarily domestic causes, namely when he is facing a low approval rating but a strong domestic economy. Nondemocracies, however, are coerced largely because of a hostile dispute with the United States. The differences reflect the characteristics that make two democracies a more affable dyad.

Chapter 7

The Decision to Modify an Economic Sanction Policy

In this chapter, I continue the empirical investigation by turning to the question of what conditions lead the president to modify an economic sanction against another country. The analysis in chapter 5 only assessed the decision to initiate an economic sanction. The next stage of analysis focuses on what the president does once sanctions have been levied. Once economic sanctions have been imposed, the president has a series of choices. He can lift, decrease, or increase the sanctions against the target.[1] Clearly, this decision cannot be modeled with a binary variable because of the multiple choices available to the president. The decisions are not interval data, however, they are ordinal. The president must decide on one of the three increasingly hostile options: completely lift, decrease, or increase the economic pressure on the target.

For example, in April 1977, President Carter initiated economic sanctions against Nicaragua by cutting aid. Two months later, he increased the economic pressure by cutting military aid, and in July, he banned sales of certain police equipment. Each of these actions, after the initial deployment, illustrates an increase in economic sanctions. Similarly, in August of that year, President Carter allowed some military credits to the Nicaraguan regime. This decision constitutes a decrease in the economic sanctions. Following Allenda's assassination and the accession of the military junta, the United States lifted all sanctions against Chile. Although less common than the incremental decreases in a sanction policy, these decisions to completely lift economic coercion do occur.

The decision to alter the economic sanction policy against a target is theoretically very similar to the initiation decision. However, the adaptation of the original hypotheses to this decision requires some discussion, which I turn to next. Following that, I discuss the differences in the data and then turn to the analysis. The results confirm the importance of the international factors and give only minimal support to the domestic influences.

Hypotheses

The basic change in the hypotheses is quite simple. Instead of asserting that changes in the independent variables will result in a change in the probability that the president will initiate economic sanctions, the assertion is that the changes will affect the probability of the president choosing to lift, decrease, or increase the economic coercion that was already deployed against the target.

At one level, the entire theoretical model should translate to the decision to modify since that decision is new just like the decision to initiate the sanctions. That is, the president may have different options, but the decision to modify is a new choice. For instance, if the president has already levied sanctions against a country and that country continues to act poorly toward the United States, the likelihood that the president will choose to levy another sanction, thereby increasing the current pressure on the target, should be affected by the same factors that affect the first decision. The same logic may be made for the other options available to the president. Those decisions should be conditioned by the same factors that affect the initial decision.

Of course, the decision to modify is dependent on the decision to initiate—one cannot change a sanction policy if there is not one there with which to begin. So perhaps the model does not fit as well as I suggest. Additionally, the sanctions themselves will also have an impact on some of the independent variables. Since they reduce trade between the United States and target they will also reduce the trade linkage variable as well as affect the trade balance between the United States and target.

Turning to the connection of the hypotheses from model I to the decision to alter economic sanctions is quite straightforward. *As the tension between the U.S. and target increases, so does the probability that the president will increase the sanctions (hypothesis 7.1).* Similarly, *an escalating dispute should make the president more likely to increase the economic pressure on the target (hypothesis 7.2).* Although the target failed to deter the United States from using sanctions in the first place, it seems logical that continued provocative, bellicose actions still send the message to the president that the target will continue to resist the sanctions. Such a signal should make the president less likely to continue the coercion since the target seems resolute in defying the United States. Therefore, *increased target provocation should decrease the likelihood that the president will increase the sanctions and more likely that he will decrease or lift them (hypothesis 7.3)*.

It is less clear why the domestic political factors of model II would influence the president. The president's approval rating and the proximity to the next election should be quite unrelated to the decision to lift or decrease sanctions against a target. The public is unlikely to hear about these decisions, much less pay any attention to them. Thus, the president should not be influenced by these factors, except that the decision to increase the level of sanctions is similar to the decision to initiate them. The decision to increase should be affected in a manner similar to the initiate decision. Hitting Libya with another set of economic restrictions after a terrorist attack in the 1980s, for example, would make President Reagan look as though he was taking action to combat state-sponsored terrorism. Because the decision to increase should be affected by the president's approval rating and proximity to elections, they are included in the model. *Lower approval ratings (hypothesis 7.4) and close proximity to an election (hypothesis 7.5) increase the probability that the president will increase the sanctions.*

Ongoing sanctions affect the U.S. economy by dampening trade with the target. Although this effect is usually very small and downright trivial when compared to the overall level of U.S. foreign trade, domestic economic indicators should influence the president because the sanctions have an economic impact on the U.S. economy. A president residing over a suffering economy with a high misery index will attempt whatever is necessary to improve the economy. While ending economic sanctions against a country is not likely to make that significant of a difference in the performance of the U.S. economy, there is no reason not to attempt such action in hopes that it may increase trade and subsequently have economic benefits. Therefore, *as the misery index rises, the probability that the president will increase the sanctions will decrease (hypothesis 7.6)*.

The trade surplus between United States and target state is significantly related to the presence of economic sanctions. The U.S. trade balance tends toward a much larger deficit with those states it is not employing sanctions against. Not surprisingly, economic coercion reduces the trade level and tends to shift the balance in the favor of the

United States. Even controlling for the general tension level between the two states, and the target's GDP per capita, sanctions have a trade balancing effect. Consequently, sanctions would partly cause changes in the trade balance; the dependent variable would be responsible for an independent variable. Therefore, I do not include the hypothesis that a trade surplus will influence the decision to modify economic sanctions.

With modification, the cognitive constraints model adapts well to the decision to alter a sanction policy. First, the president's operational code should also affect the decision to modify the economic coercion. The president's preferred tactic (conflict versus cooperative) to approaching the target, which helps explain the decision to initiate, is less appropriate in this model. Since the decision to use a more hostile tactic has been made, the president's approach to tactics is less important. Instead, I used the president's locus of control, his belief that he can control events. *Presidents with a greater sense of control over events will be more willing to decrease or lift the economic sanctions (hypothesis 7.7)*, because they will have a stronger sense that decreasing the economic pressure will bring the target into compliance. Hypothetically, a president with a strong locus of control will believe that after the sanctions are applied, they can ease up somewhat to coax the target into negotiating with the United States. A president who believes he has less control will continue to apply and even stiffen the sanctions because he believes that he does not have enough control to manage the dispute without the sanction pressure.

Second, formal advisory systems are portrayed as being more rigid. This rigidity should translate into a less flexible sanction policy, one which is less likely to lift or decrease the sanctions, but to maintain them for long periods of time. *Presidents with informal advisory systems should exhibit more flexible attitudes toward the sanctions and be more willing to modify them (hypothesis 7.8)*. The two remaining control variables, the regime type and wealth of the target are both expected to decrease the likelihood that sanctions will increase.

Data

All of the data for the independent variables is the same data from the decision to initiation economic coercion, which is detailed in chapter 5. Like before, the data are arrayed into a time series cross-section spanning two periods (1966–1992 and 1991–2000). Instead of the 50 possible countries in the initiation analysis, only those states that have been sanctioned can be included in the analysis of the decision to modify a sanction. Therefore, only 28 targets that were sanctioned are included in the analysis. The only difference is the dependent variable. The president has three options when deciding to alter an economic sanction policy against the target. He can completely lift the sanctions; he can incrementally decrease them or he can increase the economic pressure on the target by instituting another sanction such as a new trade restriction.

These three options are coded on an ordinal scale: completely lifting the sanction equals one, incremental decreases equal two, and increasing them equals three. If no sanctions had been in place against the target, the first sanction is not counted as an increase because it can only be defined as an initiation. All other cases in which no sanctions were in effect are coded as missing data. Consequently, only those states that were sanctioned are included in the analysis. Falsification of the hypotheses does not come from null cases, but from variation across time and through space.

The Decision to Modify Economic Sanctions

Now that the hypotheses have been adapted and discussed and the dependent variable defined, I turn to the analysis. I begin with a discussion of the statistical method and then proceed with the findings.

Statistical Methods

Because the data are ordinal, neither ordinary least squares (OLS) nor logit are the proper estimators. Instead, an ordered logit estimator must be used to assess the impact of the independent variables on the decision to modify an economic sanction. In the case at hand, where there are four choices, the ordered logit estimates a linear score that is divided into four groups. The probabilities associated with those groups represent the probability that the president will choose a given option. The coefficients affect that distribution and thus, the probabilities. For example, if the tension has a positive effect, then as it increases so will the probability that the president will increase the sanctioning level, and at the same time, the probabilities of lifting or decreasing the sanctions go down.[2]

A powerful advantage of using the ordered logit estimator is that it does not matter what the values of the dependent variable are, just that they are ordered from low to high. This characteristic means that the intensity of the president's decision is unimportant, only the category (lift, decrease, etc.) in which it falls matters to the estimator. For instance, if the president permitted some humanitarian aid to one target but released a large sum of development and military aid monies to another target, the model would count both equally as decreases in the sanctions. While it would be nice to have an interval measure of the intensity of the president's decision, such as the dollar value to the target, this is impractical. In the case of aid dollars, one could measure the different amounts easily. However, what is the value of a lifted travel ban? Should equal dollar amounts of military aid, development aid, and humanitarian aid be considered as having an equal impact on the target? What about the easing of an import quota? Because economic coercion can take on so many forms, it is, in effect, impossible to measure the intensity of these decisions. The ordinal logit estimator makes no assumptions about the intensity of the differences between the different options, only that they fall on an ordinal scale.

Ordinal logit can still suffer from an autoregressive process, just like logit. Diagnostic tests reveal, however, that the decision to modify economic sanctions is not temporally dependent. The president's decision is not affected by prior decisions; each time period is independent. Subsequently, the model does not require any AR(1)-type corrections.

Results, 1966–1992

I perform the analysis in stages, beginning with the foreign policy sanctions. I then turn to the Section 301 cases, and the combination of all sanctions; I discuss the differences and similarities between these different models. As before, the cognitive variables must be assessed separately due to multicolinearity. Thus, two estimations appear for each dependent variable, one with the president's locus of control and the other with his advisory system type. The results appear in tables 7.1 through 7.3.

Foreign Policy Sanctions

The results lend support to three of the hypotheses, contradict one, and provide no support for the other four. Overall, the model fits the data with a pseudo-$R^2 = 0.127$, but not very well. The model itself is significant, however (log-likelihood ratio p-value < 0.000). The variable with the largest substantive impact is the tension level between the United States and target. A one standard deviation increase in the tension level drives the probability of increasing the sanctions from 46 percent to 68 percent. The likelihood that that sanctions will be lifted or decreased falls from 53 percent to 32 percent. Like all of the analyses before, tension has a strong and ubiquitous impact on the president's decision to modify the economic coercion—more hostile disputes tend to extend and increase the level of economic coercion.

Also consistent with previous findings, the escalation level is not significant, but the provocation level is significant. The results support

Table 7.1 Foreign Policy Sanction Modification Decisions, 1966–1992

	Foreign Policy Sanctions	
Tension	0.304***	0.335***
	(0.100)	(0.105)
Escalation	0.130	0.227
	(0.592)	(0.587)
Provocation	−0.165**	−0.176**
	(0.069)	(0.071)
Presidential approval	0.018	0.019
	(0.018)	(0.018)
Number of months before election	−0.012	−0.015
	(0.026)	(0.026)
Misery index	−0.105**	−0.129***
	(0.050)	(0.047)
Operational code P4	−18.079	
	(16.558)	
Presidential advisory system		0.773*
		(0.412)
Polity score	−0.010	−0.023
	(0.046)	(0.047)
Target GDP per capita	0.000	0.000
	(0.000)	(0.000)
Observations	135	135
Pseudo-R^2	0.127	0.137

Notes: Robust standard errors in parentheses; * $p < 0.1$; ** $p < 0.05$; *** $p < 0.01$

the hypothesis that a bellicose target can signal to the United States its resolve to resist the sanctions, thereby decreasing the incentive of the president to maintain the sanctioning effort. The substantive impact is rather large, and indicates that as the provocation level increases by one standard deviation the likelihood that the president will lift or decrease the sanctions rises from 53 percent to 94 percent. In all, the international factors play the predominant role in conditioning the president's decision to use economic sanctions. They are not the only factors influencing the president, however.

The misery index appears to have a significant effect. The variable is significant and has a relatively strong overall substantive impact, almost on par with the impact of provocation. As the misery index rises by one standard deviation, the probability that the president will decrease or lift sanctions jumps from 53 percent to 64 percent. The president's approval and the proximity to elections variables do not reach statistical significance. This finding suggests that economic coercion is not salient enough in the public's mind for the president to consider what countries the United States is sanctioning when an election approaches or his approval rate suffers.

The domestic economic indicator conditions the president's decision to modify economic sanctions because it is more directly tied to the sanctions. That is, if the U.S. economy is suffering, then the president will seek to take steps to increase its performance. Removing trade restrictions imposed for political (rather than economic) reasons is one way to speed up economic growth. Admittedly, lifting the sanctions against Cuba would probably not have a strong, immediate effect on the U.S. economy as a whole. Florida's economy would directly benefit as would the travel and vacation industries, but the overwhelming size of the U.S. economy would make the influx of Cuban business seem relatively small. However small the effect may be, the president still seems to prefer to limit politically driven economic restrictions during times of domestic economic woes.[3]

The last two factors that affect the president's decision to alter economic sanctions are his locus of control over the political world and his advisory system type. As mentioned before, these variables are very collinear and so must be estimated in separate equations. Only the advisory system variable is significant, but it contradicts the hypothesis. The advisory system type shows that informal advisory systems are more likely to increase the sanction level relative to a formal advisory system type (58 percent to 39 percent, respectively). This result is difficult to explain. It is possible that informal systems prefer to continue attempting to use sanctions as a means to coerce the target because they prefer nonviolent tools and are willing to keep the pressure on to attain their goals. However, informal advisory systems are defined as being more flexible and open to information. That definition would seem to suggest that these systems would more quickly detect the failure of the sanctions and seek a different approach.

Another possible explanation is that formal advisory systems do not consider economic sanctions to be useful tools for changing the target's policies. Instead, sanctions are used to fulfill the need to create a coalition, gain a UN vote, or placate domestic demands for action. These symbolic needs can be met with an initial use of economic coercion, permitting the president to remove the sanctions relatively shortly after their imposition. Either of these explanations is feasible, but given the weak significance, substantive impact, and lack of significance in later estimations, it may be safer to conclude that the advisory system type has a negligible impact on the president's decision to alter economic sanctions.

The operational code's measure of the locus of control supports the hypothesis, but it is insignificant. It is worth noting that if the decision to modify sanctions includes the "maintain" option, then the locus of control is significant. Its substantive impact is only marginal. Still, the variable seems to indicate that presidents who believe that they have greater control in a dispute are more willing to lift sanctions. Those presidents who do not have a strong sense of control prefer to wait out the effects of the coercion rather than risk lifting it and losing control of the dispute. Before concluding that the president's beliefs do not have an impact on the decision to modify sanctions, more data should be marshaled to test the hypothesis.

Explaining the conditions that lead the president to modify an economic sanction policy is more difficult than determining what leads to the initiation of economic coercion. Nonetheless, three conclusions are apparent and appropriate.

First, international/dyadic factors are fundamental to understanding the decision. The president seems to make decisions based on the relationship with the target and not political conditions at home. Given that the demand to "do something" by the public cannot apply since sanctions were already deployed, the president is more free from domestic concerns when modifying sanctions rather than initiating them.

Second, the one domestic factor that does matter is the economic conditions in the U.S. presidents prefer not to engage in politically driven economic restrictions when the unemployment and/or inflation rates are high. The president must believe that the public would not be sympathetic to foreign policy concerns when they are struggling to make a living. Instead, the public wants the president's sympathy and, more important, his attention.

Third, cognitive constraints affect the president's decision but much less that the international factors. Once sanctions are in place, they may become more bureaucratized and less contingent on the president's cognitive preferences or abilities. One reason for the Helms-Burton sanctions against Cuba was to shake the Clinton administration a bit and force it to focus on Castro and not simply maintain the status quo (Fisk 2000). Whether Helms-Burton succeeded or not, ongoing sanctions get less of the president's attention.

Foreign Economic Policy Sanctions: The Section 301 Cases

I now turn to the results of the Section 301 analysis. The results appear in table 7.2. Not unlike the decision to initiate a foreign economic policy sanction, the decision to modify one is poorly explained by the model. In first estimation, not a single variable attains significance. In the second estimation, the tension level between the United States and target is significantly and positively associated with increases in the level of sanctioning. Neither equation reaches significance (Wald $\chi^2 = 0.802$ and 0.688, respectively).

Although the models estimating the Section 301 sanctions have higher pseudo-R^2, the insignificance of all the variables in the one case and weak significance for three in the other as well as the equation insignificance indicate that the model can explain foreign policy sanctions much better than the Section 301 sanctions. The differences in the decision-making that lead to the two types of sanctions is clearly very different. This result should not be too surprising since Section 301 sanctions follow such a different process. The Section 301 sanction is much more bureaucratic in nature compared to political sanctions, and my model of presidential decision-making emphasizes non-bureaucratic aspects of the president's decision calculus. Thus, the model is not likely to explain much. This poor performance has an important implication—foreign economic policy sanctions are different from their political counterparts and should be analyzed separately.

Table 7.2   Foreign Economic Policy Sanction Modification Decisions,
1966–1992

	Foreign Economic Policy Sanctions (Section 301)	
Tension	0.885	0.916*
	(0.747)	(0.540)
Escalation	−3.231	−1.833
	(3.420)	(2.001)
Provocation	0.081	−0.189
	(0.272)	(0.163)
Presidential approval	0.104	0.092
	(0.081)	(0.073)
Number of months before election	0.151	0.142*
	(0.129)	(0.080)
Misery index	−0.085	0.085
	(0.295)	(0.282)
Operational code P4	−78.926	
	(93.545)	
Presidential advisory system		−2.308*
		(1.313)
Polity score	−0.027	0.014
	(0.105)	(0.114)
Target GDP per capita	0.000	0.000
	(0.000)	(0.000)
Observations	25	25
Pseudo-R^2	0.387	0.402

Notes: Robust standard errors in parentheses; * $p < 0.1$

All Economic Sanctions

The final stage of the analysis for the 1966–1992 period reinforces this
conclusion. The results in the two columns of table 7.3 show that
when estimating the decision to alter both foreign policy and Section
301 sanctions, the results are almost identical to the foreign policy
sanctions. The tension, provocation, and misery index variables are all
significant and identically signed; only the advisory system variable
loses significance and the escalation variable gains significance. The
Section 301 findings appear to be virtually washed away.

Results, 1991–2000

I now turn to the analysis of the post–Cold War era. The model does
not contain the operational code and advisory system type variables

Table 7.3   Sanction Modification Decisions, 1966–1992

	All Sanctions	
Tension	0.354***	0.377***
	(0.094)	(0.097)
Escalation	−0.747*	−0.721*
	(0.450)	(0.437)
Provocation	−0.155**	−0.161***
	(0.061)	(0.062)
Presidential approval	0.022	0.023
	(0.017)	(0.016)
Number of months before election	0.014	0.013
	(0.022)	(0.022)
Misery index	−0.109***	−0.129***
	(0.041)	(0.041)
Operational code P4	−15.008	
	(14.937)	
Presidential advisory system		0.487
		(0.380)
Polity score	−0.023	0.034
	(0.040)	(0.041)
Target GDP per capita	0.000	0.000
	(0.000)	(0.000)
Observations	159	159
Pseudo-R^2	0.146	0.148

Notes: Robust standard errors in parentheses; * $p < 0.1$; ** $p < 0.05$;
*** $p < 0.01$

because there is not enough variation over the Bush and Clinton administrations. Further, the Section 301 sanctions could not be analyzed alone due to lack of observations. Therefore, I analyzed the foreign policy sanctions and then the combination of foreign policy and foreign economic policy sanctions. The results appear in table 7.4.

Foreign Policy Sanctions

The differences between the first period and the post–Cold War era are numerous. Of all the variables, only one even approaches significance, and it is in the opposite direct as the estimation of the first period. The results show that as the misery index (p-value $= 0.141$) increases, the probability increases that the president will increase the economic coercion. Unlike the other variables in previous models, this finding is not robust and drops from significance if the dates are truncated by

Table 7.4   Sanction Modification Decisions, 1991–2000

	Political Sanctions	All Sanctions
Tension	−0.005	0.157
	(0.180)	(0.154)
Escalation	−0.239	−0.828*
	(1.175)	(0.442)
Provocation	0.054	0.018
	(0.109)	(0.091)
Presidential approval	−0.017	−0.022
	(0.021)	(0.022)
Number of months before election	−0.005	−0.006
	(0.035)	(0.029)
Misery index	0.199	−0.056
	(0.135)	(0.140)
Polity score	−0.046	−0.037
	(0.041)	(0.031)
Target GDP per capita	0.000	0.000
	(0.000)	(0.000)
Observations	83	97
Pseudo-R^2	0.051	0.042

Notes: Robust standard errors in parentheses; * $p < 0.1$

one or two years.[4] These findings must be interpreted as a failure of the model to explain the post–Cold War decisions to alter economic sanctions.

If changing the status of a sanction policy is largely dependent upon the target giving in to the U.S. demands, then the decision rests on the target's actions. These actions are reflected by the tension, escalation, and especially provocation variables. Thus, if the target's actions do not influence the president's decision in the post–Cold War environment, what does? One possible answer is the goals for which the sanctions are being used. Following the end of the Cold War, many more sanctions were used to coerce the target toward democratic transitions or away from internal violence. States targeted with this type of sanction may not have tense relations with the United States; in fact, there may be very few international interactions between the two countries. If that is the case, then the president will not be affected by what the target does to the United States, but by what the target is doing within its own borders.[5] Actions internal to the target do not appear in the model. Therefore, the model that is used to explain the president's decisions to modify economic sanctions during the Cold War must be modified in the future before they can be used on data in the 1990s and beyond.

All Economic Sanctions

The last analysis combines the foreign policy and Section 301 sanction decisions. The results are similar to first equation. Only one variable barely attains significance and the model as a whole is not significant (Wald $\chi^2 = 0.169$). Clearly, the model cannot explain the president's decisions to modify sanctions. These non-results are in part a function of combining the foreign policy and foreign economic policy sanctions, but it is also a function of the different process that is driving the decisions surrounding economic coercion. I turn to some of the possible explanations for these results next.

Conclusion

So what conclusions can be drawn from these results? Primarily, during the 1966–1992 period, the hostility level of the dispute mattered most in the president's decision-making process. It is both the most powerful explanatory variable and the most constant. This finding is not surprising since one would expect that the decisions regarding an economic sanction policy are driven by the relationship between the United States and target and not the president's concerns for domestic politics. Normatively, this outcome is rather encouraging. It paints a picture of the White House making decisions based on the actual situation and not as a result of the pressures from domestic political factors. When it comes to economic sanctions, perhaps the president is likely to "do the right thing" rather than seek to placate his supporters or critics. Of course, sanctions are not salient issues to the public, so it is easier to ignore domestic politics. Still, economic sanctions can have devastating effects on the target, so it is good to see that such decisions are made primarily to coerce the target.

Provocative acts by the target do have a significant and moderately strong impact on the president's decisions. The target is able to signal the United States that it is resolved to resist the economic pressure, and the White House responds by being less likely to increase the economic coercion and more likely to lift it. While this cannot be considered deterrence since the sanctions have been already been applied, it is still a strong sign of the dominant impact model I has on the president's sanction decisions.

These international impacts are not the only ones that matter to the White House. The misery index also has a strong impact, but only for foreign policy sanctions. A suffering U.S. economy does not create incentives for the president to act, but constrains his actions. This outcome is probably a function of the president not wanting to appear as though he is placing foreign economic affairs above domestic ones, although it could be an indication that the president prefers open trade during poor economic times.

None of the other domestic political variables reach significance. This suggests that once the sanctions are in place, the White House is not concerned with what the public thinks about the sanctions. Assuming that the public is not paying attention to the sanctions and the dispute that lead to them is probably quite safe for the president. Once the initial disagreement with the target has been addressed by the president, waiting for the target to concede cannot hold the public's attention. This outcome may even be one of the reasons the president initiated the sanctions—to placate the public's demands for action.

Finally, cognitive factors have a small influence over the president's decision process for foreign policy sanctions. The president's advisory system type indicates that some cognitive effects still influence the president's decision. It is quite possible that once the sanctions are put in place, the decisions to alter them become more bureaucratized. If more control is handed over to the bureaucracy, then it seems logical that the president will be less involved in the decision. Therefore, his cognitive characteristics and the structure of his advisors will have less of an impact.

The results are different for the Section 301 sanctions. The model is unable to explain the decision calculus for modifying foreign economic policy sanctions. This failure points to the significant differences between the foreign policy and Section 301 sanctions.

All of these conclusions change once the analysis is run on the post–Cold War data.[6] No variable is consistent across the different models. These findings must be interpreted as a failure of the model to explain the post–Cold War decisions to alter economic sanctions. The most likely cause for this failure is the shift in goals that economic coercion is used to attain. With the end of the Cold War, there was a desire to promote democratization and a need to stem increasingly common ethnic conflict. Sanctions used to attain these goals rely less on the sender–target relationship and more on the conditions within the target. The theoretical model does not emphasize the target's internal political conditions and therefore, is ill suited to explain at least the sanction decisions surrounding the democratization and internal conflicts. The inability of the model to explain post–Cold War sanction modification decisions and the rather weak explanatory ability of the model for the 1966–1992 period suggest that the president's decisions are driven partly by factors not included in the model. This could also mean that domestic lobby groups have a much stronger influence on the decisions once sanctions are in place in the post–Cold War period.

One last issue with the analysis of the president's modification decisions is worth noting. Once the president attempts to economically coerce the target, the economic sanctions themselves may become an issue in the dispute between the two states. Targets of long-running economic sanctions, such as Cuba, Libya, and previously Iraq, often complain that the United States is engaging in economic warfare or imperialism. Such comments would appear in the measure of tension within the dyad. Thus, the sanctions become endogenous to the dispute. This endogeneity makes the argument that the international conditions are driving the president's decision problematic. Maybe the decisions regarding sanctions are driving international conditions toward higher tension. While this reciprocal relationship is quite likely, it should not directly affect the results or conclusion too much. Complaints by the target concerning the United States sanctions will not score very high on the tension scale because they will simply be comments and not actions. In the recent U.S. history of economic coercion, no state has attacked—directly or indirectly—the United States because of sanctions levied against it. Thus, hostility directly caused by the economic coercion does not contribute much to the overall tension between the two states.

There may be indirect effects, however. Sanctions may exacerbate the existing dispute causing the target to pursue more belligerent actions toward the United States. Thus, the endogeneity problem cannot be completely overcome. This problem with the data may explain why the model performs so poorly. It does not suggest, however, that the results are spurious. The robust nature of the tension, provocation, and misery index variables indicates that they do have an impact on the president's decision to lift, decrease, or increase the economic pressure on the target.

Chapter 8

What Kinds of Sanctions Does the President Use? Domestic Constraints and Incentives

Thus far, I have shown that economic sanction decisions are largely driven by international factors, although some domestic political considerations and cognitive constraints do play a part in the president's decision. In almost every estimation of the theoretical models, the tension level between the United States and the target/country had the biggest, positive impact on the likelihood that the White House would initiate economic coercion. The analysis also shows that the target can often deter the president from using economic sanctions by being belligerent and provocative. U.S. economic factors also influence the decision process, but they tend to have less of an impact. Poor economic conditions in the United States generally constrain the president from using economic coercion, while a large trade surplus is associated with sanction use. Finally, the president's beliefs tend to color his decisions such that less cooperatively oriented presidents tend to use sanctions more often. While the White House does tend to sanction Latin American countries more during the Cold War and sanction democracies less after it, the results paint a rather clear picture of how the president uses economic sanctions.

A yet to be addressed question is: What type of sanction does the president choose to deploy or lift? That is, when imposing or lifting economic sanctions, what type does the president select? As discussed in chapter 2, the options are almost limitless. The White House has banned travel, held up the sale of weapons, cut aid, imposed quotas, frozen assets, held up parts shipments, and so on. The list is as extensive as U.S. economic interactions are with other nations. These options can be categorized into types that provide information about the severity of the coercion. In this chapter, I show that international factors continue to have the biggest impact on the president's sanction choices to initiate, but that explaining the aspects of lifting sanctions is problematic (not unlike the difficulty of explaining the president's decisions to modify sanctions). I also use prospect theory to probe the domestic political considerations further and find that they have little impact on what type of sanction the president selects.

Below, I spell out prospect theory and use it to explain the relationship between domestic imperatives and the president's choice of economic sanctions. Next, I develop hypotheses for the president's choice of which type of sanctions to initiate and then his selection of the type of sanctions to lift. Both of these questions are tested and the conclusions discussed.

Choosing the Type of Economic Coercion

At the most basic level, economic sanctions do not directly threaten American lives—a subject with which the public is quite concerned (Jentleson 1992: 51–52). While it is difficult to conceive of the president using military force without considering domestic sentiment, it is easy to conceive of the president disregarding domestic sentiment when deciding to use economic sanctions. Because economic sanctions do not garner the same dramatic attention as military force does, they provide an interesting and hard case for testing the influence of domestic political factors on foreign policy decisions. However, the president does not entirely disregard domestic politics when using economic coercion. Nor does he ignore these factors when modifying an economic sanction policy. The misery index is inversely related to both the decisions to use and to alter economic sanctions, and the trade balance is associated with the initiation of economic coercion such that surpluses lead to an increased probability of economic coercion. These findings are particularly interesting because they are contrary to the empirical studies of the use of force, which find a positive relationship between the misery index and the president's approval and the use of force.

The fact that the decisions to use and modify sanctions are partly driven by domestic economic conditions warrants a closer look at the effects of domestic political considerations. The effects of the misery index and trade surplus did not conform to expectations, however.

Therefore, an alternative approach or angle of analysis may provide more information about the way domestic politics affects the president's decision. To gain this different angle, I use prospect theory. Prospect theory has the potential to give a richer explanation of the domestic conditions under which the president uses economic sanctions.

Prospect Theory

Prospect theory offers a unique way of explaining presidential preferences for action. The theory alters standard rational choice cost–benefit analysis by asserting that decision-makers are loss-averse, and that this desire to avoid loss, which is driven more by psychological factors rather than rational calculations, controls their propensity to accept risk. Two specific conditions determine a decision-maker's risk preferences. The first condition is whether the decision-maker faces a decision between two or more options that would benefit (increase) his current situation or two or more options that would cost (decrease) his current situation.

If the options available to the decision-maker would benefit his current situation, the decision-maker is said to be in the domain of gains. Once in the domain of gains, the decision-maker tends to be risk averse. An example best explains this assertion. Laboratory experiments show that when given a choice between (1) a 100 percent probability of $3,000 gain or (2) an 80 percent probability of $4,000 gain, people overwhelmingly chose the first and less risky option. This choice is not consistent with rational choice logic, which predicts that people would select the second option because its probable payoff is higher (Levy 1992a: 174).[1] Thus, people tend to be risk averse when in the domain of gains.

If the options would both cost or decrease the decision-maker's current status in some way, he is said to be in the domain of losses where he will tend to be risk acceptant. Reversing the above example, when told they were going to lose money and their options were (1) a 100 percent probability of a $3,000 loss or (2) an 80 percent probability of a $4,000 loss, people tended to select option two—the more risky option (Levy 1992a: 174). Once again, rational choice would predict the opposite decision, option one, which has a negative utility of $3,000 rather than $3,200. Thus, when in the domain of losses, people tend to be risk acceptant "[m]ore than the hope of gains, the specter of losses activates, energizes, and drives actors, producing great (and often misguided) efforts that risk—and frequently lead to—greater losses" (Jervis 1992: 187).[2]

The second main condition concerns the decision-maker's current situation. Prospect theory asserts that these gains and losses are measured not in net units but are relative to a reference point, often the status quo (Levy 1992a: 174). The reference point is the level the decision-maker accepts as normal. Therefore, instead of seeing a $3,000 gain as an additional $3,000, the decision-maker sees it as increasing his reference point or current situation. An example of a reference point is a gambler who counts his winnings to find out if he is ahead or behind from when he started betting. The original amount of money the gambler started with is the reference point. In the middle of the betting, he can count to see if he is ahead (domain of gains) or behind (domain of losses) his original reference point. According to prospect theory, knowledge of the domain will affect how the gambler plays.[3]

While the gambler example above (as well as the lab experiments often used to test this theory) characterizes the reference point as static, real world applications show that new gains or losses are accommodated or accepted as the new norm. The decision-maker's calculus changes to reflect the new reference point (Levy 1992a: 177). Not surprisingly, gains are normally accommodated more quickly than losses. For example, if a person receives a promotion and raise, he accommodates that new status and income rather quickly. As a result, the decision-maker will fight much harder and take much greater risks to keep the new position and salary if they are threatened than he would to get another promotion and raise. In international relations, prospect theory would assert that a state would fight much harder to keep a territory it gained in a previous adventure than to gain it in the first place (for both examples see Levy 1992b: 288).

Prospect theory applies to the decision to levy economic sanctions because sanctions carry a risk for the president. Sanctions can be either a benefit or a cost to the president domestically. As a benefit, the sanctions could be perceived as a show of strong leadership by the president, that he is more active and is fulfilling his job in general. The president could also receive considerable support from a smaller group. For example, the Helms-Burton bill that allows expatriated Cubans to sue companies using land taken from them by the Castro regime gave President Clinton a boost from that interest group.

As a cost, economic sanctions could also reduce the president's domestic support by directly damaging an exporting industry and threatening American jobs. For example, sanctions limiting exports of a product to a nation would damage the company or companies that were selling that product. If the sanctions are extensive and a whole industry is affected, the sanctions could cause the loss of American jobs. The affected industry could then mount a campaign to seriously damage the president's domestic support. Thus, levying sanctions involves the risk of whether the sanctioning effort will be domestically beneficial or costly.

Types of Economic Coercion

The type of sanction that the president chooses to use against the target can be portrayed by the intensity of its direct costs. The more direct the costs to both the target and the United States, the greater the severity of the sanctions. While specific dollar amounts would be a better measure of intensity, chapter 2 points out the pitfalls of this measure.[4] Therefore, I characterize the president's choice of the type of sanction as a series of options that increasingly cost the target.

I categorize the White House's options into two groups.[5] The least intense option available to the president is the banning of developmental, humanitarian, or military aid, imposing a travel ban, or delaying developmental loans. While economic aid or a loan may be a significant part of the target's economy and cost it dearly, the impact will tend to be less than shutting off trade with the United States. Further, limiting aid will draw little attention from the U.S. public. For example, cutting off PL 480 (food aid) is unlikely to disturb the public thereby allowing the president to use such coercion without considering domestic political factors.[6]

The second option includes sanctions that directly cost the target and U.S. markets such as banning the sale of certain products, including military hardware. These sanctions are more intense because they cut either the market for the target's goods, consequently denying their economy hard currency, or deny access to U.S. goods, which can temporarily cripple their ability to maintain their industries.[7] For the U.S. economy, cutting international trade necessarily creates losses for some firms. Limiting imports forces firms dependent upon those goods to seek them elsewhere and, mostly likely, at higher prices. Limiting exports reduces the market access to exporting firms. Trade sanctions are therefore, more intense than aid sanctions.

Choosing the Sanction to Use

Now that the sanction options available have been defined, I turn to explaining the president's decision calculus through a series of hypotheses. I first adapt the international conditions that affect the decision and then explain how prospect theory fits the domestic political factors influencing the president.[8]

The international/dyadic conditions map directly to the president's choice of sanction type. Facing a more hostile dispute will provide significant incentives for the president to use more severe economic pressure; therefore, *increased tension between the U.S. and the target increases the likelihood that the president will use more acute sanctions (hypothesis 8.1)*. An increasingly escalatory dispute will also influence the president such that *higher rates of escalation will increase the probability that the president will use more severe sanctions (hypothesis 8.2)*.

The last international condition is the provocation by the target. While provocation has been shown to deter the White House from using sanctions, if the president has already decided to initiate the coercion, then there is no reason to think that a belligerent target would influence the president's choice of sanction. A belligerent target sends a signal to the United States that it is unwilling to concede to the American demands and will resist the sanctions. Knowing the target is likely to resist the sanctions and still having decided to initiate them, the president is unlikely to consider the target's hostility when choosing the economic instrument. That is, the president has already ignored the target's provocation when deciding to initiate the economic coercion; therefore, he will not start considering such factors when choosing the instrument itself. Therefore, I do not include provocation in the model.

To assess the domestic political factors, I employ prospect theory to gain a different perspective on the way in which domestic politics affects the president's decision. Chapter 5's findings about how domestic political factors affect the president's decision to deploy economic coercion tends to contradict prospect theory's expectations. First, the president's approval is only significant in the post–Cold War era, but it does conform well to prospect theory. The finding shows that the president's job approval is negatively related to the probability that he will use economic sanctions. That is, a president is more likely to use sanctions when his approval is low and less likely when it is high. Prospect theory explains this preference to use coercion when the president has a low approval rating by asserting that the president is in the domain of losses and subsequently wants to return to his reference point. This desire makes the president risk acceptant and increases the likelihood he will use economic coercion. Conversely, a president with high approval is less likely to use sanctions because he is in the domain of gains and subsequently wants to avoid the risk of losing any approval.[9]

The second domestic finding indicates that as the U.S. economy suffers, the president is less likely to use economic sanctions. Prospect theory would predict that a president facing a high inflation and/or unemployment rates would be more likely to use coercion, rather than less. The poor economy puts the president in the domain of losses, which should make him more risk accepting and likely to use sanctions. The third finding from chapter 5, that a trade surplus increases the probability that sanctions will be used, also contradicts prospect theory. A trade surplus places the president in the domain of gains and makes him more risk averse and less likely to engage in coercion. However, the results clearly show that the president is more likely to use a sanction when the United States has surplus of trade with the target.

An obvious question at this point would be: Is there any value in pursuing prospect theory if two of the three variables do not show any signs of fitting with the theory's expectations? The fact that the domestic political factors have tended to contradict the hypotheses thus far suggests that additional tests should be used to determine if these contradictory findings are consistent across different measures of the variables. That is, testing a different conceptualization of how the domestic political factors influence the president's decision will confirm (or reject) the findings so far. If the prospect theory explanation is rejected in the tests later, then I can conclude that the results are not simply a function of how domestic politics was conceptualized and measured.

One of the components needed to determine the level of risk the president perceives is the president's perception of the probability that the sanctions will be a benefit or a cost. Unfortunately, that probability is very difficult to measure and relatively impossible to put into numeric values. An example of this difficulty is McDermott's (1992) revealing study in which she applies prospect theory to President Carter's decision to attempt a hostage rescue. She shows that each option Carter considered involved different risk levels that were determined by both probability and cost (242–245). However, she does not give the probabilities numeric values nor place them on an ordinal scale. It would be quite difficult to figure probabilities for the domestic reaction to a set of economic sanctions.

What McDermott (1992) does to solve this problem is order the risks primarily by their possible costs. I follow her lead and look at how costly the sanctions are to the United States. As defined earlier, sanctions have differing levels of severity. By exploring the different costs, I tap into the risk the president faces when deciding to levy economic sanctions.

The explanation of what type of sanction the president will select offered by prospect theory is relatively simple; the president decides which economic sanction to use based on their domestic risks (as determined by the probability of their possible costs) and the domain he occupies at the time of the decision. Only two broad concepts are fundamental to testing the explanation: the sanction's severity and the president's current domain. The first concept varies by how directly the economic sanctions affect the United States and the target. The more acute the sanctions are, the more potential costs they will have for the president at home.

Less severe sanctions that do not cost the public will appear to have little effect on the target. Subsequently, these "weaker" sanctions will be less noticeable to the public, and the president will not derive much of a benefit from using them. More costly sanctions are a greater show of leadership and may generate a greater rally effect. Ending aid to a nation does not provide the public with much to rally around. Consequently, more costly sanctions are riskier ventures—the president may derive greater benefits from them, or they may cost him dearly.

The second part of the domestic decision calculus is the domain the president occupies, which can be determined for his job approval and the U.S. economic situation. According to prospect theory, presidents whose job approval falls below its mean approval will be more likely to take risks. Assuming that more costly sanctions may bring greater domestic benefits because they are a stronger show of strength but at a greater risk, *presidents whose approval is below its reference point will be more likely to apply more extreme sanctions; conversely, presidents whose approval is above its reference point are risk averse and making them more likely to levy less domestically costly sanctions (hypothesis 8.3)*. Since the reference point is dynamic, a simple mean is not appropriate. Instead, I use a three-month moving average of the president's approval. The president compares his current approval to what it has been on average for the last quarter to determine if he is in the domain of gains or losses.

The domain for the misery index is determined similarly. If the misery index is above its mean, then the president is in the domain of losses and will be more risk acceptant. *Presidents governing over a weak economy are more likely to use more severe sanctions (hypothesis 8.4).* Similarly, when the trade balance is below its mean level, then the president is in the domain of losses. *When the trade balance is below its mean, the president will be more likely to use acute forms of economic coercion (hypothesis 8.5).* Like the approval rating, the reference points for the economic conditions are dynamic. Therefore, I use a six-month moving average of the misery index and trade balance to determine if the president is currently in the domain of losses or gains.[10] Thus, the president compares the current misery index and trade balance with the last two quarters to determine its position relative to the reference point.

The last hypothesis concerns the cognitive constraints facing the president. The president's choice of sanction instruments may be affected by his tactical preferences. *Presidents who prefer more coercive forms of diplomacy will be more likely to use more severe forms of economic pressure (hypothesis 8.6).* Finally, I include the control variables (regime type, target per capita GDP, and the U.S.–target trade link) in the model.

I use the logit estimator to assess the hypotheses.[11] The results appear in column 1 of table 8.1. The model does a reasonably good job explaining the president's choice of economic sanction with a pseudo-R^2 of 0.221. The results support two hypotheses, contradict one, and offer no support for three hypotheses. First, the tension level is significant and the most powerful variable in the model. A one standard deviation increase in the tension level increases the probability that the president will use more severe (trade) sanctions from 50 percent to 71 percent. This result complements all of the other findings that show international conditions have an almost overwhelming influence on the president's decisions. Also similar to previous findings, there is no support for the escalation variable (hypothesis 8.2). The president does not consider a rapidly escalating dispute when choosing what sanction to deploy.

The second hypothesis to receive support from the findings is the president's domain for his approval rating. Unlike previous analyses, which did not find a robust connection between the approval rating

Table 8.1   Sanction Choices, 1966–1992

	Type of Sanction Levied	Type of Sanction Lifted
Tension	0.387***	−0.014
	(0.147)	(0.141)
Escalation	0.693	−2.313**
	(0.625)	(1.039)
Provocation		0.351***
		(0.112)
Domain for presidential approval	−1.034**	−0.717
	(0.524)	(0.670)
Domain for misery index	0.083	−0.734
	(0.584)	(0.697)
Domain for U.S. trade surplus	1.631**	−1.474**
	(0.712)	(0.708)
Operational code I1	−4.425	−11.052
	(4.481)	(7.340)
Polity score	0.001	0.076
	(0.055)	(0.058)
Target GDP per capita	0.000***	0.000**
	(0.000)	(0.000)
Logged total U.S. trade with target	−0.180	−0.019
	(0.123)	(0.110)
Constant	−0.923	7.014
	(3.241)	(4.893)
Observations	89	64
Pseudo-R^2	0.221	0.277

Notes: Robust standard errors in parentheses; ** $p < 0.05$; *** $p < 0.01$

and the president's sanction decisions, these results show quite strongly that if the president is in the domain of gains (a high approval rating) he is less likely to use a more severe form of economic coercion. When in the domain of gains, the White House is most likely to use aid sanctions (53 percent probability). However, when in the more risk acceptant domain of losses, the president has a 71 percent probability that he will use more severe sanctions.[12] This effect provides strong support for prospect theory. The president does not consider his approval rating per se when deciding to initiate or choosing what type of sanction to use. However, he does consider how his current approval stands relative to the recent past.

The results do not support the hypothesis that the misery index affects the president's decisions, and they contradict the trade surplus hypothesis. Instead of a trade surplus decreasing the president's risk acceptance, it shows that he is more likely to use severe sanctions when the United States has an above average trade balance with the target. Note that this does not mean the president prefers a trade surplus when using severe sanctions. The variable indicates that when the U.S. trade balance with the target is above the average for the past two quarters, the president is likely to use trade sanctions. When the president has an above average trade surplus, he has an 85 percent probability that he will use trade sanctions. When the trade surplus is below the two-quarter average, the probability drops to 53 percent. This result is clear and convincing evidence that the president does not use foreign policy sanctions to gain a better trade balance. The results show that the president uses the sanctions when the United States already has an edge relative to the past. The Kaempfer and Lowenberg (1989) argument must be rejected for sanctions deployed by an executive.[13]

Finally, there is no support for the connection between the president's operational code and his choice of sanctions. It is possible that once the decision to use sanctions has been made, the preference for tactics has had its effect. That is, more coercively minded presidents select sanctions as a tactic, but once they do, their preference for coercion does not affect what type they deploy.

Only one of the control variables reaches significance and is in the opposite direction as one would expect: wealthier countries are sanctioned more severely. This finding is the result of how severity is defined, however. The United States does not give much, if any aid to developed countries. The only remaining option is trade sanctions. Therefore, wealthier states are more likely to experience trade sanctions because they do not regularly receive aid.

What can be concluded from these results? First, tension has proven its powerful role in the president's decision. Second, domestic factors do influence the president, but their impact is secondary to the international conditions and not as consistent. The misery index has no effect on the president's choice of sanctions, a result that is inconsistent with the decision to initiate where a suffering U.S. economy constrained the president's actions. The trade surplus did consistently increase the likelihood that sanctions would be used and used severely. This finding puts to rest the idea that political sanctions are used to offset a trade deficit. The president's job approval rating blinks in and out of significance. This non-robust finding must be interpreted as supporting some domestic political influence on the president but not much. Third, the president's belief system only affects the initial decision and does not carry over to the choice of sanction.

The Decision to Lift

Now that the president's selection of the type of sanction to impose has been analyzed, it is time to turn to the president's choice of the type of sanction to lift. Unlike the decision to levy sanctions, applying prospect theory to the decision to alter the sanctions is somewhat problematic. The act of lifting or decreasing sanctions does not entail clear benefits or costs making it impossible to determine the risk level. For example, lifting the current sanctions against Cuba could be a boon for the U.S. resort industry. However, the consequences of said action would be very costly to the president, particularly in Florida and New Jersey where there are a large number of Cuban ex-patriots. It seems entirely probable that the public's perception of why the sanctions were lifted will determine whether the domestic consequences will be costly or beneficial to the president. That is, if the public perceives that the sanctions were lifted because they were successful, the president should reap benefits, and vice versa.

Another example is the sanctions against the People's Republic of China. Initiated in October 1949 by Truman, the sanctions were slowly lifted by Nixon beginning in July 1969. Were these sanctions successful? According to Hufbauer et al. (1990a), they were an absolute failure, and yet opening China is considered one of Nixon's greatest accomplishments.

To begin to overcome this problem, I assume lifting or decreasing sanctions entails the same possible cost as levying them. Lifting a total embargo is a riskier venture than resuming nonmilitary aid because it is potentially more costly. As such, I expect presidents in the domain of gains to avoid such risks and lift lower levels of sanctions. Presidents in the domain of gains will be hesitant to act in any dramatic fashion, either lifting or levying. Presidents in the domain of losses will tend to take more dramatic actions. As such, they will tend to lift more severe sanctions.

I expect all three international factors to influence the president's decision of what type of sanction to lift. First, *the tension level should be inversely related to the type of sanction (hypothesis 8.7)*. A dispute with a higher level of tension is unlikely to elicit a dropping of severe sanctions. Only in cases where the target and United States are on relatively cooperative terms should the president be expected to lift acute trade sanctions. The second variable, escalation, should work the same way: *a rapidly escalating dispute will decrease the likelihood that the president will lift trade sanctions (hypothesis 8.8).* Third, a provocative target would likely make the president look bad both domestically and internationally if he were in the process of lifting the sanctions. If the target was issuing belligerent demands to Washington just as the sanctions were to be lifted, this would look as though the White House was kneeling to foreign demands and not the other way around. Therefore, *provocation must be expected to decrease the probability that the president will lift severe sanctions (hypothesis 8.9).*

The domestic political factors have the same effect on lifting as levying choices. *Hypothesis 8.10 asserts that a president below his current mean approval is more likely to lift more costly sanctions and a president above his current mean approval is more likely to lift less costly sanctions.* Likewise, *hypothesis 8.11 asserts that a president facing a weak economy will be more likely to risk lifting more costly sanctions.* Finally, *above average trade surpluses will increase the probability that the president will lift less severe sanctions (hypothesis 8.12).*

Cognitive constraints should also play a role when the president lifts sanctions. *Presidents who prefer more coercive forms of diplomacy will be more likely to lift less severe economic sanctions (hypothesis 8.6).* Each of the control variables is also included.

The results from the logit model appear in column 2 of table 8.1 earlier. The model successful predicts a considerable amount of variance (pseudo-$R^2 = 0.277$), but it only supports two hypotheses, contradicts one, and provides no evidence for the others. The tension level is insignificant indicating that once the president has decided to lift the economic coercion, the direct relations with the target do not affect his choices. The potential future of that relationship does, however. If the rate of escalation is low or negative, then the president is more likely to lift trade sanctions. This effect is quite pronounced. If the escalation rate increases by one standard deviation, then the probability that the president will lift trade sanctions falls from 64 percent to 45 percent (holding all other variables constant). The president considers the state of the relationship with the target as he moves to lift the sanctions. If the relationship is not becoming increasingly hostile once the dispute has been resolved, then lifting trade sanctions would seem reasonable. If relations with the target were degenerating again, then lifting only a less severe form of economic pressure is warranted.

The provocation from the target contradicts the hypothesis showing that a more bellicose target is more likely to have trade sanctions lifted rather than aid sanctions. Although its overall impact is not as strong as the escalation variable's, it is significant and nontrivial.

This is a curious finding that defies simple explanation. It is possible that as the president lifts the sanctions, the United States takes a more conciliatory position and the target may act out toward the United States. Once the dispute has been resolved and the United States is backing down its economic pressure, the target may issue statements that show its displeasure that the sanctions were used in the first place. This explanation is pure conjecture. Future studies should focus specifically on the decisions to lift coercion to determine what casual effect the target's behavior has on the president.

The only domestic politics variable that reaches significance is the trade surplus, which confirms the hypothesis. As the trade surplus exceeds its mean and the president resides in the domain of gains, then he is more likely to lift the less risky aid sanctions and not trade sanctions. This effect is quite substantial. President's lifting sanctions when the trade balance is below average (putting them in the domain of gains) have 52 percent probability of lifting trade sanctions, but the same president with a strong economy is only 19 percent likely to lift trade sanctions. Once in the domain of gains, the president is clearly reluctant to take action that would jeopardize that position, and lifting trade sanctions would directly affect the positive trade balance preferred by the president. Furthermore, the president's preference for hostile or cooperative tactics receives no support from the model. Like the choice of what sanction to levy, the president's beliefs seem to only have an impact on the larger decisions to initiate and modify economic coercion.

One issue that is not addressed in the logit model but has been shown to have an effect in previous research is the president's party. Drury (1997) shows that presidents of one party did not lift a single failing sanction if it was levied by a president of the same party. While the data for effectiveness is not available for the current dataset, the parties of the president's initiating and ending the economic coercion is available.[14] In table 8.2, I combine the two periods into one that begins in 1966 and ends in 2000 and cross tabulate the parties of the president who levied a specific sanction and who lifted that specific sanction.[15] The Fisher's exact test reveals the association is significant.[16] There is a moderately strong trend for the Oval Office to lift those sanctions deployed by a member of its own party. These results suggest that domestic political considerations do enter into the decision-making process to lift an economic sanction. The White House has a moderate preference for dealing with the policies of its own party and leaving the opposing party's policies alone.

Table 8.2   Presidential Parties that Initiated and Lifted
Economic Sanctions

Party that Levied Sanctions	Party that Lifted Sanctions		
	Democrat	Republican	Total
Democrat	8	13	21
Republican	2	17	19
Total	10	30	40

Notes: Pearson $\chi^2(1)$ = 4.0434; Probability = 0.044; gamma = 0.6790;
Fisher's exact = 0.069; 1-sided Fisher's exact = 0.048

Conclusion

The preceding analysis generated some support for prospect theory.
Once the decision to levy economic sanctions is made, prospect theory
improves the explanation of how domestic imperatives affect the president's choice of economic measures. When faced with losses, the
president tends to act in a more risk-accepting fashion and levy more
costly sanctions. When the president's approval is in the domain of
losses, nations finding themselves in dispute with the United States
should be more cautious because if sanctions are levied, they will be
more costly. Conversely, if the president is in the domain of gains, it is
better to dispute an issue with the United States because the sanctions,
if levied, would be less costly. On the other side of the dispute, the
United States must recognize that, during periods when the president
is in the domain of gains, other nations may have greater bargaining
power.

Prospect theory also receives some support when applied to the
president's selection of the type of sanctions to lift, although analysis
created as many questions as answers. When the United States has an
above average trade balance with the target, the president selects the
less risky choice and lifts aid sanctions. This confirmatory evidence
suggests that president's preference toward risk is determined partly
by domestic politics. The positive effect of provocation on the president's choice raises serious questions about how the target's actions
influence the Oval Office. Instead of leading the president to lift less
acute sanctions, a belligerent target is associated with the lifting of
trade sanctions. Additional research focusing on the target must be
undertaken to explain this result.

Three other conclusions can be drawn from the analysis. First, tension has a large and constant role in the president's decisions to use economic coercion. As hypothesized, the White House uses sanctions when the relations with the target/country deteriorate. Second, domestic political factors do play a role in the president's decisions, although it is a marginal one. It does not appear that the president is responding to rent seeking lobbyists or public demands for action but a more general concern for his domestic standing. Third, explaining and modeling the decisions to initiate and select the type of coercion is easier than the decisions to modify or lift the sanction policy. Additional factors not specified in the model must be responsible for the choices the president makes once a sanction is in place. Future research into the decision process may provide the information needed to explain these choices.

Chapter 9
Conclusions and Implications

At the International Studies Association annual meetings in 2002, a discussant on an economic sanctions panel suggested that sanction success is no longer an interesting question because sanctions simply do not work. Instead, other unanswered questions concerning economic coercion should be investigated. In this book, I have investigated and attempted to answer some of these questions, specifically: the decisions to initiate and modify a sanction policy, the selection of the type of sanction, whether a bias toward a type of country exists, the contrast between foreign policy sanctions and Section 301 sanctions, and the differences in the sanctioning decision calculus between the Cold War and post–Cold War eras.

The answers and new information revealed by this investigation have important implications for both future research and our general understanding of the president's decision to use economic coercion. In this concluding chapter, I review the findings and conclusions and place them into an overall picture of the use of economic sanctions. I proceed step-by-step through the president's decisions to use and alter sanctions, as well as discussing the characteristics of those decisions. I then discuss the implications these findings have for both our understanding of economic coercion and presidential decision-making. Finally, I suggest possible paths for future research.

Reviewing the Findings

Sanction Effectiveness

What conditions make economic sanctions effective? One would expect this question to come after the analysis of the conditions that lead the president to use and maintain economic sanctions.

That expectation is valid, but it is also the reason the question comes first in this book. Only a small handful of scholars studying economic coercion have ever assessed the conditions under which it is used. While some discuss the reasons sanctions are used or the goals they serve, most assume that the sanctions have one goal—policy change by the target—and then move on to analyze sanction effectiveness regarding those goals. Because scholars have rarely explored the conditions leading to sanction use, their analyses of effectiveness are typically flawed. True, some of the case studies are rich in information and help advance our general understanding of economic sanctions (e.g., Galtung 1967; Olson 1979; Rowe 2000), but the studies that move beyond a small number of cases begin to fail in their attempts to explain sanction effectiveness.

I illustrate this failure in the reanalysis of the large data set collected by Hufbauer et al. (1991a, 1991b). My reanalysis identified five conditions for effective sanctions: (1) distressed targets succumb to sanctions more often; (2) sanctions costly to the target tend to be more effective; (3) when several nations cooperate to sanction a target without the help of an international organization, the sanctions are less effective; (4) when the sender is concerned about national security when sanctioning, the effort is less likely to be successful; and (5) economic coercion against a democratic target tends to be more effective than nondemocratic targets. While these five findings are interesting, they are only a small portion of those originally reported by Hufbauer et al. Of the eleven policy recommendations they make, only two stand up to close analysis without conditions (1) and (2) present, and one holds up with substantial qualifications when condition (3) is met. Further, the model's predictive capacity is rather weak, making the recommendations that do hold up not as meaningful as originally suggested. These findings indicate that the conventional wisdom is unable to accurately explain sanction effectiveness.

Previous studies encountered problems explaining sanction effectiveness, because they had such a limited conception of the goals sanctions serve. Most scholars assume economic coercion has but one goal: a policy change by the target. These policy changes are most typically derived from the overt goals that the sender government lays out when levying the sanctions. While some investigators have argued this assumption is invalid (e.g., Barber 1979; Baldwin 1985; Lindsey 1986; Drezner 2001; Drury 2001), most scholars still hold onto the idea that the sender is only interested in policy change in the target. The poor performance of sanctions as instruments of policy change has led several scholars to conclude that the use of economic coercion is driven by domestic economic and political factors. Many suggest that sanctions are a reaction to a public demand for action—the "do something" hypothesis (Renwick 1981; Doxey 1987; Haass 1993), while others argue that sanctions are the result of domestic demands for trade protection (Kaempfer and Lowenberg 1988, 1989, 1992). These claims are largely untested, however.

Sanction Decisions

I contend that the reason the literature cannot explain sanction effectiveness is because we do not have an understanding of the conditions that lead to their use. The remainder of the book explores the conditions that lead the president to use and alter economic coercion. I developed a theory to explain the conditions under which the president uses economic coercion, beginning with a traditional assumption that economic sanctions are used for international reasons, and that the president made his decision based on these reasons. The first model that I explored hypothesized that the president would react to increased dispute hostility with a greater likelihood of sanction use, but target provocation could deter the president from acting.

My second model assumed that domestic political conditions affect the president's decision to sanction. This model predicted that when the president was weak domestically, he would be more likely to take more action internationally, specifically employing economic coercion. I argue that the president has a general preference for action during periods of low domestic support. It is this increased preference for action that translates into a greater likelihood of sanction use. However, this preference for action is tempered by economic conditions and enhanced by incentives to use economic coercion to offset a trade deficit with the target.

Both of these models assume that the president is unconstrained in his ability to make decisions. This assumption is rather unrealistic because of the constraints on the amount of time and information available for any given decision as well as the impact beliefs will have on the decision process. To compensate for these time and information constraints, the president organizes an advisory system through which the decision process functions. Others have argued that the system's organization affects the actual decisions made (e.g., see George 1980;

M. Hermann and C. Hermann 1989). Presidents with informal advisory systems should be more likely to use economic sanctions, because the system encourages both more innovative and incremental decision-making. Presidents with formal systems will act in just the opposite manner; they will be less innovative and more extreme and therefore are less likely to use sanctions.

To include the impact beliefs have on the decisions to use economic coercion, I model the president's operational code. Several studies have shown that the president's philosophical and instrumental beliefs condition his response to international disputes (George 1969; Walker et al. 1998; Walker and Schafer 2003). I hypothesize that a more hostile view of the world and a preference for more coercive rather than cooperative tactics will increase the president's penchant for using economic coercion.

The Decision to Use Economic Coercion

In a sanctioning episode, the first decision the president makes is to initiate economic coercion against the target nation. This decision is colored by foreign, domestic, and cognitive factors. I find that the tension level of the dispute between the United States and the target/country increases the president's propensity to use sanctions. The effects of the tension level are consistently the strongest and most robust across all of the different specifications of foreign policy sanctions. The dispute with the target is the driving force behind the decision to initiate economic pressure on the target. While a highly escalatory dispute has no effect on the White House, a bellicose, provocative target decreases the president's propensity to use sanctions. The president is reacting to the relations with the target in such a manner that he is more likely to sanction if the dispute reaches a certain level of hostility. However, if the target is particularly provocative, then it is able to deter the president from using economic coercion.

In addition to these international influences, domestic political factors also have an impact on the president, although these effects are not as robust and consistently powerful as the international factors. The president's job approval rating has a significant but marginal and inconsistent impact on the decision to use economic coercion. The White House may have a small preference for engaging in coercion when the public holds a favorable impression of the president. The findings concur with some of the use-of-force scholarship that shows the president uses the military when his overall approval rating is high. This effect is very small, however, and does not mean that the president seriously considers or is constrained by his domestic standing.

The impact of the U.S. misery index and the trade balance with the target have a much more robust and powerful influence on the president's decision. The results indicate that the misery index dampens the probability that the White House will initiate economic coercion. The president clearly considers using sanctions a less than optimal strategy when the domestic economy is suffering. The fear of being perceived as caring more about foreign affairs than domestic suffering and the negative economic impact sanctions have on the economy tend to constrain the president's use of economic coercion.

Contrary to expectations, the White House prefers a trade surplus when sanctioning the target. I suggest that this effect is driven by the president's desire to have a direct and immediate impact on the target's economy. Since the loss of goods from the United States can cause disruption in manufacturing, transportation, and consumer goods, applying sanctions to a target with which the United States has a trade surplus may make them more effective. This effect leads the president to pull the trigger on applying economic pressure more readily toward targets who receive high levels of U.S. exports.

The president's beliefs about tactical preferences also affect his decision. Presidents who prefer more coercive diplomatic tactics tend to use economic coercion more quickly. This preference only seems to affect the decision to initiate a foreign policy sanction. It is that decision, however, that requires the most attention from the president.

Now that the effects of the international, domestic, and cognitive factors have been detailed, I turn to other possible influences on the president's decision. While one might expect the president to be more likely to sanction communist nations, during the Cold War, a target's ideological orientation does not have an impact on the decision. The geographical region of the target does affect the decision—the United States sanctions Latin American nations significantly more often. Further, the White House tends to sanction its southern neighbors primarily for international reasons, and it cannot be deterred by belligerent actions. The president's belief system also has a stronger impact when considering economic coercion against Latin American states. The perception that U.S. involvement throughout Latin America is a norm in Washington D.C. makes the president less likely to consider domestic political factors and more likely that his operational code beliefs will have an impact on his decisions. That is, the historical presence of the United States in Latin America removes some of the factors that might normally affect the Oval Office's decisions. With these factors gone, others are able to play a larger role.

In the post–Cold War world, the Latin American bias disappears but is replaced by a tendency not to sanction democratic regimes. As others have shown, the liberal peace extends to the use of economic coercion by constraining the use of sanctions between democracies (Cox and Drury 2002; Lektzian and Souva 2003). In addition to this inverse relationship, the president tends to consider international political factors less when sanctioning democracies. The lower tension levels between democracies means that the president is more likely to consider domestic factors when using sanctions against another democracy. When sanctioning a nondemocracy, relations are more hostile. Consequently, the decision to use coercion is much more likely, and it is less constrained by domestic factors.

Once the president decides to use economic coercion, he must decide how severe the sanctions will be. The selection of the sanction type is influenced by both international and domestic factors. Using prospect theory, I show that when the president is in the domain of gains, he is somewhat less likely to take extreme action. When the president's approval rating is above his mean level of approval, he will levy sanctions that are less costly to domestic groups and in their impact on the target. This aversion to extreme action is a result of the president's attempt to keep from jeopardizing his favorable approval rating. If the president's approval rating is in the domain of losses, he is more likely to select sanctions that are more costly and severe to both the United States and the target nation in an attempt to regain approval. The results also show that when the trade surplus is higher than average, placing the president in the domain of gains, the White House tends to lift less severe sanctions. Although the choices associated with the type of sanction are affected by domestic factors, the most powerful effect is the relationship between the United States and the target. As with the decision to initiate, the president considers the international situation most; domestic considerations are definitely secondary.

The Decision to Modify Economic Coercion

After sanctions are in place for a month, the president can lift, decrease, or increase them.[1] Clearly, the target's actions will affect the president's decision. The president is more likely to increase the economic pressure when the tension with the target is high. As one would expect, the president does not tend to lift or decrease the sanctions if the dispute with the target is still quite hostile and unresolved. However, when the target is particularly provocative, the president is more likely to decrease or lift the sanctions. Since deterrence by the target will have failed once sanctions were used, the target can only hope to act belligerently enough to make the president believe that the sanctions are not worth his while. The findings show that the target is able to do just that.

Sanctions themselves may cause the dispute with the target to remain tense. The target commonly chafes under the pressure of the sanctions and will often focus on the sanctions rather than Washington's actual demand. In some ways this does create a reciprocal relationship where the sanctions increase the tension, which in turn, reduces the probability that the sanctions will be lifted or reduced. Increased tension caused by the sanctions will not change the U.S. demand that the target alter its behavior and may agitate the White House so that it prefers to apply more pressure. That is, the president uses economic coercion because of some issue with the target, but he later applies more pressure to punish the target for resisting.

One domestic political factor conditions the president's decision to alter an economic sanction policy. The economic misery index has a relatively strong impact on the decision to lift, decrease, or increase the economic pressure on the target. The White House prefers to reduce the level of sanctions when the U.S. economy is suffering. Instead of using a sanction as a trade barrier to benefit some domestic industry, the president seems to prefer to open up trade with other countries when the economy is not performing well. Furthermore, the president's advisory system has a small but significant effect on the decision to alter the sanction policy. Contrary to expectations, informal advisory systems are more likely to increase the level of sanctioning. Apparently, the more open flow of information creates an optimistic view of sanctions and subsequent attempts to make them effective by increasing the economic pressure.

To sum up, the president clearly considers several factors when deciding to use and alter economic sanctions. The strongest predictors of sanction use are the relations between the United States and the target. However, once a dispute reaches a certain level, other factors such as the domestic economy and the president's belief system can affect the sanction decisions. These findings are not consistent across the different types of economic coercion. The president follows a very different decision process when initiating and modifying foreign economic policy sanctions. I now turn to a discussion of the difference between foreign policy and foreign economic policy sanctions and the Cold War and post–Cold War differences in the use of economic sanctions.

Section 301 Sanctions

All of the discussion thus far has centered on foreign policy sanctions, not the Section 301 or foreign economic policy sanctions. Some scholars have argued that one theory should be able to explain the outcome of a coercion attempt regardless of the goal being sought (Drezner 2001). Just because the sender is attempting to alter an economic policy in the target should not mean that the process or mechanism of the coercion is any different when the goal is purely political. Additionally, the ubiquitous Hufbauer et al. (1990a) data for economic sanctions includes several cases that are about economic issues such as expropriation and commodity pricing. Thus, a clear and uncontested line between the two types of issues does not exist in the literature. Assessing the differences between foreign policy and foreign economic policy sanctions should help define whether a distinction between the two of them can be made. The results are quite clear for Section 301 sanctions in the analyses. The differences between them and the foreign policy sanctions are stark. When deciding to initiate a Section 301 sanction, the only significant influence on the president is the trade balance with the target. Unlike foreign policy sanctions, which are associated with trade surpluses, a trade deficit with the target increases the probability that the president will initiate such a sanction. This result suggests that the president uses the sanctions to help offset trade deficits with the target, a finding that fits well with other studies of Section 301 cases and Kaempfer and Lowenberg's (1988, 1989) argument that sanctions are used as a form of protectionism (Reinhardt 2000; Zeng 2004). Even more striking than this intuitive finding is the lack of significance for all of the other variables. The tension, provocation, misery index, and operational code—all found to have significant impacts on the president's decision to use foreign policy sanctions—are completely unrelated to the Section 301 decisions. The decisions to modify sanctions are also different as the models of political rationality fail almost completely to explain them.

The lack of influence that tension has on the decision indicates that the Section 301 sanctions are driven by a different process. Instead of a reaction to the actions of the target, they are a result of domestic industries suing for protection against what they perceive as "unfair" competition. Even though the root cause of the sanction is a policy, such as a subsidy for one of the target's industries, the direct cause is internal to the United States and not a government-to-government dispute with the target. Therefore, the White House does not consider what the target government is doing—including any provocative actions aimed at deterring the president—when it applies a Section 301 sanction. Additional evidence for this conclusion is the nonexistent or weak impact of temporal dependence. That is, prior use (or lack thereof) of a Section 301 sanction has no bearing on current decisions. This finding also suggests that the decisions are not driven by relations with the target but decision-making internal to the United States.

One might still expect that the president's belief system would affect his decision to use a foreign economic policy sanction. A president who prefers more coercive tactics or sees the world as a more hostile environment would seem also to prefer using a Section 301 sanction rather than engaging in bilateral trade talks to resolve the "unfair" trade issue. However, none of the operational code variables had any significant impact on the president's decision. Bounded rationality in the form of presidential beliefs probably plays a smaller role because of the more bureaucratized nature of the Section 301 decision process. Most Section 301 cases are started by private firms petitioning the U.S. Trade Representative (USTR). The decision process starts with the USTR not the Oval Office, and it often concludes with significantly less input from the president. Therefore, there is less opportunity for the president's beliefs to influence the decision.

Overall, these results indicate that there are no commonalities between the foreign policy and Section 301 sanction decisions. Does this conclusion mean that Drezner (2001) is wrong when he argues that one theory should be able to explain how coercion functions for either type of sanction? Although the evidence presented here is not particularly supportive of his position, it does not refute it. Just because the decision process is very different does not mean that the way in which the two types of sanctions function is. Section 301 sanctions are placed on the target for reasons different than foreign policy sanctions, but they are still a coercive tool aimed at altering the target's policy. Therefore, a rational choice theory of coercion should apply to both types of sanction.

Costs and benefits are calculated for both types of sanctions, but their determinants vary by the type of sanction. For example, the results suggest that Drezner's (2001) argument that military force is always a consideration of the sender and target may be wrong. If military power was always a consideration or at least cast a constant shadow on all coercion attempts by the United States, one would expect that the Oval Office would be involved in the decision-making more closely. Certainly the president's beliefs should be expected to have an effect. Instead, Section 301 sanctions are left more to the USTR, and thus, the shadow that the U.S. military may cast is not likely to influence the target.

Cold War and Post–Cold War Differences

Two important differences exist in the way the United States uses economic coercion across the Cold War and post–Cold War periods. First, the president is less likely to economically coerce a democracy in the post–Cold War era; such a constraint does not exist during the Cold War. The demise of the Soviet empire led to (1) the promotion of democratic government as a solution for inter- and intrastate conflict and (2) a decrease in the U.S. need to maintain a pro-American bloc against the Soviet Union. The promotion of democracy means that the United States will be less likely to punish other democratic regimes, but more importantly, that the White House will be more likely to sanction nondemocratic regimes in order to coerce them into accepting democratic reforms.

The end of the Soviet empire and the fulfillment of containment also meant that the United States no longer perceived the need to support anti-Soviet dictatorships. Sanctions such as those against leftist democratic regimes of Mossadegh in Iran and Allende in Chile were also no longer considered necessary for U.S. security. As a result, the United States became significantly less likely to use economic coercion against fellow democratic regimes.

The second important difference in the post–Cold War era is the insignificant effect that provocation has on the U.S. decision to sanction. The findings show that bellicose targets are unable to deter the president from initiating economic coercion. The increase in internal conflict after the Cold War, such as the conflicts in the Balkans, created a new reason for the United States to engage in coercion.

Sanctions used for this purpose were based on a dispute about a policy internal to the target, for example, ethnic cleansing. Therefore, belligerent actions would not change the U.S. view of the conflict, which was not with the United States but with a group within the target. Further, most of these sanctions were mandated by the UN, making it more difficult to deter the United States from using the sanctions. That is, for the target to successfully deter the sanctions, it must deter the United States, the UN, and all other nations cooperating with the UN. The greater number of senders and the political cover provided by the UN makes any provocative actions more diffuse and subsequently less effective as a deterrent.

Implications and Limitations

The findings in this book challenge some of the sanction literature's traditional conclusions about economic coercion. First, sanctions are not used for primarily domestic purposes, and therefore, domestic politics should not be blamed for their failure. The "do something" argument does not hold up as typically specified. One can argue that sanctions are used because the president feels he must "do something" in the face of the target's actions or policies, but the impetus for action is the target not the American public. If the president is using the sanctions simply because he must react to the target, then one would expect that they would often fail and that the president would have no illusions about that likely failure. Regardless, domestic politics should not be used as a scapegoat to explain the poor success rate of economic coercion.

Second, the results point to a link between trade and increased use of economic coercion. This finding does not support the argument that trade increases conflict between states, however. The positive connection between trade and interstate relations means that the president uses economic coercion more on states who are U.S. trading partners because there is greater opportunity to economically coerce those states and not because the trade creates more disputes. The correlation between the trade link and tension variables is negative and significant ($r = -0.188$) suggesting that trade makes relations between states more cooperative. While the objectives in this book do not include engaging the trade–conflict debate, the results do suggest that lower levels of conflict and more detailed measures of interstate relations are fruitful areas for future analysis.

Third, the marginal effect that domestic factors have on the president's decision to use economic coercion provides little evidence for a connection between domestic politics and the use of force. The significant and robust relationship between the misery index and the use of sanctions contradicts the expectations of diversionary war theory. The findings show that as the economy worsens, the president is less likely to use economic sanctions. This finding may be the result of another difference between economic and military coercion. Economic coercion has the potential to damage the U.S. economy, although the damage is likely to be minute. Still, the president will not want to engage in such behavior when the economy is already suffering. Therefore, economic sanctions do not offer the same diversionary qualities as the use of military force. The president tends to consider his approval seriously only when choosing the severity of the sanction; economic coercion does not have the same saliency to the public as military coercion. Consequently, one might expect that public opinion would have no effect on the president at all. The fact that there is any influence does suggest that for more salient issues that warrant military action the president seriously considers his job approval rating.

Fourth, the president's beliefs also play a role in his decision to initiate an economic sanction. The greater the president's preference for coercive tactics, the more likely he is to use economic coercion. Although beliefs do not influence the decision to use Section 301 sanctions, beliefs mattered and in the theorized direction in every model of the decision to initiate a foreign policy sanction. Given that economic sanctions are a lesser form of coercion relative to the use of military force, the significance of the operational code variables highlight the validity of the measure.

Unlike his beliefs, the president's advisory system does not have an impact on the decision process. The difference between these two variables may be explained by the precedence of the belief system. That is, the president's view of the world and tactical preferences normally precede the formation of the advisory system. Therefore, the advisory system reflects the influence of the president's cognitive constraints and personality traits (George 1979).

Like all studies, this one also has its limitations and raises or leaves unanswered several questions. First, the operational code data on the president's belief system is quite limited. The speeches used for each president did not generate enough data to have monthly or even yearly scores for the presidents. Although the findings were consistent with expectations, more precise data may yield stronger results. For example, the measure of the president's view of the world never attained significance. More data may reveal that this measure of the president's beliefs also affects his use of economic coercion. It is always possible that more data will falsify the current findings, but this outcome seems unlikely given that the current measure already produces strong results.

Second, the model is not particularly good at explaining sanction policy modification, especially in the post–Cold War era. Part of the difficulty is the model does not account for the status of the dispute. While the tension level may gauge the hostility level between the United States and target, there is no variable that indicates whether the target conceded to the U.S. demands, whether the United States dropped its demands, or some negotiated middle ground appeared over time.

The data required to model the status of the dispute would have to include information about what demands the United States made and how the target responded. The detailed and contextual nature of this information would make quantification difficult, although not impossible. The analysis of the United States and target rhetoric has been shown to be effective in understanding sanction threats (Drury and Li 2004) and would prove useful here as well. For example, coding the U.S. verbal demands and target reactions would provide useful information as to the state of the dispute and issues surrounding it. If these data could be built into the model, then we would be able to better understand how economic coercion ends. This information, along with the understanding provided in this book of how and why sanctions are used, would provide a complete picture of the sanction episode and shed even more light on the question of effectiveness.

Can the theoretical models developed here be applied empirically to nations other than the United States? If future researchers become intent on continuing the quantitative track taken here, it would be very difficult to apply the model to a non-U.S. nation. Most problematic are collecting the data for the domestic political factors model. They would be very difficult to attain for other democracies such as Britain, much less for autocracies like the Soviet Union. This failure of the model's generalizability to other nations is not as damning as it may seem at first blush. The United States is responsible for more than 68 percent of the sanctions between 1966 and 2000. Understanding what conditions lead the U.S. president to use economic sanctions alone is clearly an important contribution to our knowledge base regarding the dynamics of economic coercion.

The Overall Picture

Even considering these weaknesses, four variables have a robust significant impact on the president's decision to use economic coercion: tension, target provocation, misery index, and presidential beliefs. These findings are constant across all presidents, which is quite impressive since the variation between the different occupants of the White House is quite large.[2]

These robust findings provide a clear picture of the different models of political rationality that explain the president's decision to use economic coercion. The primary aspects of the substantive rationality models are international and domestic factors.[3] The strongest driving force behind the president's decision is international. A dispute must arise between the United States and the target/country before economic coercion is even considered. The president does not use sanctions to bolster his domestic standing or placate firms seeking trade protection. Instead, the White House uses economic coercion in reaction to the dispute with the target. Further evidence of this conclusion is the ability of the target to deter the president from initiating a sanction by acting belligerently. If the president was simply using the sanction to provide protection to a domestic industry, then the target would not be able to deter the president.

While international factors have the strongest impact, the president is constrained as well by the state of the U.S. economy. An extremely hostile dispute will override the domestic considerations. When the international tension level has passed the threshold necessary for sanctions to be used but has not grown too intense, however, then the White House considers the domestic economy. The president exhibits a true classical liberal approach to economic sanctions. By extending Kaempfer and Lowenberg's (1988, 1989) argument, one might expect the president to constrain economic relations when the U.S. economy is performing poorly. History shows that states often begin erecting trade barriers when they experience economic troubles. Instead of using sanctions as an excuse to protect a suffering economy, however, the president avoids economic coercion.

One explanation for this phenomenon is that, once elected, presidents embrace free trade. While it is true that presidents generally favor liberal trade, it is by no means a certainty, as exemplified by President George W. Bush's use of heavy steel and textile tariffs. More likely, the president prefers to focus on the domestic arena and not be seen as more concerned with foreign policy issues. Since economic sanctions are often used in disputes that are not threats to the U.S. security, it is particularly important that the president is not viewed as spending too much time on "mundane" foreign policy matters. For example, the president does not want the public to believe that he prioritizes human rights issues in Asia over jobs in America. The president may still prefer not to restrict economic activity when the misery index is high, but the primary constraint is the focus on the domestic economy and maintaining the public perception that he is not more concerned with foreign policy than the plight of his fellow Americans.

These substantive rationality factors are interpreted through boundaries set by the lens of the president's beliefs and risk preferences. The president's tactical preferences tend to color his preference for action. It is important to realize that the beliefs affect the entire dispute. While the correlations between the operational code variables and the tension and provocation variables are not large enough to induce multicolinearity, they are statistically significant. The more cooperative the president views the world, the lower the tension level with the target.[4] This finding holds even when imposing the standard time series cross-section statistical controls.

Thus, the president's beliefs influence the relations with the target as well as affect the likelihood that sanctions will be deployed. These effects are independent. That is, the president's beliefs affect both the relations with the target and his decision to use economic coercion. This dual effect by beliefs suggests that their weight in the decision process may be greater than revealed in this book. By influencing both the general relationship with the target/country and the specific decision to deploy economic sanctions, the importance of the president's psychological limits and preferences on his decision proves the value of the cognitive constraints model.

In this book, I have tried to show that understanding presidential decisions to initiate and modify economic sanctions is important to our understanding of the process of economic coercion and foreign policy decision-making. While the explanation offered in this book is not perfect, taking a comprehensive approach to decision-making, which includes both substantive and bounded models of political rationality, provides a more complete explanation of how U.S. presidents use economic coercion against other nations.

Appendix

Statistical Methods

As discussed in chapter 5, the data are arrayed into a time series cross-section, also known as a pooled time series. More specifically, the data are a binary time series cross-section (BTSCS) because the dependent variable is dichotomous (or binary; Beck et al. 1998). Additionally, the use of economic coercion is quite rare, accounting for only 1 percent of the observations. These two characteristics, the dichotomous and rare nature of the dependent variable, and the time series cross-section data cause three independent complications in the analysis.

First, TSCS data suffer from problems of cross-unit (in these data the target/country) heteroskedasticity. This means that in addition to the normal error term (ε, or epsilon) that all models have, TSCS models may also have an error term specific to the units or cross-sections (again, the target/country). Statistically, in addition to ε_{it} (where i identifies the target/country and t identifies the date), there is also v_i, which indicates the unit-specific residual.[1] This error is constant across time but varies across each target/country. A substantive example may be helpful. The United States may tend to sanction Soviet Bloc nations during the Cold War more than neutral or Western aligned nations. If this situation were the case, there would be a larger, systematic error for the Soviet Bloc countries, because the bias toward sanctioning these countries was omitted from the model. That is, if the president tends to sanction the Soviets more than other countries regardless of the other variables in the model, then that tendency (since it is not part of the model) becomes part of the error term. Further, what if there are some individual qualities of each of the targets/countries that significantly affect the decision to sanction? To be more precise, is there something about each target/country that makes the president more or less likely to use economic coercion that is not included in models I, II, and III? If that is the case, then there will be a residual specific to each target/country in addition to the more commonly understood residual that appears in all models.

The solution for this problem is to use a fixed-effects model that controls for the target/country specific residual.[2] However, fixed-effects models are not always required because not all cross-sections are so unique vis-à-vis the model being tested that they generate their own error term. In the example above, it seems feasible that the president may sanction Soviet Bloc countries more. However, it is also quite possible that the tension level between the Soviet Bloc and United States will be systematically higher and therefore, account for the tendency to sanction those communist counties more. To test the model for such a possibility, I perform Hausman's (1978) specification test that compares a fixed-effects model with a random-effects model.[3] The diagnostic statistic tests the difference between the coefficients in the two models.

If the random-effects coefficients are not significantly different from the fixed-effects coefficients (assumed to be consistent and efficient), then the addition of the fixed-effects does not influence the other variables and is therefore, unnecessary. The tests on each iteration of the model and both the 1966–1992 and 1991–2000 time periods showed that there was no significant difference between the fixed-effects and random-effects estimators. Thus, a fixed-effects model is not appropriate; the different cross-sections are not independently and significantly affecting the president's decision to initiation economic coercion.

What does this mean substantively and does it make sense? Substantively, it means that the three theoretical models can explain the systematic differences between the different targets/countries. No single target/country stands out and has an effect on the president's decision. This assertion makes sense because the models are explaining the decisions of the executive of one country, the U.S. president. If the data contained decisions of non-American executives, then one would expect that cultural, economic, and political differences between the United States and the other senders would make the decision-making process different. For example, the United States and Canada sanction rather differently. Canadian sanctions have become tied very closely to the UN, such that Ottawa tends only to initiation economic coercion when the UN has mandated it. The United States clearly does not wait for the UN before deploying economic sanctions. Therefore, if both of these (and other) senders (the United States and Canada) were included in the analysis, controls for these differences would have to be included as well, namely the fixed-effects model.[4]

While the Hausman specification test strongly supports the use of a random-effects model, one coefficient does stand out and is worth discussing. The U.S. trade surplus with the target/country showed the biggest difference of all the coefficients. Specifically, the estimate of the trade surplus variable was lower when the fixed-effects model was used. Given that most of the variation in the trade surplus variable is cross-national and not temporal, this result is not surprising. That is, while the trade balance (as a percent of U.S. GDP) with other states does fluctuate a little over time, it is rather stable, especially compared to the variance in the trade balance between countries. Therefore, the fixed-effects model depresses the impact of the cross-target/country variation found in the trade surplus (Beck and Katz 2001; Green et al. 2001). Consequently, it stands out relative to the other variables. As I mentioned above, this difference is not large enough to warrant the use of the fixed-effects model. It is illustrative of the Hausman test, however.

The second problem facing TSCS analysis is temporal dependence. Because time is included as a component in the data (the time series portion of the TSCS data matrix), there may be an autoregressive lag process running through the data. For the question herein, this temporal dependence means that past decisions to sanction (or not sanction) will have an impact on current decisions. There is good reason to believe that the data are time dependent. It seems quite probable that the president's previous decisions would affect the current decision. That is, it is possible that one sanction may promote additional sanctions, a "piling on" of economic pressure, so to speak. Unfortunately, the dichotomous or binary nature of the dependent variable complicates diagnosing and correcting this problem.

Models with continuous dependent variables can use the Durbin-Watson statistic to diagnose an autoregressive (AR) process. To correct for such an AR process, the analyst can either lag the dependent variable thereby creating a dynamic model, or use generalized least squares to perform a Prais-Winsten or Cochrane-Orcutt regression (an AR(1) model) that models the AR process. However, because the variable I am analyzing is dichotomous (sanctions–no sanctions), neither a dynamic nor an AR(1) model is appropriate. In discussing the temporal dependence problem in conflict studies, Beck et al. (1998) argue that because the dependent variable is binary, it does not contain the same amount of information that an interval level variable contains. Specifically, the binary variable cannot indicate upward or downward trends like an interval or continuous variable can.

For example, in a study with war–peace as the dependent variable, lagging the dependent variable asserts that war leads to more war, and peace leads to more peace. However, previous periods of war do not necessarily beget more war. Instead, nations will often lose their ability and desire to continue fighting and try to end the war. Thus, war may beget peace. Conversely, previous periods of peace do not necessarily beget more peace. During peacetime, nations may begin to build up hostilities toward one another, and those hostilities may lead to war. Continued peace, through a process of building hostilities, may beget war (Beck et al. 1998). In both of these scenarios, the binary variable cannot tap a nation's decreasing ability and desire to wage war or the festering hostilities between nations. It just does not contain enough information.

In the case of the decision to use economic sanctions, this same logic is applicable. For example, if the United States is engaged in a dispute with another nation and one of the president's options is to initiate economic sanctions, then the fact that sanctions are not yet in place should, at most, have an ambivalent effect.[5] On the one hand, it may be the case that the president does not want to initiate sanctions in the first place because of the domestic costs they incur. On the other hand, it is just as possible that the president will be more likely to use sanctions because he wants to put more pressure on the target. The fact that economic coercion has not yet been employed against the target may either increase or decrease the president's propensity to initiate an economic sanction.

Similarly, if the president has already enacted an economic coercion policy against a target, one could argue that he would be more likely to maintain the sanctions simply because he has already incurred the domestic costs, and they may have become the status quo, as with the sanctions against Cuba. For the same reasons, however, the president may be more likely to lift the sanctions. First, the president may want to reduce the domestic costs the sanctions are incurring. Second, the sanctions may be perceived as failing, so the president will have an incentive to lift them. This ambivalence is a result of the lack of information in the binary variable. That is, sanctions are either in place or not in place. A continuous variable, such as used in the OLS estimations above, shows upward and downward trends; a quality that lends a great deal more information. A continuous variable would inform us of increasing and decreasing trends in the number of economic sanctions levied against a given target. Dichotomous variables do not provide such information.

Thus, diagnosing and particularly solving temporal dependence in BTSCS data is not the same as interval data. To test the data for temporal dependence, I regress the residuals from the estimated model on their lagged values (i.e., $\varepsilon_{it} = \varepsilon_{it-1}$).[6] The lagged values were significant, indicating that there was a first-order autoregressive process in the data. I also tested additional lags, but none of these attained significance. There is clearly a temporal process, defined as one-month, running through the data.[7]

Because a dichotomous dependent variable does not provide enough information to be used in a dynamic model and AR(1) models are not appropriate, an alternative must be used. Beck et al. (1998) developed such an alternative method by linking the temporal dependence to the hazard in duration data so that the hazard is the onset of an economic sanction. Thus, they correctly assert that binary time series cross-section (BTSCS) data and grouped duration data are identical. They then show that a variable that counts the number of time periods (in the data herein, months) since the last event (the month in which sanctions were last initiated) provides the information needed to represent the temporal component of the data. This count variable alone, however, "may give a false impression that the baseline hazard is jagged" (Beck et al. 1998: 1270). That is, the temporal dependent effect should be a smooth shift over time, not one that jumps up or down from one time period to the next. Thus, the variable must include a smoothing function. To accomplish this, Beck et al. (1998: 1270–1271) suggest a natural cubic spline.[8] By including the variable that counts the months since the last initiation of an economic sanction as well as the three cubic splines needed to smooth the count variable, I model the temporal dependence in the data and therefore, make the model unbiased.

The final issue with the data related to the statistical technique employed is based on the distribution of the dependent variable—sanctions are rare events. Even considering the American record of using economic coercion on a regular basis compared to other nations, when time and space are included, the deployment of an economic sanction is actually quite rare. When considering political sanctions only, there have been 160 uses over the 1966–2000. When Section 301 sanctions are included in that total, 210 sanctions have been initiated by the White House. Although an average of one sanction every two months may not seem rare, this number still only accounts for, at most, 1 percent of the observations. The standard logit model assumes that the dependent variable is evenly distributed or at least somewhat so. When the dependent variable measures a rare event, then the logit estimates may "sharply underestimate the probability of rare events" as compared to the standard logit estimator (King and Zeng 2001a: 138 see also 2001b). King and Zeng's (1999a and 1999b) Rare Events Logit estimator takes the rare nature of the variable into account.[9]

However, tests revealed that there was little difference in the performance of the rare events estimator compared to the standard logit estimator. A Hausman test of the two equations showed that no significant difference existed in the coefficients. Further, sample predicted probabilities showed no substantive difference between the two estimation techniques. Therefore, standard logistic regression was used to estimate the models.[10]

Notes

1　Introduction

1. Throughout the book, I refer to the sanctioned country as the target and the sanctioning country as the sender. I also use economic sanctions and economic coercion synonymously. These terms are commonly accepted in the literature.
2. A discussion of the estimation techniques appear in the appendix.

2　Economic Coercion in Theory and Practice

1. Note this argument is opposite to Crumm (1995).
2. Considerable scholarship exists on the impact of aid on the target's foreign policy choices (see e.g., Poe 1991, 1992; Blanton 2000). Because I am only interested in negative sanctions and a large part of the aid literature investigates the quid pro quo associated with the giving of aid, I do not discuss this literature.
3. The play tells the fictitious story of how the wives of Athens withhold sex from their husbands to pressure them into ending the war with Sparta.
4. Unlike the Greek comedy, the ban did not succeed.
5. See also Kirshner (1995).
6. Dashti-Gibson, Davis, and Radcliff (1997) also find that greater costs to the target increase the likelihood of success, although only for cases in which the sender hoped to destabilize the target.
7. "But, self-reinforcement cannot grow food, although, when there *is* food, people can be, even in the face of an implacable foe, unified and integrated" (Green 1983: 82–83, emphasis original). David Rowe provides a different explanation of how the Rhodesian government was able to secure political integration (2000, 2001). Using a modified open market theory, he shows that the sanctions were the equivalent to economic shocks that created a collective action problem for Rhodesian firms—how to distribute the costs of the sanctions. Industries like tobacco requested that the government solve this problem by taking control of the market. The Smith government was thus able to control which groups gained and which lost from the sanctions. This power created dependency on the government and continued support of its apartheid policies even in the face of economic dislocation.
8. Clearly, other factors explain why neither the United States nor Cuba has backed down from their positions. Schwebach's theory does help explain how that situation and others like it started.

9. Dan Fisk (2000) suggests that the Helms-Burton sanctions had the important intended effect of deterring expropriation.
10. Section 301 sanctions refer to section 301 of the 1974 Trade Act. The legislation directed the U.S. Trade Representative, which is part of the executive branch, to determine if U.S. trading partners were trading "fairly"—meaning that their trade barriers were comparable to the United States.

3   Evaluating Sanction Effectiveness

1. In a previous edition, two of the authors do use a simple form of regression analysis on their data. The results are mixed and they conclude that the analysis adds little to their research (Hufbauer and Schott 1985: 99–102).
2. The sender can also be damaged by sanctioning an ally. However, if sanctions are considered in the first place, then it is likely that the sender is willing to risk being hurt to influence or compel the ally.
3. A good example of this is the U.S. sanctions against Great Britain and France over the Suez Crisis. Neither London nor Paris could function without oil and quickly conceded to the U.S. demands.
4. Drury (2003) does use a different level of analysis, the dyad-year rather than the sanction episode or case. This may account for the difference as the number of sanction dyads is more than five times the number of Hufbauer et al. sanction cases. Still, it is worth noting that contradictory results have been found.
5. One exception to this could be a completely state-run economy. Even in this case, however, bureaucrats running the economy will seek to increase their power by securing rents for their respective industry.
6. Empirical analysis supports this decision by showing that the target's regime type does not significantly affect the outcome of the economic coercion.
7. Simple regression analysis of a basic model confirmed that the differences were statistically inconsequential.
8. Morgan and Schweback (1997) and Drezner (2001) also limit the measure of effectiveness to the policy result variable.
9. The dummy variable indicates that at least one supplemental policy has been used. If multiple supplemental policies are used, the dummy variable takes the same value as if one policy were used.
10. Achen (1991) shows that the ordinary least squares (OLS) estimator becomes unbiased once the dependent variable has five or more values. The four values in the policy result variable are two few to avoid the estimation problems with OLS.
11. Of course, the actual effects of the independent variables are contingent upon the probability distribution of the dependent variable (Greene 1997: 926–931). That is, whether an independent variable will have a large enough substantive impact on the dependent variable to shift it from one

value to another (e.g., from limited failure to limited success) will depend on what the likelihood of the values of the dependent variable.

12. All analyses were estimated with Stata 8.2. Data and the code used to run the analyses are available from the author's website.

13. These estimated probabilities hold all other variables at their mean, or in the case of dichotomous variables, holding them at their modal value. *Clarify* (Tomz et al. 2003; King et al. 2000) and *SPost* (Long and Freese 2001) were used to derive these probabilities.

14. It is worthwhile noting that while the cost to the target as a percent of GNP is only slightly correlated with pre-sanction trade, the absolute cost is actually inversely correlated, although the coefficient is almost zero. That close trade ties do not enhance the absolute costs to the target may indicate that these absolute costs are indeed symbolic in their nature.

15. Unilateral economic sanctions are indicated when the multilateral cooperation and institutional involvement variables are both zero.

16. This statistic is a simple estimation derived by looking at which of the four outcomes the model correctly predicts as determined by a probability for that outcome that exceeds 50 %. This generates four different "percent correctly predicted" scores, one for each outcome. These scores are then averaged to estimate how many outcomes the model can predict accurately. While this method is by no means perfect, it does provide an additional measure-of-fit that does coincide with the pseudo-R^2 reasonably well.

4 Why Does the President Sanction? Beyond the Conventional Wisdom

1. Although the president can also choose to maintain the sanctions, this choice is so routine that I consider it a nondecision and do not include it in the analysis.

2. For the reader's and my sake, I do not always repeat initiate, increase, decrease, or lift. Instead, I use terms such as "use," "alter," "modify," etc. to cover the president's different choices.

3. *Wall Street Journal*, November 16, 2004, A3.

4. Another good example of economic versus military power is the U.S. invasion of Panama. The United States first initiated sanctions against the Noreaga regime with no success. This failure is the result of Noreaga having no interest in stepping down simply because the United States was placing economic pressure on his country. In fact, it is unlikely that any coercion would have resulted in deposing Noreaga. Unless there was a coup (similar to Chile in 1973), only the physical capture of Noreaga would end his reign.

5. The United States was unable, after several attempts, to kill Saddam Hussein during the 2003 invasion, even with the most advanced weaponry available.

6. Because I now narrow the focus of my argument to decisions leading to sanctions, all mentions of leaders refer the U.S. president and all mentions of the sender refer to the United States.

7. This model does not address the possibility that the president is interested in setting an international precedent or sending a signal to third-party states. While these are certainly potential uses of economic sanctions, they are too intangible to model empirically (Barber 1979). This is not to say that the goal to influence a nation other than the target is indeterminable. For example, the Helms-Burton sanctions against Cuba can be portrayed as setting a precedent against expropriation. In a conversation with the bill's author, Dan Fisk, he suggested that the long-term impact of the sanctions will be as a deterrent to future expropriation attempts against U.S. property. Unfortunately, determining whether this was part of the original intent and therefore part of the decision calculus is very murky. Fisk (2000) explains that the bill was meant to guide the Clinton administration away from engaging Cuba and setting up a plan for post-Castro Cuba. Tertiary goals, such as deterring future expropriation, may be on the minds of the decision-makers, but they will appear as externalities. Thus, developing an a priori empirical model of tertiary sanctions is infeasible and not attempted in this book.

8. The Hickenlooper Bill gave the president authority to sanction nations that expropriated U.S. assets.

9. See Hufbauer et al. (1985: 434) and Olson (1975).

10. Note that there are many costs and benefits to action; magnitude only characterizes the international ones.

11. Another possibility is that, in the face of acute provocation, the president knows sanctions will not work and skips them to consider the use of the military or covert action.

12. When the White House banned the sale of dual-use technology to China after Tiananmen, Boeing faced losing a several million-dollar contract.

13. *New York Times*, July 8, 1989, A1.

14. There are also precedents, however, showing the opposite relations (Meernik 1994).

15. This includes midterm elections since presidents have a strong desire to see their party gain or, as is more common, not lose too many seats in the House and Senate. In the cases of a lame duck president (since 1960 there have been only three: Johnson, Reagan, and Clinton), the president will still prefer that his party succeed in the coming elections and will therefore hesitate before embarking on a policy of economic coercion.

16. Beliefs are still important because they are still the lens through which the decision-maker views reality, even though that lens simply and accurately depicts reality.

17. It is important to note that Poliheuristic Theory is based on cognitive principles. Thus, although I use it to help explain the president's need to

consider domestic politics, it is not a type of substantive rationality. Instead, it is a form of bounded rationality according to Simon's typology.

18. Some argue that the military option is always available and therefore cannot be ruled out as having an effect on the relationship between the sender and target. For example, Japan may take the hypothetical American whaling sanctions more seriously because the United States has such a powerful military. However, this argument is untenable, especially because sanctions are often used in disputes over issues that will never possibly involve military hostilities. Therefore, we must consider the severity of economic coercion relative to other realistic options.

5   When Does the President Sanction? An Empirical Analysis

1. It is worth noting that there are cases in which military action was not preceded by economic coercion, although such cases are not common.
2. Note that comparing the target's regime type with the United States is nonsensical because the U.S. regime score is a constant during the period in question.
3. Many studies in the conflict literature utilize the dyad as a unit of analysis. However, since one member of the dyad is a constant, the United States, it does not make sense to discuss dyads. That is, every dyad would include the United States. Therefore, I only discuss the different targets/countries, not the different "U.S.–target/country" dyads.
4. There are also significant drawbacks and complexities to this type of data. However, because these difficulties are statistical in nature, I discuss them later in the chapter prior to the analysis.
5. I selected these 22 nations through a stratified random sample. A list of all non-sanctioned countries was stratified into geographical regions and then selected using a random number generator.
6. There are 324 months in the 27 year period for each target. Thus, 50 targets/countries, each with 324 time points, results in 16,200 total data points. The targets include Argentina, Australia, Brazil, Cambodia, Canada, Chile, China, Cuba, Dominican Republic, Egypt, El Salvador, Ethiopia, France, Gambia, Guatemala, Haiti, Iceland, India, Indonesia, Iran, Iraq, Ireland, Israel, Japan, North Korea, Kuwait, Laos, Libya, Mauritania, Mexico, Mozambique, Nepal, New Zealand, Nicaragua, Pakistan, Panama, Peru, Poland, Portugal, South Africa, Sri Lanka, Sudan, Switzerland, Syria, Thailand, Turkey, the Soviet Union/Russia, Uruguay, Venezuela, and Vietnam.
7. The four states are: Canada, Japan, Portugal, and Thailand.
8. Reagan did initiate some weak sanctions against South Africa in an attempt to head-off the more restrictive Congressional economic coercion. These decisions are included in the data.

9. I am particularly grateful to Kim Elliott for providing me with the updated sanction case list as well as all the help with the sanction data.

10. I am particularly indebted to Erick Duchesne for sharing his Section 301 data.

11. Difficulties would also arise if the numerical count of presidential decisions was used. The count data represent the number of sanctions imposed by the president and could theoretically range from zero to infinity. In reality, it ranges from zero to 14; a range that is restricted and unevenly distributed. As mentioned above, its upper value is 14, and 76 percent of its values are zero. Although ordinary least squares estimation is often preferred because of the ease of interpretation, it demands interval data which are at least reasonably distributed and not so harshly bounded. Further, a Poisson distribution would be required to estimate any models on the data because of its event count nature.

12. Inclusion of the cooperation portion of the variable adjusts the data for the offsetting effect that harmony has on conflict. That is, more cooperative relations between the United States and target should decrease the likelihood that the president will use sanctions through the same function that increased conflict in the dyad should increase that likelihood. It is important to realize that the transformation of the data is a simple mathematical transformation that does not change the substantive value of the variable in any way. Thus, there would be no difference in the estimated parameters if I had not transformed the data. Intuitively, however, it is helpful to think of the variable as one that increases as tension increases.

13. IDEA, unlike WEIS, also codes internal events such as protests, riots, and even animal attacks. Obviously, these events are not included in the data. Instead, only those international events between the United States and each target/country are used.

14. According to IDEA, China used chemical weapons on Taiwan in February and March, 1993, December, 1994, February, 1995, twice on August, 1998, and in June, 2000. Taiwan chemically attacked China twice in August, 1998.

15. Prior to my transformation, the score is -10.

16. King and Lowe (2003) do find that the accuracy of the machine coding is equivalent to the human coding, and when the machine did make errors, it was usually in finding more events. This result fits with the anecdotal evidence of the chemical weapons attacks in Asia.

17. An additional reason to aggregate the scores by month is to smooth out the relations within the dyad. That is, tempers may temporarily increase for a couple of days even between two very cooperative states such as the United States and Canada. This flare-up would appear as a significant but short-lived dispute between the two states, while in reality, it was merely one or two officials taking exception to some issue. By aggregating the data, only those disputes that occur for more than a month will drive up the tension

level between the two nations. While a higher level of aggregation would have a greater smoothing effect, too much information would be lost.

18. Burbach (1995) provides the data up to December 1994. The remaining six years of data come directly from the Gallup Poll Monthly (2000).

19. The moving averages were mostly needed during presidential election periods.

20. Johnson's and Reagan's lame duck years are included because they would have been concerned about the strength of their respective parties and presidential candidates Humphrey and Bush.

21. These trade data come from Kristian Gleditsch's Expanded Trade Data version 4.1 (see Gleditsch 2002 for a detailed description).

22. For presidents after Carter, I used Hermann and Preston's coding rules to determine Reagan, Bush, and Clinton's advisory system types. Rosati (2004) also provided data on the advisory systems.

23. The actual procedure was: ln(imports + exports + 1). The one was added to keep all cases of zero trade from becoming missing values once the natural log was taken. All missing values as reported in the Gleditsch trade data (the source for imports and exports) were, of course, counted as missing.

24. This colinearity is not surprising to Alexander George, who argues that presidents form their advisory systems based on their personal characteristics.

25. As mentioned previously, all analyses were performed with *Stata 8.2*.

26. See the appendix for more details of the statistical methods used in the data analysis.

27. Logit models estimate that sanction initiation occurs once the probabilities pass the half-way mark, 50%. All probabilities were calculated using J. Scott Long and Jeremy Freese's *SPost* software for *Stata*.

28. Recall that Galtung's argument asserted that political integration would occur because the target's population would feel unjustly punished by the sender. A preemptive sanction that sought to hold the government hostage should enhance Galtung's effect.

29. The insignificance of the electoral proximity variable runs opposite to the findings in the military force literature (see, e.g., Meernik 1994: 134–136; Ostrom and Job 1986) and thus, underscores a critical difference between the use of military and economic sanctions. That is, the president is expected to use force more often before an election because he supposedly expects the public to rally in his favor (recall the discussion of Lian and Oneal 1993). The findings indicate that the president has no such expectations for economic sanctions. During election periods, the president is clearly under more stress and may be more risk averse because of the impending election. Since the conventional wisdom indicates that the president will always get a boost after using military force, the president can safely use force during an election period and expect a boost. Economic sanctions, however, do not have the same dramatic effect

because they do not involve risking American lives, and the president cannot, therefore, expect that they will absolutely boost his approval and not backfire. The conventional wisdom that surrounds economic sanctions is that they are ineffective, making them a rather poor policy about which to rally the public. Further, the cost economic coercion imposes on U.S. corporations as a result of the interrupted trade is an unpopular idea among powerful campaign contributors. The combination of a sanction's perceived ineffectiveness and possible domestic costs could easily inhibit their use by the president.

30. The several mentions of economic sanctions in the 2004 presidential and vice presidential debates seem to contradict this statement. However, sanctions did not overshadow the debate and were mostly connected to the Iraq War issue.

31. Some technologies are unique to the United States and therefore irreplaceable.

32. I do not display the equation with the president's image of the political universe to avoid redundancy.

33. As is clear from the table and discussion above, even with these variables included, the variables of interest still reach significance and have substantive impacts.

34. I consider Reagan to have averaged fewer sanction initiations than Bush since he had twice as long in office.

35. The operational code variables and advisory system type could not be included in the model with the presidential dummies because of the multicolinearity.

36. This effect is particularly interesting given that trade surplus and GDP per capita are negatively correlated ($r = -0.267$; note that this correlation, although significant, is not high enough to cause problems with multicolinearity). Even though the United States is more likely to have a deficit with a wealthy state, the target/country wealth dampens the probability of a sanction while the deficit increases it. The effects are competing.

37. In addition to the four sanctions against Argentina, the United States also sanctioned Guatemala and Portugal once each. The United States had a trade surplus with both of these countries at the time.

38. For example, in October, 1991, the U.S. Trade Representative initiated an investigation of "Chinese trade practices affecting U.S. exports, including quantitative restrictions (QRs), important licensing requirements, technical barriers to trade . . ." etc. (Bayard and Elliott 1994: 460–461).

39. For example, in September, 1983, the Air Courier Conference of America filed a complaint against Argentina for a rule that required time-sensitive documents to be delivered only by the Argentine postal service (Bayard and Elliott 1994: 415).

40. The entire period (1966–1992) is used because the foreign policy sanction data begin in 1966. The addition of the Section 301 data simply means there are more sanctions occurring after 1974.

41. In all of the analyses appearing below, I altered the start date of the Cold War by one year. There were only very minor changes in the results. For this reason, I do not go through all of the potential iterations.

42. This is not to say that they were more effective, only more salient to the public.

43. Alternative explanations do not fair any better. The completion of the Uruguay Round did not diminish the number of Section 301 sanctions; during both periods, there was an average of two sanctions per year. Therefore, Section 301 sanctions were not be replaced (yet, at least) by settling the trade disputes under World Trade Organization auspices.

6   Is There a Target Selection Bias?

1. Because the analysis in chapter 5 shows that the decision calculus leading to Section 301 sanctions is clearly different from foreign policy sanctions, I only test the model on the decision to use the latter type of sanction.

2. Hostility levels between the United States and communist targets/ countries are significantly higher, statistically speaking. A means difference test shows that average tension levels are more than one point higher (p-value < 0.000).

3. The communist states are: Chile between 1970 and 1973, China, Cuba after 1959, Ethiopia between 1974 and 1991, Kampuchea between 1976 and 1988, Laos after 1975, Nicaragua between 1981 and 1990, North Korea, North Vietnam, Poland before 1988, and the Soviet Union.

4. The Latin American states are: Argentina, Brazil, Chile, Cuba, Dominican Rep., El Salvador, Guatemala, Haiti, Mexico, Nicaragua, Panama, Peru, Uruguay, and Venezuela.

5. Polity scores of −10 to 0 were coded as nondemocratic, while scores of 1 and above were coded as democracies.

6. It makes no sense to include the communist variable in the post–Cold War era since U.S.–Soviet conflict had ended. Similarly, it is only logical to include the democratic variable in the post–Cold War era since it is during that period that I expect an effect from the regime type of the target/ country.

7. In both time periods (shown in tables 6.1 and 6.2), an autoregressive process existed. Therefore, I included the time since last decision and Spline variables to control for the temporal dependence.

8. One could argue that Chile was merely a left-leaning regime and not communist under Allende. Removing Chile from the communist group does not, however, affect the results.

9. Because the presidential advisory system type is not significant in the original model, I do not include it in the estimation in table 6.1.

10. A complementing explanation is the importance of Latin America to U.S. companies. Three (Brazil, Chile, and Peru) of the four expropriation

disputes that led to economic sanctions were with Latin American countries. U.S. corporations are not part of the domestic component of the model. For example, when ITT (International Telephone and Telegraph) pushed for action against Allende in Chile, it did not do so through elections or Nixon's job approval rating. Instead, such lobbying activity (when successful) would only appear as greater tension between the United States and the target.

11. The data show that 44% of the targets/counties were democratic in the first period while 69% were in the post–Cold War era.

12. This result fits with Dixon's (1994) argument that democracies tend to resolve their disputes more quickly and peacefully and with Lektzian and Souva's (2003) and Cox and Drury's (2002) findings that show the democratic peace extends to economic coercion.

13. It is important to note that defining a democracy as having a higher Polity score did have an impact on the results (Wolfson et al. 2004). When democratic states are defined as having a Polity score of 6 or above, the tension level and rate of escalation do become significant in the expected directions. However, their substantive impacts are trivial. Thus, while tension may influence the president, it only has a very marginal impact at most.

7   The Decision to Modify an Economic Sanction Policy

1. Over the entire period (1966–2000), the president lifted sanctions 40 times, decreased them 103 times, and increased them 120 times. Note that I do not refer to target/country here. All of the countries in these data have been sanctioned at one point. If the United States has never sanctioned a country, then the president cannot modify the sanction against them by definition. Therefore, all references are simply to the target. Also recall that although the president can also choose to maintain the sanctions (rather than lift, decrease, or increase them), this choice is a nondecision. Therefore, I do not include it in the analysis.

2. More specifically, the actual effects of the independent variables are contingent on the actual probability distribution (Greene 1997: 926–931).

3. One might argue that only Republican presidents hold the idea that foreign trade increases economic performance. However, once in the Oval Office, every president begins to prefer liberal trade. A good example of this was the unanimous support of former presidents for NAFTA during the period that President Clinton negotiated its passage through Congress.

4. I tested the effect of dropping 1991 to see if selecting an alternative date for the end of the Cold War mattered. I also dropped both 1991 and 1992 to see if the effect was the inclusion of only half of President Bush's tenure. In both cases, the misery index was insignificant (all of the other variables were insignificant as well).

5. For example, the United States was reluctant to cut humanitarian aid to the Sudan in the late-1980s and early-1990s. It was not until the situation inside Sudan became too violent that the United States withdrew the aid. Thus, the decision was based largely on what was going on inside Sudan, not on the U.S.–Sudan relationship.

6. There is one exception. The model cannot explain the president's decision to modify Section 301 sanctions in either period.

8   What Kinds of Sanctions Does the President Use? Domestic Constraints and Incentives

1. Multiplying the probability by the payoff reveals that option two has a higher probable payoff by $200.

2. Risk is defined as the cost multiplied by the probability that it will occur. Thus, if P equals the probability of a gain, $(1-P)$ is the probability of a loss. Risk then equals Cost multiplied by $(1-P)$. Because of the difficulty in determining the probabilities the president may assign to different sanction options, as well as the possibility that such a limited selection of options may have the same probabilities, I hold the probability constant and use the cost to determine the risk level (see Gallhofer and Saris 1979, for a discussion of the different decision-making models using probability and costs).

3. Sayings such as "chasing the money" in which a gambler continues to engage in risky betting to regain losses fit well with prospect theory. Similarly, the adage that one should not count one's money during gambling for fear that it will adversely affect one's betting makes sense.

4. For example, how can one measure the economic impact of a travel ban or the direct consequences of a loan that is delayed?

5. Originally, I used four groups (aid, military aid, trade, total sanctions). However, these groups were unevenly distributed and the distinctions that separated them less clear than those dividing the sanctions into two groups.

6. Although military aid will affect U.S. military industries, it is not as direct a cost a limited trade or banning the sale of military goods. Therefore, I include military aid with the other types of aid.

7. For example, sanctioning proprietary spare parts to a factory may make it impossible for that factory to keep producing.

8. Like the decision to modify sanctions that are already imposed, choosing the type of economic coercion implies that the president has already decided to initiate economic coercion.

9. Election proximity never reaches significance in any of the models. Therefore, I do not include it in this model. However, I did run the analyses appearing below with the election proximity variable separately; it did not reach significance nor did it affect the other variables.

10. A longer time period is used because economic indicators tend to move more slowly and are viewed over longer stretches of time. The approval rating is

seen as almost a real-time indicator that the president compares from month-to-month. The misery and trade balance statistics do not fluctuate as much.

11. I do not analyze the post–Cold War era because there are too few cases for the analysis.

12. It is worth noting that this variable was also tested in the initiation models appearing in chapter 5 and was not significant, just like the approval rating itself. Thus, approval only matters when the type of sanction is being selected.

13. Recall that Kaempfer and Lowenberg concede that executive sanctions will be less likely to be influenced, while legislative initiated sanctions are more driven by groups seeking trade protection.

14. These data contain many cases in which sanctions were applied for very brief periods or switched on and off as part of an overall coercive strategy. Coding the effectiveness of these cases would be needed to repeat Drury's (1997) analysis but impossible using the Hufbauer et al. (1990a) scheme.

15. Only 40 cases appear because the table only includes those sanctions that were both initiated and ended within 1966–2000.

16. Fisher's Exact test is needed in a 2-by-2 table when the expected cell frequencies fall below 5 (Garson 1976: 254–256).

9   Conclusions and Implications

1. As discussed in chapter 7, the president can also maintain them. However, maintaining sanctions is almost exclusively the default option that does not require action on behalf of the president. Therefore, I only consider changes to the status quo policy.

2. Recall that President Carter initiated twice as many sanctions in four years than the next most sanction prone president.

3. Recall that substantive rationality is determined by "the choosing organism's goals and objective characteristics of the situation" (Simon 1985: 294) and not the characteristics or limits of the organism itself.

4. The data limitations make it impossible to determine if the level of tension is not also driving the president's view of the world. However, the president's operational code scores are general, while the tension level is specific to the target/country. Thus, the overall tension level tends to be more stable which would seem to indicate that the president's beliefs are affecting his actions toward specific targets.

Appendix

1. The full equation is written as: $y_{it} = \alpha + \mathbf{x}_{it}\boldsymbol{\beta} + v_i + \varepsilon_{it}$. Where y_{it} is the dependent variable for each target/country month, $\mathbf{x}_{it}\boldsymbol{\beta}$ is the set of independent variables for each target/country month, v_i is the unit (target/country) specific error term or residual, and ε_{it} is the error term common to the entire model.

2. This method is also known as the Least Squares Dummy Variable (LSDV) model. In the LSDV, dummy variables are added for each of the cross-sections. These variables control for the presence of v_i.

3. The random-effects model assumes that the unit-specific error (v_i) is zero or some insignificant value.

4. This does not mean that there is not some bias toward sanctioning different types of countries. Instead, it says that no bias exists for each individual country. The potential bias that the type of target/country may have is explored in chapter 7.

5. Clearly, this is not true for the control countries because they were never sanctioned. A lack of sanctions in the past for these countries can predict no future sanctions. However, countries that were sanctioned cannot be predicted in such a manner. Because (1) the method used to control for the temporal dependence must be the same throughout the model and (2) the inclusion of the 22 control countries is important so the hypotheses can be falsified across space as well as time, I must use the Beck, Katz, and Tucker method described below. Further, the Beck, Katz, and Tucker method accurately controls the temporal dependence in both the 28 sanctioned countries and the 22 control countries.

6. See Greene (1997: 595) for a discussion of this testing procedure.

7. I also performed a Wooldridge (2002) test for serial correlation. This test assumes that the dependent variable is composed of interval data and thus, violates some assumptions, but it confirms that Greene (1997) residual test that an AR(1) process exists and must be corrected.

8. A cubic spline is calculated from a set of cubic polynomials that "tie" themselves (so to speak) to the time variable. This process of forcing the ties or "knots" to fit with the time variable has the effect of making the data smooth (Beck et al. 1998: 1270).

9. This method also allows the data to be weighted to account for incomplete data collection. That is, since only a sample of the sanctioned and non-sanctioned countries is included in the data, the data only represent approximately one quarter of the total population of states in the world. King and Zeng's (1999a and 1999b) software can correct for this sampling, particularly when the data are largely selected on the dependent variable, through a weighting technique. That is, when data are selected because sanctions occurred, rather than through a random selection process, there is a potential, significant bias. Different weighting schemes were estimated and had no differential impact on the statistical or substantive outcome. The lack of any substantive differences in the weighting schemes is most likely the result of the control group being randomly selected and the sanctions themselves being levied by only one state, the United States. The effect is that the data contain a rather close estimation of the population of U.S. executive sanctions.

10. It is worth discussing the advantage logit brings to decision-making models. Logistic analysis is based on the idea that there is an interval level

variable underlying the dichotomy, but we do not have a sensitive enough measure to capture the variable's latent interval nature. Thus, logistic analysis estimates the probability of the dependent variable being a one or a zero given the properties of the independent variables. This form of estimation uniquely captures the nature of decision-making because the decision-making process can be characterized as inherently probabilistic. That is, when making a decision, people tend to be influenced by conditions, and those conditions (the independent variables) will increase or decrease the person's penchant for deciding one way or another. For example, if the president is deciding to levy sanctions or not, higher levels of tension between the United States and the target will make the president more likely (increasing the probability) to use sanctions, while lower tension levels should decrease the probability. Because logistic analysis estimates these probabilities, it is uniquely suited to decision-making analysis.

Bibliography

Achen, C. 1991. "The Polichotomous Linear Probability Model." Paper presented at the 1991 Annual Political Methodology Society meeting, Berkeley, CA.

Aldrich, J., J. Sullivan, and E. Borgida. 1989. "Foreign Affairs and Issue Voting: Do Presidential Candidates Waltz Before a Blind Audience?" *American Political Science Review*, 83: 123–142.

Azar, E. 1980. "The Conflict and Peace Data Bank (COPDAB) Project." *Journal of Conflict Resolution*, 24: 143–152.

Baldwin, David A. 1985. *Economic Statecraft*. Princeton: Princeton University Press.

Barber, James. 1979. "Economic Sanctions as a Policy Instrument." *International Affairs*, 55: 367–384.

Bayard, Thomas O. and Kimberly Ann Elliott. 1994. *Reciprocity and Retaliation in U.S. Trade Policy*. Washington, DC: Institute for International Economics.

Bayard, Thomas O., Joseph Pelzman, and Jorge Perez-Lopez. 1983. "Stakes and Risks in Economic Sanctions." *World Economy*, 6 (1, March): 73–87.

Beck, Nathanial and Jonathan Katz. 2001. "Throwing out the Baby with the Bath Water: A Comment on Green, Kim, and Yoon." *International Organization*, 55(Spring): 487–495.

Beck, Nathaniel, Jonathan N. Katz, and Richard Tucker. 1998. "Taking Time Seriously: Time-Series-Cross-Section Analysis with a Binary Dependent Variable." *American Journal of Political Science*, 42(3): 1260–1288.

Blanchard, Jean-Marc F. and Norrin M. Ripsman. 1999/2000. "Asking the Right Question: *When* Do Economic Sanctions Work Best?" *Security Studies*, 9(1/2, Autumn/Winter): 219–235.

Blanton, S. L. 2000. "Promoting Human Rights and Democracy in the Developing World: U.S. Rhetoric versus U.S. Arms Exports." *American Journal of Political Science*, 44: 123–131.

Blessing, James A. 1981. "The Suspension of Foreign Aid: A Macro Analysis." *Polity*, 8(3, Spring): 524–535.

Bolks, Sean M. and Dina Al-Sowayel. 2000. "How Long Do Economic Sanctions Last? Examining the Sanctioning Process through Duration." *Political Research Quarterly*, 53(2): 241–265.

Bond, Doug, Joe Bond, J. Craig Jenkins, Churl Oh, and Charles L. Taylor. 2001. "Integrated Data for Events Analysis (IDEA): An Event Form Typology for Automated Events Data Development." Unpublished manuscript, Harvard University, Cambridge, Mass. Boston, MA: Northeastern University Press.

Brody, R. 1991. *Assessing the President*. Stanford: Stanford University Press.

Bueno De Mesquita, Bruce and David Lalman. 1992. *War and Reason*. New Haven: Yale University Press.

Bueno De Mesquita, Bruce and Randolph Siverson. 1995. "War and the Survival of Political Leaders: A Comparative Study of Regime Types and Political Accountability." *American Political Science Review*, 89(4): 841–853.

Burbach, D. 1995. *Presidential Approval, 1949–1994*. Data made available on the internet.

Chan, Steve. 1997. "In Search of Democratic Peace: Problems and Promise." *International Studies Review*, 41(1): 59–91.

Chan, Steve. 2000. "Economic Sanction: The U.S. Debate on MFN Status for China," in *Sanctions as Economic Statecraft: Theory and Practice*, edited by Chan, Steve and A. Cooper Drury. London: Macmillan/St. Martins.

Chan, Steve and A. Cooper Drury, editors. 2000. *Sanctions as Economic Statecraft: Theory and Practice*. London: Macmillan Press.

Cox, Dan and A. Cooper Drury. 2002. "Democratic Sanctions: The Connection between the Democratic Peace and Economic Sanctions." Paper presented at the Annual Meeting of the International Studies Association, New Orleans, LA.

Crumm, Eileen M. 1995. "The Value of Economic Incentives in International Politics." *Journal of Peace Research*, 32(3, August): 131–330.

Dashti-Gibson, J., P. Davis, and B. Radcliff. 1997. "On the Determinants of the Success of Economic Sanctions: an Empirical Analysis." *American Journal of Political Science*, 41: 608–618.

Dassel, Kurt. 1998. "Civilians, Soldiers, and Strife: Domestic Sources of International Aggression." *International Security*, 23(1): 107–140.

Dassel, Kurt and Eric Reinhardt. 1999. "Domestic Strife and the Initiation of Violence at Home and Abroad." *American Journal of Political Science*, 43(1): 56–85.

Davidson, Jason and George Shambaugh. 2000. "Who's Afraid of Economic Incentives? The Efficacy/Externalities Tradeoff," in *Sanctions as Economic Statecraft: Theory and Practice*, edited by Chan, Steve and A. Cooper Drury. London: Macmillan/St. Martins.

Deese D. 1983. "The Vulnerability of Modern Nations: Economic Diplomacy in East–West Relations," in *Dilemmas of Economic Coercion: Sanctions in World Politics*, edited by Miroslav Nincic and Peter Wallensteen. New York: Praeger.

DeRouen, Karl, Jr. 1995. "The Indirect Link: Politics, the Economy, and the Use of Force." *Journal of Conflict Resolution*, 39(4): 671–695.

Dixon, William J. 1994. "Democracy and the Peaceful Settlement of International Conflicts." *American Political Science Review*, 88(1): 14–32.

Doxey, M. 1971. *Economic Sanctions and International Enforcement*. London: Oxford University Press.

Doxey, M. 1980. *Economic Sanctions and International Enforcement*. London: Oxford University Press.

Doxey, M. 1987. *International Sanctions in Contemporary Perspective.* London: Macmillan Press Ltd.

Doyle, Michael W. 1986. "Liberalism and World Politics." *American Political Science Review*, 80(4): 1151–1169.

Drezner, Daniel W. 1997. "Allies, Adversaries, and Economic Coercion: Russian Foreign Economic Policy since 1991." *Security Studies*, 6(1): 65–111.

Drezner, Daniel W. 1998. "Conflict Expectations and the Paradox of Economic Coercion." *International Studies Quarterly*, 42(4): 709–731.

Drezner, Daniel W. 1999. *The Sanctions Paradox: Economic Statecraft and International Relations.* Cambridge, U.K.: Cambridge University Press.

Drezner, Daniel W. 2000. "Bargaining, Enforcement, and Multilateral Sanctions: When is Cooperation Counterproductive?" *International Organization*, 54(1, Winter): 73–102.

Drezner, Daniel W. 2000. "The Trouble with Carrots: Transaction Costs, Conflict Expectations, and Economic Inducements," *Security Studies*, 9(1/2): 188–218.

Drezner, Daniel W. 2001. "Outside the Box: Explaining Sanctions in Pursuit of Foreign Economic Goals." *International Interactions*, 26(4): 379–410.

Drezner, Daniel W. 2003. "The Hidden Hand of Economic Coercion," *International Organization,* 57(3): 643–659.

Drukker, D. M. 2003. "Testing for Serial Correlation in Linear Panel-Data Models." *The Stata Journal*, 2(3): 1–10.

Drury, A. Cooper. 1997. *Economic Sanctions and Presidential Decisions: Models of Political Rationality.* Ph.D. Dissertation, Arizona State University.

Drury, A. Cooper. 1998. "Revisiting *Economic Sanctions Reconsidered.*" *Journal of Peace Research*, 35(4): 497–510.

Drury, A. Cooper. 2001. "Sanctions as Coercive Diplomacy: The U.S. President's Decision to Initiate Economic Sanctions," *Political Research Quarterly,* 54(4): 485–508.

Drury, A. Cooper. 2003. "Democracy, Autocracy, and Economic Sanctions: How Regime Type Affects the Use of Economic Coercion." Paper presented at the Annual Meeting of the American Political Science Association, Philadelphia, PA.

Drury, A. Cooper and Yitan Li. 2004. "U.S. Economic Sanction Threats against China: Failing to leverage better Human Rights." Paper presented at the Annual Meeting of the *International Studies Association-Midwest,* St. Louis, MO.

Duchesne, Erick. 1997. *International Bilateral Trade and Investment Negotiations: Theory, Formal Model, and Empirical Evidence.* Ph.D. Dissertation, Michigan State University.

Eaton, Jonathan and Maxim Engers. 1999. "Sanctions: Some Simply Analytics." *American Economic Review*, 89(2, May): 409–414.

Eland, I. 1995. "Economic Sanctions as Tools of Foreign Policy," in *Economic Sanctions: Panacea of Peacebuilding in a Post–Cold War World?* edited by D. Cortright and G. Lopez. Boulder: Westview Press.

Elliott, Kimberly Ann and Gary Clyde Hufbauer. 1999. "Same Song, Same Refrain? Economic Sanctions in the 1990s." *American Economic Review*, 89(2, May): 403–408.

Elliott, Kimberly Ann and J. David Richardson. 1997. "Determinants and Effectiveness of 'Aggressively Unilateral' U.S. Trade Actions," in *The Effects of U.S. Trade Protection and Promotion Policies*, edited by Robert C. Feenstra. Chicago, IL: University of Chicago Press, 215–246.

Feenstra, Robert C., ed. 1997. *The Effects of U.S. Trade Protection and Promotion Policies*. Chicago: University of Chicago Press.

Feis, Herbert. 1950. *The Diplomacy of the Dollar, 1919–1932*. New York: W. W. Norton and Company

Fisk, Daniel W. 2000. "Economic Sanctions: The Cuba Embargo Revisited," in *Sanctions as Economic Statecraft: Theory and Practice*, edited by Chan, Steve and A. Cooper Drury. London: Macmillan/St. Martin's.

Forsythe, David. 1992. "Democracy, War, and Covert Action." *Journal of Peace Research*, 29(4): 385–395.

Gallhofer, I. N. and W. E. Saris. 1979. "Strategy Choices of Foreign Policy Decision Makers: The Netherlands, 1914." *Journal of Conflict Resolution*, 23: 425–445.

Galtung, J. 1967. "On the Effects of International Economic Sanctions, with Examples from the Case of Rhodesia." *World Politics*, 19: 378–416.

Galtung, J. 1983. "On the Effects of International Economic Sanctions: With Examples from the Case of Rhodesia." in *Dilemmas of Economic Coercion: Sanctions in World Politics*, edited by Miroslav Nincic and Peter Wallensteen. New York: Praeger, 17–60.

Garson, G. 1976. *Political Science Methods*. Boston: Holbrook Press.

Gelpi, Christopher. 1997. "Democratic Diversions: Governmental Structure and the Externalization of Domestic Conflict." *The Journal of Conflict Resolution*, 41(2): 255–282.

George, A. 1969. "The Operational Code: A Neglected Approach to the Study of Political Leaders and Decision Making." *International Studies Quarterly*, 23: 190–222.

George, A. 1979. "The Causal Nexus Between Beliefs and Behavior," in *Psychological Models in International Politics*, edited by L. Falkowski. Boulder, CO: Westview Press, 95–124.

George, A. 1980. *Presidential Decisionmaking in Foreign Policy*. Boulder: Westview Press.

George, A. 1991. *Forceful Persuasion: Coercive Diplomacy as an Alternative to War*. Washington, D.C.: United States Institute for Peace.

George, A. 1993. *Bridging the Gap: Theory and Practice in Foreign Policy*. Washington, D.C.: United States Institute for Peace.

George, A., David K. Hall, and William R. Simons. 1971. *The Limits of Coercive Diplomacy: Laos–Cuba–Vietnam*. Boston: Little, Brown and Company.

Gilbert, Felix. 1961. *To the Farewell Address*. Princeton: Princeton University Press.

Gilpin, Robert. 1984. "Structural Constraints on Economic Leverage: Market-Type Systems," in *Strategic Dimensions of Economic Behavior*, edited by McCormich, Gordon H. and Richard E. Bissell. New York: Praeger, 105–128.

Gilpin, Robert. 2001. *Global Political Economy: Understanding the International Economic Order*. Princeton, NJ: Princeton University Press.

Gleditsch, Kristian S. 2002. "Expanded Trade and GDP Data." *Journal of Conflict Resolution*, 46: 712–724.

Goldstein, J. and J. Freeman. 1991. "U.S.–Soviet–Chinese Relations: Routine, Reciprocity, or Rational Expectations?" *American Political Science Review*, 85: 17–35.

Green, Donald P., Soo Yeon Kim, and David H. Yoon. 2001. "Dirty Pool." *International Organization*, 55(Spring): 441–468.

Green, J. 1983. "Strategies for Evading Economic Sanctions," in *Dilemmas of Economic Coercion: Sanctions in World Politics*, edited by Miroslav Nincic and Peter Wallensteen. New York: Praeger, 61–83.

Greene, William H. 1997. *Econometric Analysis*, Third Edition. New Jersey: Prentice Hall.

Haas, Ernest B. and S. Whiting Allen. 1956. *Dynamics of International Relations*. New York: McGraw Hill.

Haass, Richard N. 1993. *Economic Sanctions and American Diplomacy*. New York: Brookings Institution Press.

Hart, Robert A., Jr. 2000. "Democracy and the Successful Use of Economic Sanctions." *Political Research Quarterly*, 53(2, June): 267–284.

Hausman, J. 1978. "Specification Tests in Econometrics." *Econometrica*, 46: 1251–1272.

Hermann, M. and C. Hermann. 1989. "Who Makes Foreign Policy Decisions and How: An Empirical Inquiry." *International Studies Quarterly*, 33: 361–387.

Hermann, Margaret and Thomas Preston. 1994. Presidents, Advisors, and Foreign Policy: The Effect of Leadership Style on Executive Arrangements. *Political Psychology*, 15: 75–96.

Hufbauer, G. and J. Schott. 1985. *Economic Sanctions Reconsidered: History and Current Policy*. Washington, D.C.: Institute for International Economics.

Hufbauer, G., J. Schott, and K. Elliott. 1990a. *Economic Sanctions Reconsidered: History and Currant Policy*. Washington, D.C.: Institute for International Economics.

Hufbauer, G., J. Schott, and K. Elliott. 1990b. *Economic Sanctions Reconsidered: Supplemental Case Histories*. Washington, D.C.: Institute for International Economics.

Hufbauer, G., J. Schott, and K. Elliott. Forthcoming. *Economic Sanctions Reconsidered*. Third edition. Washington, D.C.: Institute for International Economics.

James, P. and J. Oneal. 1991. "The Influence of Domestic and International Politics on the President's Use of Force." *Journal of Conflict Resolution*, 35: 307–332.

James, P. and A. Hristoulas. 1994. "Domestic Politics and Foreign Policy: Evaluating a Model of Crisis Activity." *The Journal of Politics*, 56: 327–348.

James, P. and Glenn E. Mitchell II. 1995. "Targets of Covert Pressure: The Hidden Victims of the Democratic Peace." *International Interactions*, 21(1): 85–107.

Jentleson, Bruce. 1992. "The Pretty Prudent Public: Post Post-Vietnam American Opinion on the Use of Military Force." *International Studies Quarterly*, 36: 49–74.

Jervis, Robert. 1992. "Political Implications of Loss Aversion." *Political Psychology*, 13: 187–204.

Johnson, R. 1974. *Managing the Whitehouse*. New York: Harper and Row.

Kaempfer, William H. and Anton D. Lowenberg. 1988. "The Theory of International Economic Sanctions: A Public Choice Perspective." *American Economic Review*, 78(4): 786–794.

Kaempfer, William H. 1989. "The Theory of International Economic Sanctions: A Public Choice Approach: Reply." *American Economic Review*, 79(5): 1304–1306.

Kaempfer, William H. 1992. *International Economic Sanctions: A Public Choice Perspective*. Boulder, CO: Westview Press.

Kaempfer, William H., James A. Lehman, and Anton D. Lowenberg. 1987. "Divestment, Investment Sanctions, and Disinvestment: An Evaluation of Anti-Apartheid Policy Instruments." International Organization, 41(3, Summer): 457–473.

Keohane, Robert O. and Joseph S. Nye. 1977. *Power and Interdependence: World Politics in Transition*. Boston: Little, Brown and Company.

King, Gary and Langche Zeng. 1999a. "Logistic Regression in Rare Events Data," Department of Government, Harvard University, available from <http://GKing.Harvard.Edu>.

King, Gary and Langche Zeng. 1999b. "Estimating Absolute, Relative, and Attributable Risks in Case-Control Studies," Department of Government, Harvard University, available from <http://GKing.Harvard.Edu>.

King, Gary and Langche Zeng. 2001a. "Logistic Regression in Rare Events Data." *Political Analysis*, 9(2, Spring): 137–163.

King, Gary and Langche Zeng. 2001b. "Explaining Rare Events in International Relations." *International Organization*, 55(3, Summer): 693–715.

King, Gary, Michael Tomz, and Jason Wittenberg. 2000. "Making the Most of Statistical Analyses: Improving Interpretation and Presentation." *American Journal of Political Science*, 44(2): 347–361.

King, Gary, Robert Keohane, and Sydney Verba. 1994. *Designing Social Inquiry*. Princeton: Princeton University Press.

King, Gary and Will Lowe. 2003. "An Automated Information Extraction Tool for International Conflict Data with Performance as Good as Human Coders: A Rare Events Evaluation Design." *International Organization* 57(Summer): 617–642.

Kirshner, Jonathan. 1995. *Currency and Coercion: The Political Economy of International Monetary Power*. Princeton: Princeton University Press.

Knorr, Klaus. 1977. "International Economic Leverage and its Uses," in *Economic Issues and National Security*, edited by Knorr, Klaus and Frank N. Trager. Lawrence: Allen Press.

Knorr, Klaus and Frank N. Trager, eds. 1977. *Economic Issues and National Security*. Lawrence: Allen Press.

Krasner, Stephen D. 1977. "Domestic Constraints on International Economic Leverage," in *Economic Issues and National Security*, edited by Knorr, Klaus and Frank Trager. Lawrence: Allen Press.

Lacy, Dean and Emerson M. S. Niou. 2004. "A Theory of Economic Sanctions and Issue Linkage: The Roles of Preferences, Information, and Threats." *Journal of Politics*, 66: 25–42.

Lektzian, David and Mark Souva. 2001. "Institutions and International Cooperation: An Event History Analysis of the Effects of Economic Sanctions." *Journal of Conflict Resolution*, 45(1, February): 61–79.

Lektzian, David and Mark Souva. 2003. "The Economic Peace Between Democracies: Economic Sanctions and Domestic Institutions." *Journal of Peace Research*, 40(6): 641–660.

Leng, Russel. 1993. *Interstate Crisis Behavior, 1816–1980: Realism Versus Reciprocity*. Cambridge: Cambridge University Press.

Levy, J. 1989. "Diversionary Theory of War," in *Hand Book of War Studies*, edited by Manus I. Midlarsky. Winchester, MA.: Unwin Hyman, Inc.

Levy, J. 1992a. "An Introduction to Prospect Theory." *Political Psychology*, 13: 171–186.

Levy, J. 1992b. "Prospect Theory and International Relations: Theoretical Applications and Analytical Problems." *Political Psychology*, 13: 283–310.

Levy, Philip I. 1999. "Sanctions on South Africa: What did they Do?" *American Economic Review*, 89(2, May): 415–420.

Li, C. P. 1993. "The Effectiveness of Sanction Linkages: Issues and Actors." *International Studies Quarterly*, 37: 349–370.

Li, Yitan and A. Cooper Drury. 2004. "Granting MFN Status to China: Implications and Practices of Sanction Threats." *International Studies Perspectives*, 5: 378–394.

Lian, Bradley and John R. Oneal. 1993. "Presidents, the Use of Military Force, and Public Opinion." *The Journal of Conflict Resolution*, 37: 2.

Light, Paul. 1991. *The President's Agenda*. Baltimore: Johns Hopkins University Press.

Lindsey, James M. 1986. "Trade Sanctions as Policy Instruments: A Re-examination." *International Studies Quarterly*, 30: 153–173.

Long, J. Scott and Jeremy Freese. 2001. *Regression Models for Categorical Dependent Variables Using Stata.* College Station, TX: Stata Press.

Losman, David L. 1979. *International Economic Sanctions: The Cases of Cuba, Israel, and Rhodesia.* Albuquerque: University of New Mexico Press.

Mansfield, Edward D. 1995. "International Institutions and Economic Sanctions." *World Politics*, 47(July): 575–605.

Mansfield, Edward D., Helen V. Milner, and B. Peter Rosendorff. 2000. "Free to Trade? Democracies, Autocracies, and International Trade Negotiations." *American Political Science Review*, 94: 305–322.

Marcich, Marino. 1998. "Sanctions Reform." National Association of Manufacturers.

Marshall, Monty G. and Jaggers, Keith. 2000. *Polity IV Project: Political Regime Characteristics and Transitions, 1800–1999* <www.cidcm.umd.edu/inser/polity>.

Martin, Lisa L. 1992. *Coercive Cooperation: Explaining Multilateral Economic Sanctions.* Princeton, NJ: Princeton University Press.

Mastanduno, Michael. 1992. *Economic Containment: COCOM and the Politics of East-West Trade.* Ithaca, NY: Cornell University Press.

Mastanduno, Michael. 1998. "Economics and Security in Statecraft and Scholarship." *International Organization*, 52(4, Autumn): 825–854.

Mastanduno, Michael. 1999/2000. "Economic Statecraft, Interdependence, and National Security: Agendas for Research." *Security Studies*, 9(1/2, Autumn/Winter): 288–316.

McCormich, Gordon H. and Richard E. Bissell. 1984. *Strategic Dimensions of Economic Behavior.* New York: Praeger.

McDermott, R. 1992. "Prospect Theory in International Relations: The Iranian Hostage Rescue Mission." *Political Psychology*, 13: 237–263.

Meernik, J. 1994. Presidential Decision Making and the Political Use of Force. *International Studies Quarterly*, 38: 121–138.

Meernik, James and Peter Waterman. 1996. "The Myth of the Diversionary Use of Force by American Presidents." *Political Research Quarterly*, 49: 573–590.

Miers, Anne C. and T. Clifton Morgan. 2002. "Multilateral Sanctions and Foreign Policy Success: Can Too Many Cooks Spoil the Broth?" *International Interactions*, 28: 117–136.

Miller, Ross A. 1995. "Domestic Structures and the Diversionary Use of Force." *American Journal of Political Science*, 39(3): 760–785.

Mintz, Alex, editor. 2003. *Integrating Cognitive and Rational Theories of Foreign Policy Decision Making.* New York: Palgrave Macmillan.

Morgan, C. 1990. "Power, Resolve and Bargaining In International Crises: A Spatial Theory." *International Interactions*, 15: 279–302.

Morgan, C. 1994. *Untying the Knot of War: A Bargaining Theory of International Crises.* Ann Arbor: The University of Michigan Press.

Morgan, C. 1995. "Clinton's Chinese Puzzle: Domestic Politics and the Effectiveness of Economic Sanctions." *Issues and Studies*, 31(8): 19–45.

Morgan C. and Kenneth N. Bickers. 1992: "Domestic Discontent and the External Use of Force." *Journal of Conflict Resolution*, 36(1): 25–52.

Morgan, C. and Valerie L. Schwebach. 1996. "Economic Sanctions as an Instrument of Foreign Policy: The Role of Domestic Politics." *International Interactions*, 36: 25–52.

Morgan, C. and Valerie L. Schwebach. 1997. "Fools Suffer Gladly: The Use of Economic Sanctions in International Crises." *International Studies Quarterly*, 41: 27–50.

Morgan, C. and Anne Miers. 1999. "When Threats Succeed: A Formal Model of Threat and Use of Economic Sanctions." Presented at the Annual Meeting of the *American Political Science Association*, Atlanta, GA.

Mueller, J. 1973. *War, Presidents, and Public Opinion*. New York: John Wiley.

Myers, Steve Lee. "Converting the Dollar into a Bludgeon." *New York Times*, April 20, 1997.

Naylor, R. T. 2001. *Economic Warfare: Sanctions, Embargo Busting, and Their Human Cost*. Boston: Northeastern University Press.

Neustadt, R. 1980. *Presidential Power*. New York: Macmillan Publishing Company.

Newnham, Randall E. 2000. "More Flies with Honey: Positive Economic Linkage in German Ostpolitik from Bismarck to Kohl." *International Studies Quarterly*, 44(1, March): 73–96.

Newnham, Randall. 2004. " 'Nukes for Sale Cheap?' Purchasing Peace with North Korea." *International Studies Perspectives*, 5(2): 164–178.

Nincic, Miroslav. 1997. "Loss Aversion and the Domestic Context of Military Intervention." *Political Research Quarterly*, 50(1): 97–120.

Nincic and Peter Wallensteen. 1983. in *Dilemmas of Economic Coercion: Sanctions in World Politics*, edited by Nincic and Wallensteen. New York: Praeger pp. 155–182.

Noland, Marcus. 1997. "Chasing Phantoms: The Political Economy of the USTR." *International Organization*, 51(3, Summer): 365–387.

Nooruddin, Irfan. 2002. "Modeling Selection Bias in Studies of Sanctions Efficacy," *International Interactions*, 28(1): 59–75.

Nossal, Kim Richard. 1989. "International Sanctions as International Punishment," *International Organization*, 43(2): 301–322.

Olson, Richard Stuart. 1975. "Economic Coercion in International Disputes: The United States and Peru in the IPC Expropriation Dispute of 1968–1971." *Journal of Developing Areas*, 9(April): 395–413.

Olson, Richard Stuart. 1977. "Expropriation and International Economic Coercion: Ceylon and the 'West' 1961–1965." *Journal of Developing Areas*, 11(2): 205–226.

Olson, Richard Stuart. 1979a. "Economic Coercion in World Politics: With a Focus on North–South Relations." *World Politics*, 31: 471–494.

Olson, Richard Stuart. 1979b. "Expropriation and Economic Coercion in World Politics: A Retrospective Look at Brazil in the 1960s." *Journal of Developing Areas*, 13(3): 247–262.

Ostrom, Charles and Brian Job. 1986. "The President and the Political Use of Force." *American Political Science Review*, 80(2): 541–566.

Pape, Robert. 1997. "Why Economic Sanctions Do Not Work." *International Security*, 22(2): 90–136.

Pape, Robert. 1998a. "Why Economic Sanctions Still Do Not Work." *International Security*, 23(1): 66–77.

Pape, Robert. 1998b. "Evaluating Economic Sanctions," *International Security*, 23(2): 195–198.

Poe, Steven C. 1991. "Human Rights and the Allocation of U.S. Military Assistance." *Journal of Peace Research*, 28: 205–216.

Poe, Steven C. 1992. "Human Rights and Economic Aid under Ronald Reagan and Jimmy Carter." *American Journal of Political Science*, 36: 147–168.

Reinhardt, Eric. 1999. "Aggressive Multilateralism: The Determinants of GATT/WTO Dispute Initiation, 1948–1998." Paper presented at the Annual Meeting of the International Studies Association, Washington, DC, February 17–20.

Reinhardt, Eric. 2000. "To GATT or Not To GATT: Which Trade Disputes Does the U.S. Litigate, 1975–1999?" Emory University working paper.

Renwick, R. 1981. *Economic Sanctions*. Rensselaer: Hamilton Printing Company.

Rosati, Jerel A. 2004. *The Politics of United States Foreign Policy*. Belmont: Wadsworth.

Rowe, David M. 1999/2000. "Economic Sanctions Do Work: Economic Statecraft and the Oil Embargo of Rhodesia." *Security Studies*, 9(1/2, Autumn/Winter): 254–287.

Rowe, David M. 2000. "Economic Sanctions, Domestic Politics and the Decline of Rhodesia Tobacco, 1965–79," in *as Economic Statecraft: Theory and Practice*, edited by Chan, Steve and A. Cooper Drury. London: Macmillan/St. Martin's, 131–157.

Rowe, David M. 2001. *Manipulating the Market: Understanding Economic Sanctions, Institutional Change, and the Political Unity of White Rhodesia*. Ann Arbor: University of Michigan Press.

Schreiber, Anna P. 1973. "Economic Coercion as an Instrument of Foreign Policy: U.S. Economic Measures against Cuba and the Dominican Republic." *World Politics*, 25(April): 387–413.

Schwebach, Valerie L. 2000. "Sancitons as Signals: A Line in the Sand of a Lack of Resolve?" in *Sanctions as Economic Statecraft: Theory and Practice*, edited by Chan, Steve and A. Cooper Drury. London: Macmillan/St. Martin's, 187–211.

Seeler, H. J. 1982. "Wirtschaftssanktionen als zweifelhaftes Instrument der Aussenpolitik." *Europa-Archiv*, 20: 611–618.

Seldon, Zachary, 1999. *Economic Sanctions as Instruments of American Foreign Policy*. West Port, CN: Praeger.

Shambaugh, George E. 1999. *States, Firms, and Power: Successful Sanctions in United States Foreign Policy*. Albany, New York: State University of New York Press.

Simon, Herbert. 1985 "Human Nature in Politics: The Dialogue of Psychology with Political Science." *American Political Science Review*, 79: 293–304.

Simon, Marc V. 1996. "When Sanctions Can Work: Economic Sanctions and the Theory of Moves." *International Interactions*, 21(3): 203–228.

Sislin, John. 1994. "Arms as Influence: The Determinants of Successful Influence." *Journal of Conflict Resolution*, 38(4, December): 665–689.

Smith, Alastair. 1996. "The Success and Use of Economic Sanctions." *International Interactions*, 21(3): 229–245.

Snyder, G. and P. Diesing. 1977. *Conflict Among Nations*. Princeton: Princeton University Press.

Snyder, Richard C., H. W. Bruck, and Burton Sapin. 1962. *Foreign Policy Decision-Making; An Approach to the Study of International Politics*. New York: Free Press of Glencoe.

StataCorp. 2004. *Stata Statistical Software: Release 8.2*. College Station, TX: Stata Corporation.

Tomz, Michael, Jason Wittenberg, and Gary King. 2003. CLARIFY: Software for Interpreting and Presenting Statistical Results. Version 2.1. Stanford University, University of Wisconsin, and Harvard University. January 5. Available at <http://gking.harvard.edu/>.

Tversky, Amos and Daniel Kahneman. 1992. "Advances in Prospect Theory: Cumulative Representation of Uncertainty." *Journal of Risk and Uncertainty*, 5: 297–323.

van Bergeijk, Peter A. G. 1994. *Economic Diplomacy, Trade and Commercial Policy: Positive and Negative Sanctions in a New World Order*. Hants, England: Edward Elgar Publishing Company.

Walker, Stephen G. and Mark Schafer. 2003. "Theodore Roosevelt and Woodrow Wilson: Realist and Idealist Archetypes?" Paper presented at the Annual Meeting of the *International Society of Political Psychology*, Boston, MA, July 5–9.

Walker, Stephen G., Mark Schafer, and Michael Young. 1998. "Systematic Procedures for Operational Code Analysis." *International Studies Quarterly*, 42: 175–190.

Wallensteen, Peter. 1968. "The Characteristics of Economic Sanctions." *Journal of Peace Research*, 3: 248–267.

Wallensteen, Peter, Carina Staibano, and Mikael Eriksson. 2004. *Routes to Democracy in Burma/Myanmar: The Uppsala Pilot Study on Dialogue and International Strategies*. Uppsala University, Department of Peace and Conflict Research.

Weiss, Thomas G., 1999. "Sanctions as a Foreign Policy Tool: Weighing Humanitarian Impulses." *Journal of Peace Research*, 36(5): 499–510.

Wolfson, Murray, Zagros Madjd-Sadjadi, and Patrick James. 2004. "Identifying National Types: A Cluster Analysis of Politics, Economics and Conflict." *Journal of Peace Research*, 41: 607–623.

Wooldridge, J. M. 2002. *Econometric Analysis of Cross Section and Panel Data*. Cambridge, MA: The MIT Press.

Zeng, Ka. 2004. *Trade Threats, Trade Wars: Bargaining, Retaliation, and American Coercive Diplomacy*. Ann Arbor: University of Michigan Press.

Index